THE
LIFE AND LETTERS
OF
WALTER H. PAGE

From a painting by P. A. LASZLO

Walter H. Page

THE
LIFE AND LETTERS OF
WALTER H. PAGE

BY
BURTON J. HENDRICK

VOLUME
I

GARDEN CITY   NEW YORK
DOUBLEDAY, PAGE & COMPANY
1922

PREFATORY NOTE

Among the many who have assisted in the preparation of this Biography especial acknowledgment is made to Mr. Irwin Laughlin, First Secretary and Counsellor of the London Embassy under Mr. Page. Mr. Page's papers show the high regard which he entertained for Mr. Laughlin's abilities and character, and the author similarly has found Mr. Laughlin's assistance indispensable. Mr. Laughlin has had the goodness to read the manuscript and make numerous suggestions, all for the purpose of reënforcing the accuracy of the narrative. The author gratefully remembers many long conversations with Viscount Grey of Fallodon, in which Anglo-American relations from 1913 to 1916 were exhaustively canvassed and many side-lights thrown upon Mr. Page's conduct of his difficult and delicate duties. The British Foreign Office most courteously gave the writer permission to examine a large number of documents in its archives bearing upon Mr. Page's ambassadorship and consented to the publication of several of the most important.

B. J. H.

CONTENTS
VOLUME I

LIST OF ILLUSTRATIONS

THE
LIFE AND LETTERS
OF
WALTER H. PAGE

THE LIFE AND LETTERS OF WALTER H. PAGE

CHAPTER I

A RECONSTRUCTION BOYHOOD

I

THE earliest recollections of any man have great biographical interest, and this is especially the case with Walter Page, for not the least dramatic aspect of his life was that it spanned the two greatest wars in history. Page spent his last weeks in England, at Sandwich, on the coast of Kent; every day and every night he could hear the pounding of the great guns in France, as the Germans were making their last desperate attempt to reach Paris or the Channel ports. His memories of his childhood days in America were similarly the sights and sounds of war. Page was a North Carolina boy; he has himself recorded the impression that the Civil War left upon his mind.

"One day," he writes, "when the cotton fields were white and the elm leaves were falling, in the soft autumn of the Southern climate wherein the sky is fathomlessly clear, the locomotive's whistle blew a much longer time than usual as the train approached Millworth. It did not stop at so small a station except when there was somebody to get off or to get on, and so long a blast meant that someone was coming. Sam and I ran down the avenue of elms to see who it was. Sam was my Negro companion,

philosopher, and friend. I was ten years old and Sam
said that he was fourteen. There was constant talk
about the war. Many men of the neighbourhood had
gone away somewhere—that was certain; but Sam and I
had a theory that the war was only a story. We had
been fooled about old granny Thomas's bringing the baby
and long ago we had been fooled also about Santa Claus.
The war might be another such invention, and we sometimes suspected that it was. But we found out the truth
that day, and for this reason it is among my clearest early
recollections.

"For, when the train stopped, they put off a big box
and gently laid it in the shade of the fence. The only
man at the station was the man who had come to change
the mail-bags; and he said that this was Billy Morris's
coffin and that he had been killed in a battle. He asked
us to stay with it till he could send word to Mr. Morris,
who lived two miles away. The man came back presently and leaned against the fence till old Mr. Morris
arrived, an hour or more later. The lint of cotton was
on his wagon, for he was hauling his crop to the gin when
the sad news reached him; and he came in his shirt
sleeves, his wife on the wagon seat with him.

"All the neighbourhood gathered at the church, a
funeral was preached and there was a long prayer for our
success against the invaders, and Billy Morris was buried.
I remember that I wept the more because it now seemed
to me that my doubt about the war had somehow done
Billy Morris an injustice. Old Mrs. Gregory wept more
loudly than anybody else; and she kept saying, while the
service was going on, 'It'll be my John next.' In a
little while, sure enough, John Gregory's coffin was put
off the train, as Billy Morris's had been, and I regarded
her as a woman gifted with prophecy. Other coffins, too,

were put off from time to time. About the war there, could no longer be a doubt. And, a little later, its realities and horrors came nearer home to us, with swift, deep experiences.

"One day my father took me to the camp and parade ground ten miles away, near the capital. The General and the Governor sat on horses and the soldiers marched by them and the band played. They were going to the front. There surely must be a war at the front, I told Sam that night. Still more coffins were brought home, too, as the months and the years passed; and the women of the neighbourhood used to come and spend whole days with my mother, sewing for the soldiers. So precious became woollen cloth that every rag was saved and the threads were unravelled to be spun and woven into new fabrics. And they baked bread and roasted chickens and sheep and pigs and made cakes, all to go to the soldiers at the front."[1]

The quality that is uppermost in the Page stock, both in the past and in the present generation, is that of the builder and the pioneer. The ancestor of the North Carolina Pages was a Lewis Page, who, in the latter part of the eighteenth century, left the original American home in Virginia, and started life anew in what was then regarded as the less civilized country to the south. Several explanations have survived as to the cause of his departure, one being that his interest in the rising tide of Methodism had made him uncongenial to his Church of England relatives; in the absence of definite knowledge, however, it may safely be assumed that the impelling motive was that love of seeking out new things, of constructing a new home in the wilderness, which has never forsaken his

---

[1] From "The Southerner," Chapter I. The first chapter in this novel is practically autobiographical, though fictitious names have been used.

descendants. His son, Anderson Page, manifesting this same love of change, went farther south into Wake County, and acquired a plantation of a thousand acres about twelve miles north of Raleigh. He cultivated this estate with slaves, sending his abundant crops of cotton and tobacco to Petersburg, Virginia, a traffic that made him sufficiently prosperous to give several of his sons a college education. The son who is chiefly interesting at the present time, Allison Francis Page, the father of the future Ambassador, did not enjoy this opportunity. This fact in itself gives an insight into his character. While his brothers were grappling with Latin and Greek and theology—one of them became a Methodist preacher of the hortatory type for which the South is famous—we catch glimpses of the older man battling with the logs in the Cape Fear River, or penetrating the virgin pine forest, felling trees and converting its raw material to the uses of a growing civilization. Like many of the Page breed, this Page was a giant in size and in strength, as sound morally and physically as the mighty forests in which a considerable part of his life was spent, brave, determined, aggressive, domineering almost to the point of intolerance, deeply religious and abstemious—a mixture of the frontiersman and the Old Testament prophet. Walter Page dedicated one of his books[1] to his father, in words that accurately sum up his character and career. "To the honoured memory of my father, whose work was work that built up the commonwealth." Indeed, Frank Page —for this is the name by which he was generally known— spent his whole life in these constructive labours. He founded two towns in North Carolina, Cary and Aberdeen; in the City of Raleigh he constructed hotels and other buildings; his enterprising and restless spirit opened

---

[1] "The Rebuilding of Old Commonwealths." (1902.)

up Moore County—which includes the Pinehurst region; he scattered his logging camps and his sawmills all over the face of the earth; and he constructed a railroad through the pine woods that made him a rich man.

Though he was not especially versed in the learning of the schools, Walter Page's father had a mind that was keen and far-reaching. He was a pioneer in politics as he was in the practical concerns of life. Though he was the son of slave-holding progenitors and even owned slaves himself, he was not a believer in slavery. The country that he primarily loved was not Moore County or North Carolina, but the United States of America. In politics he was a Whig, which meant that, in the years preceding the Civil War, he was opposed to the extension of slavery and did not regard the election of Abraham Lincoln as a sufficient provocation for the secession of the Southern States. It is therefore not surprising that Walter Page, in the midst of the London turmoil of 1916, should have found his thoughts reverting to his father as he remembered him in Civil War days. That gaunt figure of America's time of agony proved an inspiration and hope in the anxieties that assailed the Ambassador. "When our Civil War began," wrote Page to Col. Edward M. House—the date was November 24, 1916, one of the darkest days for the Allied cause—"every man who had a large and firm grip on economic facts foresaw how it would end—not when but how. Young as I was, I recall a conversation between my father and the most distinguished judge of his day in North Carolina. They put down on one side the number of men in the Confederate States, the number of ships, the number of manufactures, as nearly as they knew, the number of skilled workmen, the number of guns, the aggregate of wealth and of possible production. On the other side they put down the best estimate they could make of all these things in the Northern States. The Northern States made two (or I shouldn't wonder if it were three) times as good a showing in men and resources as the Confederacy had. 'Judge,' said my father, 'this is the most foolhardy enterprise that man ever undertook.' But Yancey of Alabama was about that time making five-hour speeches to thousands of people all over the South, declaring that one Southerner could whip five Yankees, and the awful slaughter began and darkened our childhood and put all our best men where they would see the sun no more. Our people had at last to accept worse terms than they could have got at the beginning. This World War, even more than our Civil War, is an economic struggle. Put down on either side the same items that my father and the judge put down and add the items up. You will see the inevitable result."

If we are seeking an ancestral explanation for that moral ruggedness, that quick perception of the difference between right and wrong, that unobscured vision into men and events, and that deep devotion to America and to democracy which formed the fibre of Walter Page's being, we evidently need look no further than his father. But the son had qualities which the older man did not possess—an enthusiasm for literature and learning, a love of the beautiful in Nature and in art, above all a gentleness of temperament and of manner. These qualities he held in common with his mother. On his father's side Page was undiluted English; on his mother's he was French and English. Her father was John Samuel Raboteau, the descendant of Huguenot refugees who had fled from France on the Revocation of the Edict of Nantes; her mother was Esther Barclay, a member of a family which gave the name of Barclaysville to a small town half way between Raleigh and Fayetteville, North Carolina. It is a member of this tribe to whom Page once referred as the "vigorous Barclay who held her receptions to notable men in her bedroom during the years of her bedridden condition." She was the proprietor of the "Half Way House," a tavern located between Fayetteville and Raleigh; and in her old age she kept royal state, in the fashion which Page describes, for such as were socially entitled to this consideration. The most vivid impression which her present-day descendants retain is that of her fervent devotion to the Southern cause. She carried the spirit of secession to such an extreme that she had the gate to her yard painted to give a complete presentment of the Confederate Flag. Walter Page's mother, the granddaughter of this determined and rebellious lady, had also her positive quality, but in a somewhat more subdued form. She did not die until 1897, and so the recollection of her is fresh and vivid. As a mature woman she was undemonstrative and soft spoken; a Methodist of old-fashioned Wesleyan type, she dressed with a Quaker-like simplicity, her brown hair brushed flatly down upon a finely shaped head and her garments destitute of ruffles or ornamentation. The home which she directed was a home without playing cards or dancing or smoking or wine-bibbing or other worldly frivolities, yet the memories of her presence which Catherine Page has left are not at all austere. Duty was with her the prime consideration of life, and fundamental morals the first conceptions which she instilled in her children's growing minds, yet she had a quiet sense of humour and a real love of fun.

She had also strong likes and dislikes, and was not especially hospitable to men and women who fell under her disapproval. A small North Carolina town, in the years preceding and following the Civil War, was not a fruitful soil for cultivating an interest in things intellectual, yet those who remember Walter Page's mother remember her always with a book in her hand. She would read at her knitting and at her miscellaneous household duties, which were rather arduous in the straitened days that followed the war, and the books she read were always substantial ones. Perhaps because her son Walter was in delicate health, perhaps because his early tastes and temperament were not unlike her own, perhaps because he was her oldest surviving child, the fact remains that, of a family of eight, he was generally regarded as the child with whom she was especially sympathetic. The picture of mother and son in those early days is an altogether charming one. Page's mother was only twenty-four when he was born; she retained her youth for many years after that event, and during his early childhood, in appearance and manner, she was little more than a girl. When Walter was a small boy, he and his mother used to take long walks in the woods, sometimes spending the entire day, fishing along the brooks, hunting wild flowers, now and then pausing while the mother read pages of Dickens or of Scott. These experiences Page never forgot. Nearly all his letters to his mother—to whom, even in his busiest days in New York, he wrote constantly —have been accidentally destroyed, but a few scraps indicate the close spiritual bond that existed between the two. Always he seemed to think of his mother as young. Through his entire life, in whatever part of the world he might be, and however important was the work in which he might be engaged, Page never failed to write her a long and affectionate letter at Christmas.

"Well, I've gossiped a night or two"—such is the

conclusion of his Christmas letter of 1893, when Page was thirty-eight, with a growing family of his own—"till I've filled the paper—all such little news and less non-sense as most gossip and most letters are made of. But it is for you to read between the lines. That's where the love lies, dear mother. I wish you were here Christmas; we should welcome you as nobody else in the world can be welcomed. But wherever you are and though all the rest have the joy of seeing you, which is denied to me, never a Christmas comes but I feel as near you as I did years and years ago when we were young. (In those years *big* fish bit in old Wiley Bancom's pond by the rail-road: they must have been two inches long!)—I would give a year's growth to have the pleasure of having you here. You may be sure that every one of my children along with me will look with an added reverence toward the picture on the wall that greets me every morning, when we have our little Christmas frolics—the picture that little Katharine points to and says 'That's my grand-mudder.'—The years, as they come, every one, deepen my gratitude to you, as I better and better understand the significance of life and every one adds to an affection that was never small. God bless you.

"WALTER."

Such were the father and mother of Walter Hines Page; they were married at Fayetteville, North Carolina, July 5, 1849; two children who preceded Walter died in infancy. The latter was born at Cary, August 15, 1855. Cary was a small village which Frank Page had created; in honour of the founder it was for several years known as Page's Station; the father himself changed the name to Cary, as a tribute to a temperance orator who caused something of a commotion in the neighbourhood in the

early seventies.   Cary was not then much of a town and
has not since become one; but it was placed amid the
scene of important historical events.   Page's home was
almost the last stopping place of Sherman's army on its
march through Georgia and the Carolinas, and the Confederacy came to an end, with Johnston's surrender of the
last Confederate Army, at Durham, only fifteen miles from
his native village.   Walter, a boy of ten, his brother Robert,
aged six, and the negro "companion" Tance—who figures
as Sam in the extract quoted above—stood at the second-
story window and watched Sherman's soldiers pass their
house, in hot pursuit of General "Joe" Wheeler's cavalry.
The thing that most astonished the children was the vast
size of the army, which took all day to file by their home.
They had never realized that either of the fighting forces
could embrace such great numbers of men.   Nor did the
behaviour of the invading troops especially endear them to
their unwilling hosts.   Part of the cavalry encamped in the
Page yard; their horses ate the bark off the mimosa trees;
an army corps built its campfires under the great oaks, and
cut their emblems on the trunks; the officers took possession of the house, a colonel making his headquarters in the
parlour.   Several looting cavalrymen ran their swords
through the beds, probably looking for hidden silver; the
hearth was torn up in the same feverish quest; angry at
their failure, they emptied sacks of flour and scattered the
contents in the bedrooms and on the stairs; for days the
flour, intermingled with feathers from the bayonetted
beds, formed a carpet all over the house.   It is therefore perhaps not strange that the feelings which Walter entertained for Sherman's "bummers," despite his
father's Whig principles, were those of most Southern communities.   One day a kindly Northern soldier, sympathizing with the boy because of the small rations left for the

local population, invited him to join the officers' mess at dinner. Walter drew proudly back.

"I'll starve before I'll eat with the Yankees," he said.

"I slept that night on a trundle bed by my mother's," Page wrote years afterward, describing these early scenes, "for her room was the only room left for the family, and we had all lived there since the day before. The dining room and the kitchen were now superfluous, because there was nothing more to cook or to eat. . . . A week or more after the army corps had gone, I drove with my father to the capital one day, and almost every mile of the journey we saw a blue coat or a gray coat lying by the road, with bones or hair protruding—the unburied and the forgotten of either army. Thus I had come to know what war was, and death by violence was among the first deep impressions made on my mind. My emotions must have been violently dealt with and my sensibilities blunted—or sharpened? Who shall say? The wounded and the starved straggled home from hospitals and from prisons. There was old Mr. Sanford, the shoemaker, come back again, with a body so thin and a step so uncertain that I expected to see him fall to pieces. Mr. Larkin and Joe Tatum went on crutches; and I saw a man at the post-office one day whose cheek and ear had been torn away by a shell. Even when Sam and I sat on the river-bank fishing, and ought to have been silent lest the fish swim away, we told over in low tones the stories that we had heard of wounds and of deaths and of battles.

"But there was the cheerful gentleness of my mother to draw my thoughts to different things. I can even now recall many special little plans that she made to keep my mind from battles. She hid the military cap that I had worn. She bought from me my military buttons and put them away. She would call me in and tell me pleasant stories of her own childhood. She would put down her work to make puzzles with me, and she read gentle books to me and kept away from me all the stories of the war and of death that she could. Whatever hardships befell her (and they must have been many) she kept a tender manner of resignation and of cheerful patience.

"After a while the neighbourhood came to life again. There were more widows, more sonless mothers, more empty sleeves and wooden legs than anybody there had ever seen before. But the mimosa bloomed, the cotton was planted again, and the peach trees blossomed; and the barnyard and the stable again became full of life. For, when the army marched away, they, too, were as silent as an old battlefield. The last hen had been caught under the corn-crib by a 'Yankee' soldier, who had torn his coat in this brave raid. Aunt Maria told Sam that all Yankees were chicken thieves whether they 'brung freedom or no.'

"Every year the cotton bloomed and ripened and opened white to the sun; for the ripening of the cotton and the running of the river and the turning of the mills make the thread not of my story only but of the story of our Southern land—of its institutions, of its misfortunes and of its place in the economy of the world; and they will make the main threads of its story, I am sure, so long as the sun shines on our white fields and the rivers run—a story that is now rushing swiftly into a happier narrative of a broader day. The same women who had guided the spindles in war-time were again at their tasks—they at least were left; but the machinery was now old and worked ill. Negro men, who had wandered a while looking for an invisible 'freedom,' came back and went to work on the farm from force of habit. They now received wages and bought their own food. That was the only apparent difference that freedom had brought them.

"My Aunt Katharine came from the city for a visit, my Cousin Margaret with her. Through the orchard, out into the newly ploughed ground beyond, back over the lawn which was itself bravely repairing the hurt done by horses' hoofs and tent-poles, and under the oaks, which bore the scars of camp-fires, we two romped and played gentler games than camp and battle. One afternoon, as our mothers sat on the piazza and saw us come loaded with apple-blossoms, they said something (so I afterward learned) about the eternal blooming of childhood and of Nature—how sweet the early summer was in spite of the harrying of the land by war; for our gorgeous pageant of the seasons came on as if the earth had been the home of unbroken peace."[1]

II

And so it was a tragic world into which this boy Page had been born. He was ten years old when the Civil War came to an end, and his early life was therefore cast in a desolate country. Like all of his neighbours, Frank Page had been ruined by the war. Both the Southern and Northern armies had passed over the Page territory; compared with the military depredations with which Page became familiar in the last years of his life, the Federal troops did not particularly misbehave, the attacks on hen roosts and the destruction of feather beds representing the extreme of their "atrocities"; but no country can entertain two great fighting forces without feeling the effects for a prolonged period. Life in this part of North Carolina again became reduced to its

[1] "The Southerner," Chapter I.

fundamentals. The old homesteads and the Negro huts were still left standing, and their interiors were for the most part unharmed, but nearly everything else had disappeared. Horses, cattle, hogs, livestock of all kinds had vanished before the advancing hosts of hungry soldiers; and there was one thing which was even more a rarity than these. That was money. Confederate veterans went around in their faded gray uniforms, not only because they loved them, but because they did not have the wherewithal to buy new wardrobes. Judges, planters, and other dignified members of the community became hack drivers from the necessity of picking up a few small coins. Page's father was more fortunate than the rest, for he had one asset with which to accumulate a little liquid capital; he possessed a fine peach orchard, which was particularly productive in the summer of 1865, and the Northern soldiers, who drew their pay in money that had real value, developed a weakness for the fruit. Walter Page, a boy of ten, used to take his peaches to Raleigh, and sell them to the "invader"; although he still disdained having companionable relations with the enemy, he was not above meeting them on a business footing; and the greenbacks and silver coin obtained in this way laid a new basis for the family fortunes.

Despite this happy windfall, life for the next few years proved an arduous affair. The horrors of reconstruction which followed the war were more agonizing than the war itself. Page's keenest inspiration in after life was democracy, in its several manifestations; but the form in which democracy first unrolled before his astonished eyes was a phase that could hardly inspire much enthusiasm. Misguided sentimentalists and more malicious politicians in the North had suddenly endowed the Negro with the ballot. In practically all Southern States that meant government by Negroes—or what was even worse, government by a combination of Negroes and the most vicious white elements, including that which was native to the soil and that which had imported itself from the North for this particular purpose. Thus the political vocabulary of Page's formative years consisted chiefly of such words as "scalawag," "carpet bagger," "regulator," "Union League," "Ku Klux Klan," and the like. The resulting confusion, political, social, and economic, did not completely amount to the destruction of a civilization, for underneath it all the old sleepy ante-bellum South still maintained its existence almost unchanged. The two most conspicuous and contrasting figures were the Confederate veteran walking around in a sleeveless coat and the sharp-featured New England school mar'm, armed with that spelling book which was overnight to change the African from a genial barbarian into an intelligent and conscientious social unit; but more persistent than these forces was that old dreamy, "unprogressive" Southland—the same country that Page himself described in an article on "An Old Southern Borough" which, as a young man, he contributed to the *Atlantic Monthly*. It was still the country where the "old-fashioned gentleman" was the controlling social influence, where a knowledge of Latin and Greek still made its possessor a person of consideration, where Emerson was a "Yankee philosopher" and therefore not important, where Shakespeare and Milton were looked upon almost as contemporary authors, where the Church and politics and the matrimonial history of friends and relatives formed the staple of conversation, and where a strong prejudice still existed against anything that resembled popular education. In the absence of more substantial employment, stump speaking, especially eloquent in praise of the South and its achievements in war, had become the leading industry.

"Wat" Page—he is still known by this name in his old home—was a tall, rangy, curly-headed boy, with brown hair and brown eyes, fond of fishing and hunting, not especially robust, but conspicuously alert and vital. Such of his old playmates as survive recall chiefly his keenness of observation, his contagious laughter, his devotion to reading and to talk. He was also given to taking long walks in the woods, frequently with the solitary companionship of a book. Indeed, his extremely efficient family regarded him as a dreamer and were not entirely clear as to what purpose he was destined to serve in a community which, above all, demanded practical men. Such elementary schools as North Carolina possessed had vanished in the war; the prevailing custom was for the better-conditioned families to join forces and engage a teacher for their assembled children. It was in such a primary school in Cary that Page learned the elementary branches, though his mother herself taught him to read and write. The boy showed such aptitude in his studies that his mother began to hope, though in no aggressive fashion, that he might some day become a Methodist clergyman; she had given him his middle name, "Hines," in honour of her favourite preacher—a kinsman. At the age of twelve Page was transferred to the Bingham School, then located at Mebane. This was the Eton of North Carolina, from both a social and an educational standpoint. It was a military school; the boys all dressed in gray uniforms built on the plan of the Confederate army; the hero constantly paraded before their imaginations was Robert E. Lee; discipline was rigidly military; more important, a high standard of honour was insisted upon. There was one thing a boy could not do at

Bingham and remain in the school; that was to cheat in class-rooms or at examinations. For this offence no second chance was given. "I cannot argue the subject," Page quotes Colonel Bingham saying to the distracted parent whose son had been dismissed on this charge, and who was begging for his reinstatement. "In fact, I have no power to reinstate your boy. I could not keep the honour of the school—I could not even keep the boys, if he were to return. They would appeal to their parents and most of them would be called home. They are the flower of the South, Sir!" And the social standards that controlled the thinking of the South for so many years after the war were strongly entrenched. "The son of a Confederate general," Page writes, "if he were at all a decent fellow, had, of course, a higher social rank at the Bingham School than the son of a colonel. There was some difficulty in deciding the exact rank of a judge or a governor, as a father; but the son of a preacher had a fair chance of a good social rating, especially of an Episcopalian clergyman. A Presbyterian preacher came next in rank. I at first was at a social disadvantage. My father had been a Methodist—that was bad enough; but he had had no military title at all. If it had become known among the boys that he had been a 'Union man'—I used to shudder at the suspicion in which I should be held. And the fact that my father had held no military title did at last become known!"

A single episode discloses that Page maintained his respect for the Bingham School to the end. In March, 1918, as American Ambassador, he went up to Harrow and gave an informal talk to the boys on the United States. His hosts were so pleased that two prizes were established to commemorate his visit. One was for an essay by Harrow boys on the subject: "The Drawing

Together of America and Great Britain by Common Devotion to a Great Cause." A similar prize on the same subject was offered to the boys of some American school, and Page was asked to select the recipient. He promptly named his old Bingham School in North Carolina.

It was at Bingham that Page gained his first knowledge of Greek, Latin, and mathematics, and he was an outstanding student in all three subjects. He had no particular liking for mathematics, but he could never understand why any one should find this branch of learning difficult; he mastered it with the utmost ease and always stood high. In two or three years he had absorbed everything that Bingham could offer and was ready for the next step. But political conditions in North Carolina now had their influence upon Page's educational plans. Under ordinary conditions he would have entered the State University at Chapel Hill; it had been a great headquarters in ante-bellum days for the prosperous families of the South. But by the time that Page was ready to go to college the University had fallen upon evil days. The forces which then ruled the state, acting in accordance with the new principles of racial equality, had opened the doors of this, one of the most aristocratic of Southern institutions, to Negroes. The consequences may be easily imagined. The newly enfranchised blacks showed no inclination for the groves of Academe, and not a single representative of the race applied for matriculation. The outraged white population turned its back upon this new type of coeducation; in the autumn of 1872 not a solitary white boy made his appearance. The old university therefore closed its doors for lack of students and for the next few years it became a pitiable victim to the worst vices of the reconstruction era. Politicians were awarded the presidency and the professorships as

political pap, and the resources of the place, in money and
books, were scattered to the wind. Page had therefore
to find his education elsewhere. The deep religious feelings of his family quickly settled this point. The young
man promptly betook himself to the backwoods of North
Carolina and knocked at the doors of Trinity College,
a Methodist Institution then located in Randolph County.
Trinity has since changed its abiding place to Durham
and has been transformed into one of the largest and most
successful colleges of the new South; but in those days
a famous Methodist divine and journalist described it
as "a college with a few buildings that look like tobacco
barns and a few teachers that look as though they ought
to be worming tobacco." Page spent something more
than a year at Trinity, entering in the autumn of 1871,
and leaving in December, 1872. A few letters, written
from this place, are scarcely more complimentary than
the judgment passed above. They show that the young
man was very unhappy. One long letter to his mother
is nothing but a boyish diatribe against the place. "I do
not care a horse apple for Trinity's distinction," he writes,
and then he gives the reasons for this juvenile contempt.
His first report, he says, will soon reach home; he warns
his mother that it will be unfavourable, and he explains
that this bad showing is the result of a deliberate plot.
The boys who obtain high marks, Page declares, secure
them usually by cheating or through the partisanship of
the professors; a high grade therefore really means that
the recipient is either a humbug or a bootlicker. Page
had therefore attempted to keep his reputation unsullied
by aiming at a low academic record! The report on that
three months' work, which still survives, discloses that
Page's conspiracy against himself did not succeed, for his
marks are all high. "Be sure to send him back" is the

annotation on this document, indicating that Page had made a better impression on Trinity than Trinity had made on Page.

But the rebellious young man did not return. After Christmas, 1872, his schoolboy letters reveal him at Randolph-Macon College in Ashland, Va. Here again the atmosphere is Methodistical, but of a somewhat more genial type. "It was at Ashland that I first began to unfold," said Page afterward. "Dear old Ashland!" Dr. Duncan, the President, was a clergyman whose pulpit oratory is still a tradition in the South, but, in addition to his religious exaltation, he was an exceedingly lovable, companionable, and stimulating human being. Certainly there was no lack of the religious impulse. "We have a preacher president," Page writes his mother, "a preacher secretary, a preacher chaplain, and a dozen preacher students and three or more preachers are living here and twenty-five or thirty yet-to-be preachers in college!" In this latter class Page evidently places himself; at least he gravely writes his mother—he was now eighteen—that he had definitely made up his mind to enter the Methodist ministry. He had a close friend— Wilbur Fisk Tillett—who cherished similar ambitions, and Page one day surprised Tillett by suggesting that, at the approaching Methodist Conference, they apply for licensing as "local preachers" for the next summer. His friend dissuaded him, however, and henceforth Page concentrated on more worldly studies. In many ways he was the life of the undergraduate body. His desire for an immediate theological campaign was merely that passion for doing things and for self-expression which were always conspicuous traits. His intense ambition as a boy is still remembered in this sleepy little village. He read every book in the sparse college library; he talked

Allison Francis Page (1824-1899), father of Walter H. Page

Catherine Raboteau Page (1831–1897), mother of
Walter H. Page

to his college mates and his professors on every imaginable subject; he led his associates in the miniature parliament —the Franklin Debating Society—to which he belonged; he wrote prose and verse at an astonishing rate; he explored the country for miles around, making frequent pilgrimages to the birthplace of Henry Clay, which is the chief historical glory of Ashland, and to that Hanover Court House which was the scene of the oratorical triumph of Patrick Henry; he flirted with the pretty girls in the village, and even had two half-serious love affairs in rapid succession; he slept upon a hard mattress at night and imbibed more than the usual allotment of Greek, Latin, and mathematics in the daytime. One year he captured the Greek prize and the next the Sutherlin medal for oratory. With a fellow classicist he entered into a solemn compact to hold all their conversation, even on the most trivial topics, in Latin, with heavy penalties for careless lapses into English. Probably the linguistic result would have astonished Quintilian, but the experiment at least had a certain influence in improving the young man's Latinity. Another favourite dissipation was that of translating English masterpieces into the ancient tongue; there still survives among Page's early papers a copy of Bryant's "Waterfowl" done into Latin iambics. As to Page's personal appearance, a designation coined by a fellow student who afterward became a famous editor gives the suggestion of a portrait. He called him one of the "seven slabs" of the college. And, as always, the adjectives which his contemporaries chiefly use in describing Page are "alert" and "positive."

But Randolph-Macon did one great thing for Page. Like many small struggling Southern colleges it managed to assemble several instructors of real mental distinction. And at the time of Page's undergraduate life it possessed at least one great teacher. This was Thomas R. Price, afterward Professor of Greek at the University of Virginia and Professor of English at Columbia University in New York. Professor Price took one forward step that has given him a permanent fame in the history of Southern education. He found that the greatest stumbling block to teaching Greek was not the conditional mood, but the fact that his hopeful charges were not sufficiently familiar with their mother tongue. The prayer that was always on Price's lips, and the one with which he made his boys most familiar, was that of a wise old Greek: "O Great Apollo, send down the reviving rain upon our fields; preserve our flocks; ward off our enemies; and—build up our speech!" "It is irrational," he said, "absurd, almost criminal, to expect a young man, whose knowledge of English words and construction is scant and inexact, to put into English a difficult thought of Plato or an involved period of Cicero." Above all, it will be observed, Price's intellectual enthusiasm was the ancient tongue. A present-day argument for learning Greek and Latin is that thereby we improve our English; but Thomas R. Price advocated the teaching of English so that we might better understand the dead languages. To-day every great American educational institution has vast resources for teaching English literature; even in 1876, most American universities had their professors of English; but Price insisted on placing English on exactly the same footing as Greek and Latin. He himself became head of the new English school at Randolph-Macon; and Page himself at once became the favourite pupil. This distinguished scholar—a fine figure with an imperial beard that suggested the Confederate officer—used to have Page to tea at least twice a week and at these meetings the young man was first introduced in an understanding way to Shakespeare, Milton, Wordsworth, Tennyson, and the other writers who became the literary passions of his maturer life. And Price did even more for Page; he passed him on to another place and to another teacher who extended his horizon. Up to the autumn of 1876 Page had never gone farther North than Ashland; he was still a Southern boy, speaking with the Southern drawl, living exclusively the thoughts and even the prejudices of the South. His family's broad-minded attitude had prevented him from acquiring a too restricted view of certain problems that were then vexing both sections of the country; however, his outlook was still a limited one, as his youthful correspondence shows. But in October of the centennial year a great prospect opened before him.

III

Two or three years previously an eccentric merchant named Johns Hopkins had died, leaving the larger part of his fortune to found a college or university in Baltimore. Johns Hopkins was not an educated man himself and his conception of a new college did not extend beyond creating something in the nature of a Yale or Harvard in Maryland. By a lucky chance, however, a Yale graduate who was then the President of the University of California, Daniel Coit Gilman, was invited to come to Baltimore and discuss with the trustees his availability for the headship of the new institution. Dr. Gilman promptly informed his prospective employers that he would have no interest in associating himself with a new American college built upon the lines of those which then existed. Such a foundation would merely be a duplication of work already well done elsewhere and therefore a waste of money and effort. He proposed that this large endowment should be used, not for the erection of expensive architecture, but primarily for seeking out, in all parts of the world, the best professorial brains in certain approved branches of learning.   In the same spirit he suggested that a similarly selective process be adopted in the choice of students: that only those American boys who had displayed exceptional promise should be admitted and that part of the university funds should be used to pay the expenses of twenty young men who, in undergraduate work at other colleges, stood head and shoulders above their contemporaries.   The bringing together of these two sets of brains for graduate study would constitute the new university.   A few rooms in the nearest dwelling house would suffice for headquarters.   Dr. Gilman's scheme was approved; he became President on these terms; he gathered his faculty not only in the United States but in England, and he collected his first body of students, especially his first twenty fellows, with the same minute care.

It seems almost a miracle that an inexperienced youth in a little Methodist college in Virginia should have been chosen as one of these first twenty fellows, and it is a sufficient tribute to the impression that Page must have made upon all who met him that he should have won this great academic distinction.   He was only twenty-one at the time—the youngest of a group nearly every member of which became distinguished in after life.   He won a Fellowship in Greek.   This in itself was a great good fortune; even greater was the fact that his new life brought him into immediate contact with a scholar of great genius and lovableness.   Someone has said that America has produced four scholars of the very first rank—Agassiz in natural science, Whitney in philology, Willard Gibbs in physics, and Gildersleeve in Greek.   It was the last of these who now took Walter Page in charge.

The atmosphere of Johns Hopkins was quite different from anything which the young man had previously known. The university gave a great shock to that part of the American community with which Page had spent his life by beginning its first session in October, 1876, without an opening prayer. Instead Thomas H. Huxley was invited from England to deliver a scientific address—an address which now has an honoured place in his collected works. The absence of prayer and the presence of so audacious a Darwinian as Huxley caused a tremendous excitement in the public prints, the religious press, and the evangelical pulpit. In the minds of Gilman and his abettors, however, all this was intended to emphasize the fact that Johns Hopkins was a real university, in which the unbiased truth was to be the only aim. And certainly this was the spirit of the institution. "Gentlemen, you must light your own torch," was the admonition of President Gilman, in his welcoming address to his twenty fellows; intellectual independence, freedom from the trammels of tradition, were thus to be the directing ideas. One of Page's associates was Josiah Royce, who afterward had a distinguished career in philosophy at Harvard. "The beginnings of Johns Hopkins," he afterward wrote, "was a dawn wherein it was bliss to be alive. The air was full of noteworthy work done by the older men of the place and of hopes that one might find a way to get a little working power one's self. One longed to be a doer of the word, not a hearer only, a creator of his own infinitesimal fraction of the product, bound in God's name to produce when the time came."

A choice group of five aspiring Grecians, of whom Page was one, periodically gathered around a long pine table in a second-story room of an old dwelling house on Howard Street, with Professor Gildersleeve at the head. The process of teaching was thus the intimate contact of mind with mind. Here in the course of nearly two years' residence, Page was led by Professor Gildersleeve into the closest communion with the great minds of the ancient world and gained that intimate knowledge of their written word which was the basis of his mental equipment. "Professor Gildersleeve, splendid scholar that he is!" he wrote to a friend in North Carolina. "He makes me grow wonderfully. When I have a chance to enjoy Æschylus as I have now, I go to work on those immortal pieces with a pleasure that swallows up everything." To the extent that Gildersleeve opened up the literary treasures of the past—and no man had a greater appreciation of his favourite authors than this fine humanist—Page's life was one of unalloyed delight. But there was another side to the picture. This little company of scholars was composed of men who aspired to no ordinary knowledge of Greek; they expected to devote their entire lives to the subject, to edit Greek texts, and to hold Greek chairs at the leading American universities. Such, indeed, has been the career of nearly all members of the group. The Greek tragedies were therefore read for other things than their stylistic and dramatic values. The sons of Germania then exercised a profound influence on American education; Professor Gildersleeve himself was a graduate of Göttingen, and the necessity of "settling hoti's business" was strong in his seminar. Gildersleeve was a writer of English who developed real style; as a Greek scholar, his fame rests chiefly upon his work in the field of historical syntax. He assumed that his students could read Greek as easily as they could read French, and the really important tasks he set them had to do with the most abstruse fields of philology. For work of this kind Page had little interest and less inclination. When Professor Gildersleeve would assign him the adverb πρίν, and direct him to study the peculiarities of its use from Homer down to the Byzantine writers, he found himself in pretty deep waters. Was it conceivable that a man could spend a lifetime in an occupation of this kind? By pursuing such studies Gildersleeve and his most advanced pupils uncovered many new facts about the language and even found hitherto unsuspected beauties; but Page's letters show that this sort of effort was extremely uncongenial. He fulminates against the "grammarians" and begins to think that perhaps, after all, a career of erudite scholarship is not the ideal existence. "Learn to look on me as a Greek drudge," he writes, "somewhere pounding into men and boys a faint hint of the beauty of old Greekdom. That's most probably what I shall come to before many years. I am sure that I have mistaken my lifework, if I consider Greek my lifework. In truth at times I am tempted to throw the whole thing away. . . . But without a home feeling in Greek literature no man can lay claim to high culture." So he would keep at it for three or four years and "then leave it as a man's work." Despite these despairing words Page acquired a living knowledge of Greek that was one of his choicest possessions through life. That he made a greater success than his self-depreciation would imply is evident from the fact that his Fellowship was renewed for the next year.

But the truth is that the world was tugging at Page more insistently than the cloister. "Speaking grammatically," writes Prof. E. G. Sihler, one of Page's fellow students of that time, in his "Confessions and Convictions of a Classicist," "Page was interested in that one of the main tenses which we call the Present." In his after life, amid all the excitements of journalism, Page could take a brief vacation and spend it with Ulysses by the sea; but actuality and human activity charmed him even more than did the heroes of the ancient world. He went somewhat into Baltimore society, but not extensively; he joined a club whose membership comprised the leading intellectual men of the town; probably his most congenial associations, however, came of the Saturday night meetings of the fellows in Hopkins Hall, where, over pipes and steins of beer, they passed in review all the questions of the day. Page was still the Southern boy, with the strange notions about the North and Northern people which were the inheritance of many years' misunderstandings. He writes of one fellow student to whom he had taken a liking. "He is that rare thing," he says, "a Yankee Christian gentleman." He particularly dislikes one of his instructors, but, as he explains, he is a native of Connecticut, and Connecticut, I suppose, is capable of producing any unholy human phenomenon." Speaking of a beautiful and well mannered Greek girl whom he had met, he writes: "The little creature might be taken for a Southern girl, but never for a Yankee. She has an easy manner and even an air of gentility about her that doesn't appear north of Mason and Dixon's Line. Indeed, however much the Southern race (I say race intentionally: Yankeedom is the home of another race from us) however much the Southern race owes its strength to Anglo-Saxon blood, it owes its beauty and gracefulness to the Southern climate and culture. Who says that we are not an improvement on the English? An improvement in a happy combination of mental graces and Saxon force?" This sort of thing is especially entertaining in the youthful Page, for it is precisely against this kind of complacency that, as a mature man, he directed his choicest ridicule. As an editor and writer his energies were devoted to reconciling North and South, and Johns Hopkins itself had much to do with opening his eyes. Its young men and its professors were gathered from all parts of the country; a student, if his mind was awake, learned more than Greek and mathematics; he learned much about that far-flung nation known as the United States.

And Page did not confine his work exclusively to the curriculum. He writes that he is regularly attending a German Sunday School, not, however, from religious motives, but from a desire to improve his colloquial German. "Is this courting the Devil for knowledge?" he asks. And all this time he was engaging in a delightful correspondence—from which these quotations are taken —with a young woman in North Carolina, his cousin. About this time this cousin began spending her summers in the Page home at Cary; her great interest in books made the two young people good friends and companions. It was she who first introduced Page to certain Southern writers, especially Timrod and Sidney Lanier, and, when Page left for Johns Hopkins, the two entered into a compact for a systematic reading and study of the English poets. According to this plan, certain parts of Tennyson or Chaucer would be set aside for a particular week's read- ing; then both would write the impressions gained and the criticisms which they assumed to make, and send the product to the other. The plan was carried out more faithfully than is usually the case in such arrangements; a large number of Page's letters survive and give a complete history of his mental progress. There are lengthy dis- quisitions on Wordsworth, Browning, Byron, Shelley, Matthew Arnold, and the like. These letters also show that Page, as a relaxation from Greek roots and syntax, was indulging in poetic flights of his own; his efforts, which he encloses in his letters, are mainly imitations of the particular poet in whom he was at the moment interested. This correspondence also takes Page to Germany, in which country he spent the larger part of the summer of 1877. This choice of the Fatherland as a place of pilgrimage was probably merely a reflection of the enthusiasm for German educational methods which then prevailed in the United States, especially at Johns Hopkins. Page's letters are the usual traveller's descriptions of unfamiliar customs, museums, libraries, and the like; so far as enlarging his outlook was concerned the experience does not seem to have been especially profitable.

He returned to Baltimore in the autumn of 1877, but only for a few months. He had pretty definitely abandoned his plan of devoting his life to Greek scholarship. As a mental stimulus, as a recreation from the cares of life, his Greek authors would always be a first love, as they proved to be; but he had abandoned his early ambition of making them his everyday occupation and means of livelihood. Of course there was only one career for a man of his leanings, and, more and more, his mind was turning to journalism. For only one brief period did he again listen to the temptations of a scholar's existence. The university of his native state invited him to lecture in the summer school of 1878; he took Shakespeare for his subject, and made so great a success that there was some discussion of his settling down permanently at Chapel Hill in the chair of Greek. Had the offer definitely been made Page would probably have accepted, but difficulties arose. Page was no longer orthodox in his religious views; he had long outgrown dogma and could only smile at the recollection that he had once thought of becoming a clergyman. But a rationalist at the University of North Carolina in 1878 could hardly be endured. The offer, therefore, fortunately was not made. Afterward Page was much criticized for having left his native state at a time when it especially needed young men of his type. It may therefore be recorded that, if there were any blame at all, it rested upon North Carolina. He refers to his disappointment in a letter in February, 1879—a letter that proved to be a prophecy. "I shall some day buy a home," he says, "where I was not allowed to work for one, and be laid away in the soil that I love. I wanted to work for the old state; it had no need for it, it seems."

CHAPTER II

JOURNALISM

I

THE five years from 1878 to 1883 Page spent in various places, engaged, for the larger part of the time, in several kinds of journalistic work. It was his period of struggle and of preparation. Like many American public men he served a brief apprenticeship—in his case, a very brief one—as a pedagogue. In the autumn of 1878 he went to Louisville, Kentucky, and taught English for a year at the Boys' High School. But he presently found an occupation in this progressive city which proved far more absorbing. A few months before his arrival certain energetic spirits had founded a weekly paper, the *Age*, a journal which, they hoped, would fill the place in the Southern States which the very successful New York *Nation*, under the editorship of Godkin, was then occupying in the North. Page at once began contributing leading articles on literary and political topics to this publication; the work proved so congenial that he purchased—on notes—a controlling interest in the new venture and became its directing spirit. The *Age* was in every way a worthy enterprise; in the dignity of its make-up and the high literary standards at which it aimed it imitated the London *Spectator*. Perhaps Page obtained a thousand dollars' worth of fun out of his investment; if so, that represented his entire profit. He now learned a lesson which was emphasized in his after career as editor and publisher, and that was that the Southern States pro-

32

vided a poor market for books or periodicals. The net result of the proceeding was that, at the age of twenty-three, he found himself out of a job and considerably in debt.

He has himself rapidly sketched his varied activities of the next five years:

"After trying in vain," he writes, "to get work to do on any newspaper in North Carolina, I advertised for a job in journalism—any sort of a job. By a queer accident —a fortunate one for me—the owner of the St. Joseph, Missouri, *Gazette*, answered the advertisement. Why he did it, I never found out. He was in the same sort of desperate need of a newspaper man as I was in desperate need of a job. I knew nothing about him: he knew nothing about me. I knew nothing about newspaper work. I had done nothing since I left the University but teach English in the Louisville, Kentucky, High School for boys one winter and lecture at the summer school at Chapel Hill one summer. I made up my mind to go into journalism. But journalism didn't seem in any hurry to make up its mind to admit me. Not only did all the papers in North Carolina decline my requests for work, but such of them in Baltimore and Louisville as I tried said 'No.' So I borrowed $50 and set out to St. Joe, Missouri, where I didn't know a human being. I became a reporter. At first I reported the price of cattle—went to the stockyards, etc. My salary came near to paying my board and lodging, but it didn't quite do it. But I had a good time in St. Joe for somewhat more than a year. There were interesting people there. I came to know something about Western life. Kansas was across the river. I often went there. I came to know Kansas City, St. Louis—a good deal of the West. After a while I was made editor of the paper. What a rousing political campaign or two we had!

Then—I had done that kind of a job as long as I cared to. Every swashbuckling campaign is like every other one. Why do two? Besides, I knew my trade. I had done everything on a daily paper from stockyard reports to political editorials and heavy literary articles. In the meantime I had written several magazine articles and done other such jobs. I got leave of absence for a month or two. I wrote to several of the principal papers in Chicago, New York, and Boston and told them that I was going down South to make political and social studies and that I was going to send them my letters. I hoped they'd publish them.

"That's all I could say. I could make no engagement; they didn't know me. I didn't even ask for an engagement. I told them simply this: that I'd write letters and send them; and I prayed heaven that they'd print them and pay for them. Then off I went with my little money in my pocket—about enough to get to New Orleans. I travelled and I wrote. I went all over the South. I sent letters and letters and letters. All the papers published all that I sent them and I was rolling in wealth! I had money in my pocket for the first time in my life. Then I went back to St. Joe and resigned; for the (old) New York *World* had asked me to go to the Atlanta Exposition as a correspondent. I went. I wrote and kept writing. How kind Henry Grady was to me! But at last the Exposition ended. I was out of a job. I applied to the *Constitution*. No, they wouldn't have me. I never got a job in my life that I asked for! But all my life better jobs have been given me than I dared ask for. Well— I was at the end of my rope in Atlanta and I was trying to make a living in any honest way I could when one day a telegram came from the New York *World* (it was the old *World*, which was one of the best of the dailies in its

literary quality) asking me to come to New York. I had
never seen a man on the paper—had never been in New
York except for a day when I landed there on a return
voyage from a European trip that I took during one vacation when I was in the University. Then I went to New
York straight and quickly. I had an interesting experience
on the old *World*, writing literary matter chiefly, an editorial now and then, and I was frequently sent as a correspondent on interesting errands. I travelled all over the
country with the Tariff Commission. I spent one winter
in Washington as a sort of editorial correspondent while
the tariff bill was going through Congress. Then, one
day, the *World* was sold to Mr. Pulitzer and all the staff
resigned. The character of the paper changed."

What better training could a journalist ask for than
this? Page was only twenty-eight when these five years
came to an end; but his life had been a comprehensive
education in human contact, in the course of which he had
picked up many things that were not included in the routine of Johns Hopkins University. From Athens to St.
Joe, from the comedies of Aristophanes to the stockyards
and political conventions of Kansas City—the transition
may possibly have been an abrupt one, but it is not likely
that Page so regarded it. For books and the personal
relation both appealed to him, in almost equal proportions,
as essentials to the fully rounded man. Merely from the
standpoint of geography, Page's achievement had been an
important one; how many Americans, at the age of
twenty-eight, have such an extensive mileage to their
credit? Page had spent his childhood—and his childhood
only—in North Carolina; he had passed his youth in
Virginia and Maryland; before he was twenty-three he had
lived several months in Germany, and, on his return
voyage, he had sailed by the white cliffs of England, and,

from the deck of his steamer, had caught glimpses of that Isle of Wight which then held his youthful favourite Tennyson. He had added to these experiences a winter in Kentucky and a sojourn of nearly two years in Missouri. His Southern trip, to which Page refers in the above, had taken him through Tennessee, Mississippi, Alabama, Georgia, and Louisiana; he had visited the West again in 1882, spending a considerable time in all the large cities, Chicago, Omaha, Denver, Leadville, Salt Lake, and from the latter point he had travelled extensively through Mormondom. The several months spent in Atlanta had given the young correspondent a glimpse into the new South, for this energetic city embodied a Southern spirit that was several decades removed from the Civil War. After this came nearly two years in New York and Washington, where Page gained his first insight into Federal politics; in particular, as a correspondent attached to the Tariff Commission—an assignment that again started him on his travels to industrial centres—he came into contact, for the first time, with the mechanism of framing the great American tariff. And during this period Page was not only forming a first-hand acquaintance with the passing scene, but also with important actors in it. The mere fact that, on the St. Joseph *Gazette*, he succeeded Eugene Field—"a good fellow named Page is going to take my desk," said the careless poet, "I hope he will succeed to my debts too"—always remained a pleasant memory. He entered zealously into the life of this active community; his love of talk and disputation, his interest in politics, his hearty laugh, his vigorous handclasp, his animation of body and of spirit, and his sunny outlook on men and events—these are the traits that his old friends in this town, some of whom still survive, associate with the juvenile editor. In his Southern trip Page called—self-

Walter H. Page in 1876, when he was a Fellow of Johns Hopkins
University, Baltimore, Md.

Basil L. Gildersleeve, Professor of Greek, Johns Hopkins University, 1876-1915

invited—upon Jefferson Davis and was cordially received. At Atlanta, as he records above, he made friends
with that chivalric champion of a resurrected South,
Henry Grady; here also he obtained fugitive glimpses
of a struggling and briefless lawyer, who, like Page, was
interested more in books and writing than in the hum-
drum of professional life, and who was then engaged
in putting together a brochure on *Congressional Government* which immediately gave him a national standing.
The name of this sympathetic acquaintance was Woodrow Wilson.

Another important event had taken place, for, at St.
Louis, on November 15, 1880, Page had married Miss
Willia Alice Wilson. Miss Wilson was the daughter of a
Scotch physician, Dr. William Wilson, who had settled
in Michigan, near Detroit, in 1832. When she was a
small child she went with her sister's family—her father
had died seven years before—to North Carolina, near
Cary; and she and Page had been childhood friends and
schoolmates. At the time of the wedding, Page was
editor of the St. Joseph *Gazette;* the fact that he had
attained this position, five months after starting at the
bottom, sufficiently discloses his aptitude for journalistic
work.

Page had now outgrown any Southern particularism
with which he may have started life. He no longer found
his country exclusively in the area south of the Potomac;
he had made his own the West, the North—New York,
Chicago, Denver, as well as Atlanta and Raleigh. It is
worth while insisting on this fact, for the cultivation of a
wide-sweeping Americanism and a profound faith in democracy became the qualities that will loom most largely in
his career from this time forward. It is necessary only to
read the newspaper letters which he wrote on his Southern

trip in 1881 to understand how early his mind seized this new point of view. Many things which now fell under his observant eye in the Southern States greatly irritated him and with his characteristic impulsiveness he pictured these traits in pungent phrase. The atmosphere of shiftlessness that too generally prevailed in some localities; the gangs of tobacco-chewing loafers assembled around railway stations; the listless Negroes that seemed to overhang the whole country like a black cloud; the plantation mansions in a sad state of disrepair; the old unoccupied slave huts overgrown with weeds; the unpainted and broken-down fences; the rich soil that was crudely and wastefully cultivated with a single crop—the youthful social philosopher found himself comparing these vestigia of a half-moribund civilization with the vibrant cities of the North, the beautiful white and green villages of New England, and the fertile prairie farms of the West. "Even the dogs," he said, "look old-fashioned." Oh, for a change in his beloved South—a change of almost any kind! "Even a heresy, if it be bright and fresh, would be a relief. You feel as if you wished to see some kind of an effort put forth, a discussion, a fight, a runaway, anything to make the blood go faster." Wherever Page saw signs of a new spirit—and he saw many—he recorded them with an eagerness which showed his loyalty to the section of his birth. The splitting up of great plantations into small farms he put down as one of the indications of a new day. A growing tendency to educate, not only the white child, but the Negro, inspired a similar tribute. But he rejoiced most over the decreasing bitterness of the masses over the memories of the Civil War, and discovered, with satisfaction, that any remaining ill-feeling was a heritage left not by the Union soldier, but by the carpetbagger.

And one scene is worth preserving, for it illustrates not only the zeal of Page himself for the common country, but the changing attitude of the Southern people. It was enacted at Martin, Tennessee, on the evening of July 2, 1881. Page was spending a few hours in the village grocery, discussing things in general with the local yeomanry, when the telegraph operator came from the post office with rather more than his usual expedition and excitement. He was frantically waving a yellow slip which bore the news that President Garfield had been shot. Garfield had been an energetic and a successful general in the war and his subsequent course in Congress, where he had joined the radical Republicans, had not caused the South to look upon him as a friend. But these farmers responded to this shock, not like sectionalists, but like Americans. "Every man of them," Page records, "expressed almost a personal sorrow. Little was said of politics or of parties. Mr. Garfield was President of the United States—that was enough. A dozen voices spoke the great gratification that the assassin was not a Southern man. It was an affecting scene to see weatherbeaten old countrymen so profoundly agitated—men who yesterday I should have supposed hardly knew and certainly did not seem to care who was President. The great centres of population, of politicians, and of thought may be profoundly agitated to-night, but no more patriotic sorrow and humiliation is felt anywhere by any men than by these old backwoods ex-Confederates."

Page himself was so stirred by the news that he ascended a cracker barrel, and made a speech to the assembled countrymen, preaching to responsive ears the theme of North and South, now reunited in a common sorrow. Thus, by the time he was twenty-six, Page, at any rate in respect to his Americanism, was a full-grown man.

II

A few years afterward Page had an opportunity of discussing this, his favourite topic, with the American whom he most admired. Perhaps the finest thing in the career of Grover Cleveland was the influence which he exerted upon young men. After the sordid political transactions of the reconstruction period and after the orgy of partisanship which had followed the Civil War, this new figure, acceding to the Presidency in 1885, came as an inspiration to millions of zealous and intelligent young college-bred Americans. One of the first to feel the new spell was Walter Page; Mr. Cleveland was perhaps the most important influence in forming his public ideals. Of everything that Cleveland represented—civil service reform; the cleansing of politics, state and national; the reduction in the tariff; a foreign policy which, without degenerating into truculence, manfully upheld the rights of American citizens; a determination to curb the growing pension evil; the doctrine that the Government was something to be served and not something to be plundered—Page became an active and brilliant journalistic advocate. It was therefore a great day in his life when, on a trip to Washington in the autumn of 1885, he had an hour's private conversation with President Cleveland, and it was entirely characteristic of Page that he should make the conversation take the turn of a discussion of the so-called Southern question.

"In the White House at Washington," Page wrote about this visit, "is an honest, plain, strong man, a man of wonderfully broad information and of most uncommon industry. He has always been a Democrat. He is a distinguished lawyer and a scholar on all public questions. He is as frank and patriotic and sincere as any man that ever won the high place he holds. Within less than a year he has done so well and so wisely that he has disappointed his enemies and won their admiration. He is as unselfish as he is great. He is one of the most industrious men in the world. He rises early and works late and does not waste his time—all because his time is now not his own but the Republic's, whose most honoured servant he is. I count it among the most inspiring experiences in my life that I had the privilege, at the suggestion of one of his personal friends, of talking with him one morning about the complete reuniting of the two great sections of our Republic by his election. I told him, and I know I told him the truth, when I said that every young man in the Southern States who, without an opportunity to share either the glory or the defeat of the late Confederacy, had in spite of himself suffered the disadvantages of the poverty and oppression that followed war, took new hope for the full and speedy realization of a complete union, of unparalleled prosperity and of broad thinking and noble living from his elevation to the Presidency. I told him that the men of North Carolina were not only patriotic but ambitious as well; and that they were Democrats and proud citizens of the State and the Republic not because they wanted offices or favours, but because they loved freedom and wished the land that had been impoverished by war to regain more than it had lost. 'I have not called, Mr. President, to ask for an office for myself or for anybody else,' I remarked; 'but to have the pleasure of expressing my gratification, as a citizen of North Carolina, at the complete change in political methods and morals that I believe will date from your Administration.' He answered that he was glad to see all men who came in such a spirit and did not come to beg—especially young men of the South of to-day; and he talked and encouraged me to talk freely as if he had been as small a man as I am, or I as great a man as he is.

"From that day to this it has been my business to watch every public act that he does, to read every public word he speaks, and it has been a pleasure and a benefit to me (like the benefit that a man gets from reading a great history—for he is making a great history) to study the progress of his Administration; and at every step he seems to me to warrant the trust that the great Democratic party put in him."

The period to which Page refers in this letter represented the time when he was making a serious and harassing attempt to establish himself in his chosen profession in his native state. He went south for a short visit after resigning his place on the New York *World*, and several admirers in Raleigh persuaded him to found a new paper, which should devote itself to preaching the Cleveland ideals, and, above all, to exerting an influence on the development of a new Southern spirit. No task could have been more grateful to Page and there was no place in which he would have better liked to undertake it than in the old state which he loved so well. The result was the *State Chronicle* of Raleigh, practically a new paper, which for a year and a half proved to be the most unconventional and refreshing influence that North Carolina had known in many a year. Necessarily Page found himself in conflict with his environment. He had little interest in the things that then chiefly interested the state, and North Carolina apparently had little interest in the things that chiefly occupied the mind of the youthful journalist. Page was interested in Cleveland, in the reform of the civil service; the Democrats of North Carolina little appreciated their great national leader and were especially hostile to his belief that service to a party did not in itself establish a qualification for public office. Page was interested in uplifting the common people, in helping every farmer to own his own acres, and in teaching the most modern and scientific way of cultivating them; he was interested in giving every boy and girl at least an elementary education, and in giving a university training to such as had the aptitude and the ambition to obtain it; he believed in industrial training —and in these things the North Carolina of those days had little concern. Page even went so far as to take an open stand for the pitiably neglected black man: he insisted that he should be taught to read and write, and instructed in agriculture and the manual trades. A man who advocated such revolutionary things in those days was accused—and Page was so accused—of attempting to promote the "social equality" of the two races. Page also declaimed in favour of developing the state industrially; he called attention to the absurdity of sending Southern cotton to New England spinning mills, and he pointed out the boundless but unworked natural resources of the state, in minerals, forests, waterpower, and lands.

North Carolina, he informed his astonished compatriots, had once been a great manufacturing colony; why could the state not become one again? But the matter in which the buoyant editor and his constituents found themselves most at variance was the spirit that controlled North Carolina life. It was a spirit that found comfort for its present poverty and lack of progress in a backward look at the greatness of the state in the past and the achievements of its sons in the Civil War. Though Page believed that the Confederacy had been a ghastly error, and though he abhorred the institution of slavery and attributed to it all the woes, economic and social, from which his section suffered, he rendered that homage to the soldiers of the South which is the due of brave, self-sacrificing and conscientious men; yet he taught that progress lay in regarding the four dreadful years of the Civil War as the closed chapter of an unhappy and mistaken history and in hastening the day when the South should resume its place as a living part of the great American democracy. All manifestations of a contrary spirit he ridiculed in language which was extremely readable but which at times outraged the good conservative people whom he was attempting to convert. He did not even spare the one figure which was almost a part of the Southerner's religion, the Confederate general, especially that particular type who used his war record as a stepping stone to public office, and whose oratory, colourful and turgid in its celebrations of the past, Page regarded as somewhat unrelated, in style and matter, to the realities of the present. The image-breaking editor even asserted that the Daughters of the Confederacy were not entirely a helpful influence in Southern regeneration; for they, too, were harping always upon the old times and keeping alive sectional antagonisms and hatreds. This he regarded as an unworthy occupation for high-minded Southern women, and he said so, sometimes in language that made him very unpopular in certain circles.

Altogether it was a piquant period in Page's life. He found that he had suddenly become a "traitor" to his country and that his experiences in the North had completely "Yankeeized" him. Even in more mature days, Page's pen had its javelin-like quality; and in 1884, possessed as he was of all the fury of youth, he never hesitated to return every blow that was rained upon his head. As

a matter of fact he had a highly enjoyable time.   The
State Chronicle during his editorship is one of the most
cherished recollections of older North Carolinians to-day.
Even those who hurled the liveliest epithets in his direction have long since accepted the ideas for which Page
was then contending; "the only trouble with him," they
now ruefully admit, "was that he was forty years ahead
of his time."   They recall with satisfaction the satiric
accounts which Page used to publish of Democratic Conventions—solemn, long-winded, frock-coated, white-neck-
tied affairs that displayed little concern for the reform of
the tariff or of the civil service, but an energetic interest in
pensioning Confederate veterans and erecting monuments
to the Southern heroes of the Civil War.   One editorial
is joyfully recalled, in which Page referred to a public
officer who was distinguished for his dignity and his
family tree, but not noted for any animated administration of his duties, as "Thothmes II."   When this be-
wildered functionary searched the Encyclopædia and
learned that "Thothmes II" was an Egyptian king of the
XVIIIth dynasty, whose dessicated mummy had recently been disinterred from the hot sands of the desert,
he naturally stopped his subscription to the paper.
The metaphor apparently tickled Page, for he used it in
a series of articles which have become immortal in the
political annals of North Carolina.   These have always
been known as the "Mummy letters."   They furnished
a vivid but rather aggravating explanation for the
existing backwardness and chauvinism of the commonwealth.   All the trouble, it seems, was caused by the
"mummies."   "It is an awfully discouraging business,"
Page wrote, "to undertake to prove to a mummy that it
is a mummy.   You go up to it and say, 'Old fellow, the
Egyptian dynasties crumbled several thousand years ago:

you are a fish out of water. You have by accident or the Providence of God got a long way out of your time. This is America.' The old thing grins that grin which death set on its solemn features when the world was young; and your task is so pitiful that even the humour of it is gone. Give it up."

Everything great in North Carolina, Page declared, belonged to a vanished generation. "Our great lawyers, great judges, great editors, are all of the past. . . . In the general intelligence of the people, in intellectual force and in cultivation, we are doing nothing. We are not doing or getting more liberal ideas, a broader view of this world. . . . The presumptuous powers of ignorance, heredity, decayed respectability and stagnation that control public action and public expression are absolutely leading us back intellectually."

But Page did more than berate the mummified aristocracy which, he declared, was driving the best talent and initiative from the state; he was not the only man in Raleigh who expressed these unpopular views; at that time, indeed, he was the centre and inspiration of a group of young progressive spirits who held frequent meetings to devise ways of starting the state on the road to a new existence. Page then, as always, exercised a great fascination over young men. The apparently merciless character of his ridicule might at first convey the idea of intolerance; the fact remains, however, that he was the most tolerant of men; he was almost deferential to the opinions of others, even the shallow and the inexperienced; and nothing delighted him more than an animated discussion. His liveliness of spirits, his mental and physical vitality, the constant sparkle of his talk, the sharp edge of his humour, naturally drew the younger men to his side. The result was the organization of the Wautauga Club, a gathering

which held monthly meetings for the discussion of ways
and means of improving social and educational conditions in North Carolina. The very name gives the key
to its mental outlook. The Wautauga colony was one of
the last founded in North Carolina—in the extreme west,
on a plateau of the Great Smoky Mountains; it was
always famous for the energy and independence of its
people. The word "Wautauga" therefore suggested the
breaker of tradition; and it provided a stimulating name
for Page's group of young spiritual and economic path-
finders. The Wautauga Club had a brief existence of a
little more than two years, the period practically covering
Page's residence in the state; but its influence is an important fact at the present time. It gave the state ideas
that afterward caused something like a revolution in its
economic and educational status. The noblest monument
to its labours is the State College in Raleigh, an institution
which now has more than a thousand students, for the
most part studying the mechanic arts and scientific agriculture. To this one college most North Carolinians
to-day attribute the fact that their state in appreciable
measure is realizing its great economic and industrial
opportunities. From it in the last thirty years thousands
of young men have gone: in all sections of the commonwealth they have caused the almost barren acres to yield
fertile and diversified crops; they have planted everywhere new industries; they have unfolded unsuspected
resources and everywhere created wealth and spread
enlightenment. This institution is a direct outcome of
Page's brief sojourn in his native state nearly forty years
ago. The idea originated in his brain; the files of the
State Chronicle tell the story of his struggle in its behalf;
the activities of the Wautauga Club were largely concentrated upon securing its establishment.

The State College was a great victory for Page, but final success did not come until three years after he had left the state. For a year and a half of hard newspaper work convinced Page that North Carolina really had no permanent place for him. The *Chronicle* was editorially a success: Page's articles were widely quoted, not only in his own state but in New England and other parts of the Union. He succeeded in stirring up North Carolina and the South generally, but popular support for the *Chronicle* was not forthcoming in sufficient amount to make the paper a commercial possib'lity. Reluctantly and sadly Page had to forego his hope of playing an active part in rescuing his state from the disasters of the Civil War. Late in the summer of 1885, he again left for the North, which now became his permanent home.

III

And with this second sojourn in New York Page's opportunity came. The first two years he spent in newspaper work, for the most part with the *Evening Post*, but, one day in November, 1887, a man whom he had never seen came into his office and unfolded a new opportunity. Two years before a rather miscellaneous group had launched an ambitious literary undertaking. This was a monthly periodical, which, it was hoped, would do for the United States what such publications as the *Fortnightly* and the *Contemporary* were doing for England. The magazine was to have the highest literary quality and to be sufficiently dignified to attract the finest minds in America as contributors; its purpose was to exercise a profound influence in politics, literature, science, and art. The projectors had selected for this publication a title that was almost perfection—the *Forum*—but that, after nearly two years' experimentation, represented about the limit of their achievement. The *Forum* had hardly made an impression on public thought and had attracted very few readers, although it had lost large sums of money for its progenitors. These public-spirited gentlemen now turned to Page as the man who might rescue them from their dilemma and achieve their purpose. He accepted the engagement, first as manager and presently as editor, and remained the guiding spirit of the *Forum* for eight years, until the summer of 1895.

That the success of a publication is the success of its editors, and not of its business managers and its "backers," is a truth that ought to be generally apparent; never has this fact been so eloquently illustrated as in the case of the *Forum* under Page. Before his accession it had had not the slightest importance; for the period of his editorship it is doubtful if any review published in English exercised so great an influence, and certainly none ever obtained so large a circulation. From almost nothing the *Forum*, in two or three years, attracted 30,000 subscribers—something without precedent for a publication of this character. It had accomplished this great result simply because of the vitality and interest of its contents. The period covered was an important one, in the United States and Europe; it was the time of Cleveland's second administration in this country, and of Gladstone's fourth administration in England; it was a time of great controversy and of a growing interest in science, education, social reform and a better political order. All these great matters were reflected in the pages of the *Forum*, whose list of contributors contained the most distinguished names in all countries. Its purpose, as Page explained it, was "to provoke discussion about subjects of contemporary interest, in which the magazine is not a partisan, but merely the instrument." In the highest sense, that is, its purpose was journalistic; practically everything that it printed was related to the thought and the action of the time. So insistent was Page on this programme that his pages were not "closed" until a week before the day of issue. Though the *Forum* dealt constantly in controversial subjects it never did so in a narrow-minded spirit; it was always ready to hear both sides of a question and the magazine "debate," in which opposing writers handled vigorously the same theme, was a constant feature.

Page, indeed, represented a new type of editor. Up to that time this functionary had been a rather solemn, inaccessible high priest; he sat secluded in his sanctuary, and weeded out from the mass of manuscripts dumped upon his desk the particular selections which seemed to be most suited to his purpose. To solicit contributions would have seemed an entirely undignified proceeding; in all cases contributors must come to him. According to Page, however, "an editor must know men and be out among men." His system of "making up" the magazine at first somewhat astounded his associates. A month or two in advance of publication day he would draw up his table of contents. This, in its preliminary stage, amounted to nothing except a list of the main subjects which he aspired to handle in that number. It was a hope, not a performance. The subjects were commonly suggested by the happenings of the time—an especially outrageous lynching, the trial of a clergyman for heresy, a new attack upon the Monroe Doctrine, the discovery of a new substance such as radium, the publication of an epoch-making book. Page would then fix upon the inevitable men who could write most readably and most authoritatively upon these topics, and "go after" them. Sometimes he would write one of his matchless editorial letters; at other times he would make a personal visit; if necessary, he would use any available friends in a wire-pulling campaign. At all odds he must "get" his man; once he had fixed upon a certain contributor nothing could divert him from the chase. Nor did the negotiations cease after he had "landed" his quarry. He had his way of discussing the subject with his proposed writer, and he discussed it from every possible point of view. He would take him to lunch or to dinner; in his quiet way he would draw him out, find whether he really knew much about the subject, learn the attitude that he was likely to take, and delicately slip in suggestions of his own. Not infrequently this preliminary interview would disclose that the much sought writer, despite appearances, was not the one who was destined for that particular job; in this case Page would find some way of shunting him in favour of a more promising candidate. But Page was no mere chaser of names; there was nothing of the literary tuft-hunter about his editorial methods. He liked to see such men as Theodore Roosevelt, Woodrow Wilson, William Graham Sumner, Charles W. Eliot, Frederic Harrison, Paul Bourget, and the like upon his title page—and here these and many other similarly distinguished authors appeared—but the greatest name could not attain a place there if the letter press that followed were unworthy. Indeed Page's habit of throwing out the contributions of the great, after paying a stiff price for them, caused much perturbation in his counting room. One day he called in one of his associates.

"Do you see that waste basket?" he asked, pointing to a large receptacle filled to overflowing with manuscripts. "All our Cleveland articles are there!"

He had gone to great trouble and expense to obtain a series of six articles from the most prominent publicists

and political leaders of the country on the first year of
Mr. Cleveland's second administration.   It was to be the
"feature" of the number then in preparation.

"There isn't one of them," he declared, "who has got
the point.   I have thrown them all away and I am going
to try to write something myself."

And he spent a couple of days turning out an article
which aroused great public interest.   When Page commissioned an article, he meant simply that he would pay
full price for it; whether he would publish it depended
entirely upon the quality of the material itself.   But
Page was just as severe upon his own writings as upon
those of other men.   He wrote occasionally—always under
a nom-de-plume; but he had great difficulty in satisfy-
ing his own editorial standards.   After finishing an article
he would commonly send for one of his friends and read
the result.

"That is superb!" this admiring associate would sometimes say.

In response Page would take the manuscript and,
holding it aloft in two hands, tear it into several bits, and
throw the scraps into the waste basket.

"Oh, I can do better than that," he would laugh and in
another minute he was busy rewriting the article, from
beginning to end.

Page retired from the editorship of the *Forum* in 1895.
The severance of relations was half a comedy, half a
tragedy.   The proprietors had only the remotest relation
to literature; they had lost much money in the enterprise
before Page became editor and only the fortunate accident
of securing his services had changed their losing venture
into a financial success.   In a moment of despair, before the
happier period had arrived, they offered to sell the property to Page and his friends.   Page quickly assembled a

new group to purchase control, when, much to the amazement of the old owners, the *Forum* began to make money. Instead of having a burden on their hands, the proprietors suddenly discovered that they had a gold mine. They therefore refused to deliver their holdings and an inevitable struggle ensued for control. Page could edit a magazine and turn a shipwrecked enterprise into a profitable one; but, in a tussle of this kind, he was no match for the shrewd business men who owned the property. When the time came for counting noses Page and his friends found themselves in a minority. Of course his resignation as editor necessarily followed this little unpleasantness. And just as inevitably the *Forum* again began to lose money, and soon sank into an obscurity from which it has never emerged.

The *Forum* had established Page's reputation as an editor, and the competition for his services was lively. The distinguished Boston publishing house of Houghton, Mifflin & Company immediately invited him to become a part of their organization. When Horace E. Scudder, in 1898, resigned the editorship of the *Atlantic Monthly*, Page succeeded him. Thus Page became the successor of James Russell Lowell, James T. Fields, William D. Howells, and Thomas Bailey Aldrich as the head of this famous periodical. This meant that he had reached the top of his profession. He was now forty-three years old.

No American publication had ever had so brilliant a history. Founded in 1857, in the most flourishing period of the New England writers, its pages had first published many of the best essays of Emerson, the second series of the Biglow papers as well as many other of Lowell's writings, poems of Longfellow and Whittier, such great successes as Holmes's "Autocrat of the Breakfast Table," Mrs. Howe's "Battle Hymn of the Republic," and the

early novels of Henry James.   If America had a literature,
the *Atlantic* was certainly its most successful periodical
exponent.   Yet, in a sense, the *Atlantic*, by the time Page
succeeded to the editorship, had become the victim of
its dazzling past.   Its recent editors had lived too exclusively in their back numbers.   They had conducted
the magazine too much for the restricted audience of
Boston and New England.   There was a time, indeed,
when the business office arranged the subscribers in two
classes—"Boston" and "foreign"; "Boston" representing
their local adherents, and "foreign" the loyal readers who
lived in the more benighted parts of the United States.
One of its editors had been heard to boast that he never
solicited a contribution; it was not his business to be
a literary drummer!   Let the truth be fairly spoken:
when Page made his first appearance in the *Atlantic*
office, the magazine was unquestionably on the decline.
Its literary quality was still high; the momentum that
its great contributors had given it was still keeping the
publication alive; entrance into its columns still represented the ultimate ambition of the aspiring American
writer; but it needed a new spirit to insure its future.
What it required was the kind of editing that had suddenly
made the *Forum* one of the greatest of English-written
reviews.   This is the reason why the canny Yankee proprietors had reached over to New York and grasped Page
as quickly as the capitalists of the *Forum* let him slip between their fingers.

Page's sense of humour discovered a certain ironic
aspect in his position as the dictator of this famous New
England magazine.   The fact that his manner was im-
patiently energetic and somewhat startling to the placid
atmosphere of Park Street was not the thing that really
signified its break with its past.   But here was a South-

erner firmly entrenched in a headquarters that had long been sacred to the New England abolitionists. One of the first sights that greeted Page, as he came into the office, was the angular and spectacled countenance of William Lloyd Garrison, gazing down from a steel engraving on the wall. One of Garrison's sons was a colleague, and the anterooms were frequently cluttered with dusky gentlemen patiently waiting for interviews with this benefactor of their race. Page once was careless enough to inform Mr. Garrison that "one of your niggers" was waiting outside for an audience. "I very much regret, Mr. Page," came the answer, "that you should insist on spelling 'Negro' with two 'g's'." Despite the mock solemnity of this rebuke, perennial good-nature and raillery prevailed between the son of Garrison and his disrespectful but ever sympathetic Southern friend. Indeed, one of Page's earliest performances was to introduce a spirit of laughter and genial coöperation into a rather solemn and self-satisfied environment. Mr. Mifflin, the head of the house, even formally thanked Page "for the hearty human way in which you take hold of life." Mr. Ellery Sedgwick, the present editor of the *Atlantic*, has described the somewhat disconcerting descent of Page upon the editorial sanctuary of James Russell Lowell:

"Were a visitant from another sphere to ask me for the incarnation of those qualities we love to call American, I should turn to a familiar gallery of my memory and point to the living portrait that hangs there of Walter Page. A sort of foursquareness, bluntness, it seemed to some; an uneasy, often explosive energy; a disposition to underrate fine drawn nicenesses of all sorts; ingrained Yankee common sense, checking his vaulting enthusiasm; enormous self-confidence, impatience of failure—all of these were in him; and he was besides affectionate to a fault, devoted to his country, his family, his craft—a strong, bluff, tender man.

"Those were the decorous days of the old tradition, and Page's entrance into the 'atmosphere' of Park Street has taken on the dignity of legend. There were all kinds of signs and portents, as the older denizens will tell you. Strange breezes floated through the office, electric emanations, and a pervasive scent of tobacco, which—so the local historian says—had been unknown in the vicinity since the days of Walter Raleigh, except for the literary aroma of Aldrich's quarantined sanctum upstairs. Page's coming marked the end of small ways. His first requirement was, in lieu of a desk, a table that might have served a family of twelve for Thanksgiving dinner. No one could imagine what that vast, polished tableland could serve for until they watched the editor at work. Then they saw. Order vanished and chaos reigned. Huge piles of papers, letters, articles, reports, books, pamphlets, magazines, congregated themselves as if by magic. To work in such confusion seemed hopeless, but Page eluded the congestion by the simple expedient of moving on. He would light a fresh cigar, give the editorial chair a hitch, and begin his work in front of a fresh expanse of table, with no clutter of the past to disturb the new day's litter.

"The motive power of his work was enthusiasm. Never was more generous welcome given to a newcomer than Page held out to the successful manuscript of an unknown. I remember, though I heard the news second hand at the time, what a day it was in the office when the first manuscript from the future author of 'To Have and To Hold,' came in from an untried Southern girl. He walked up and down, reading paragraphs aloud and slapping the crisp manuscript to enforce his commendation. To take a humbler instance, I recall the words of over generous praise with which he greeted the first paper I ever sent to an editor quite as clearly as I remember the monstrous effort which had brought it into being. Sometimes he would do a favoured manuscript the honour of taking it out to lunch in his coat-pocket, and an associate vividly recalls eggs, coffee, and pie in a near-by restaurant, while, in a voice that could be heard by the remotest lunchers, Page read passages which many of them were too startled to appreciate. He was not given to overrating, but it was not in his nature to understate. 'I tell you,' said he, grumbling over some unfortunate proof-sheets from Manhattan, 'there isn't one man in New York who can write English—not from the Battery to Harlem Heights.' And if the faults were moral rather than literary, his disapproval grew in emphasis. There is more than tradition in the tale of the Negro who, presuming on Page's deep interest in his race, brought to his desk a manuscript copied word for word from a published source. Page recognized the deception, and seizing the rascal's collar with a firm editorial grip, rejected the poem, and ejected the poet, with an energy very invigorating to the ancient serenities of the office.

"Page was always effervescent with ideas. Like an editor who would have made a good fisherman, he used to say that you had to cast a dozen times before you could get a strike. He was forever in those days sending out ideas and suggestions and invitations to write. The result was electric, and the magazine became with a suddenness (of which only an editor can appreciate the wonder) a storehouse of animating thoughts. He avoided the mistake common to our craft of editing a magazine for the immediate satisfaction of his colleagues. 'Don't write for the office,' he would say. 'Write for outside,' and so his magazine became a living thing. His phrase suggests one special gift that Page had, for which his profession should do him especial honour. He was able, quite beyond the powers of any man of my acquaintance, to put compendiously into words the secrets of successful editing. It was capital training just to hear him talk. 'Never save a feature,' he used to say. 'Always work for the next number. Forget the others. Spend everything just on that.' And to those who know, there is divination in the principle. Again he understood instinctively that to write well a man must not only have something to say, but must long to say it. A highly intelligent representative of the coloured race came to him with a philosophic essay. Page would have none of it. 'I know what you are thinking of,' said Page. 'You are thinking of the barriers we set up against you, and the handicap of your lot. If you will write what it feels like to be a Negro, I will print that.' The result was a paper which has seemed to me the most moving expression of the hopeless hope of the race I know of.

"Page was generous in his coöperation. He never drew a rigid line about his share in any enterprise, but gave and took help with each and all. A lover of good English, with an honest passion for things tersely said, Page esteemed good journalism far above any second-rate manifestation of more pretentious forms; but many of us will regret that he was not privileged to find some outlet for his energies in which aspiration for real literature might have played an ampler part. For the literature of the past Page had great respect, but his interest was ever in the present and the future. He was forever fulminating against bad writing, and hated the ignorant and slipshod work of the hack almost as much as he despised the sham of the man who affected letters, the dabbler and the poet-aster. His taste was for the roast beef of literature, not for the side dishes and the trimmings, and his appreciation of the substantial work of others was no surer than his instinct for his own performance. He was an admirable writer of exposition, argument, and narrative—solid and thoughtful, but never dull. . . . I came into close relations with him and from him I learned more of my profession than from any one I have ever known. Scores of other men would say the same."

But the fact that a new hand had seized the *Atlantic* was apparent in other places than in the *Atlantic* office itself. One of Page's contributors of the *Forum* days, Mr. Courtney DeKalb, happened to be in St. Louis when the first number of the magazine under its new editor made its appearance. Mr. DeKalb had been out of the country for some time and knew nothing of the change. Happening accidentally to pick up the *Atlantic*, the table of contents caught his eye. It bore the traces of an unmistakable hand. Only one man, he said to himself, could assemble such a group as that, and above all, only Page could give such an enticing turn of the titles. He therefore sat down and wrote his old friend congratulating him on his accession to the *Atlantic Monthly*. The change that now took place was indeed a conspicuous, almost a startling one. The *Atlantic* retained all its old literary flavour, for to its traditions Page was as much devoted as the highest caste Bostonian; it still gave up much of its space to a high type of fiction, poetry, and reviews of contemporary literature, but every number contained also an assortment of articles which celebrated the prevailing activities of men and women in all worth-while fields of effort. There were discussions of present-day politics, and these even became personal dissections of presidential candidates; there were articles on the racial characters of the American population: Theodore Roosevelt was permitted to discuss the New York police; Woodrow Wilson to pass in review the several elements that made the Nation; Booker T. Washington to picture the awakening of the Negro; John Muir to enlighten Americans upon a national beauty and wealth of which they had been woefully ignorant, their forests; William Allen White to describe certain aspects of his favourite Kansas; E. L. Godkin to review the dangers and the hopes of American democracy; Jacob Riis to tell about the Battle with the Slum; and W. G. Frost to reveal for the first time the archaic civilization of the Kentucky mountaineers.   The latter article illustrated Page's genius at rewriting titles.   Mr. Frost's theme was that these Kentucky mountaineers were really Elizabethan survivals; that their dialect, their ballads, their habits were really a case of arrested development; that by studying them present-day Americans could get a picture of their distant forbears.   Page gave vitality to the presentation by changing a commonplace title to this one: "Our Contemporary Ancestors."

There were those who were offended by Page's willingness to seek inspiration on the highways and byways and even in newspapers, for not infrequently he would find hidden away in a corner an idea that would result in valuable magazine matter.   On one occasion at least this practice had important literary consequences.   One day he happened to read that a Mrs. Robert Hanning had died in Toronto, the account casually mentioning the fact that Mrs. Hanning was the youngest sister of Thomas Carlyle. Page handed this clipping to a young assistant, and told him to take the first train to Canada.   The editor could easily divine that a sister of Carlyle, expatriated for forty-six years on this side of the Atlantic, must have received a large number of letters from her brother, and it was safe to assume that they had been carefully preserved. Such proved to be the fact; and a new volume of Carlyle letters, of somewhat more genial character than the other collections, was the outcome of this visit.[1] And another fruit of this journalistic habit was "The Memoirs of a Revolutionist," by Prince Peter Kropotkin. In 1897 the great Russian nihilist was lecturing in Boston. Page met him, learned from his own lips his story, and persuaded him to put it in permanent form. This willingness of Page to admit such a revolutionary person into the pages of the *Atlantic* caused some excitement in conventional circles. In fact, it did take some courage, but Page never hesitated; the man was of heroic mould, he had a great story to tell, he wielded an engaging pen, and his purposes were high-minded. A great book of memoirs was the result.

Mr. Sedgwick refers above to Page's editorial fervour when Miss Mary Johnston's "Prisoners of Hope" first fell out of the blue sky into his Boston office. Page's joy was not less keen because the young author was a Virginia girl, and because she had discovered that the early period of Virginia history was a field for romance. When, a few months afterward, Page was casting about for an *Atlantic* serial, Miss Johnston and this Virginia field seemed to be an especially favourable prospect. "Prisoners of Hope" had been published as a book and had made a good success, but Miss Johnston's future still lay ahead of her. With Page to think meant to act, and so, instead of writing a formal letter, he at once jumped on a train for Birmingham, Alabama, where Miss Johnston

---

[1] "Letters of Thomas Carlyle to his Youngest Sister." Edited by Charles Townsend Copeland. Houghton, Mifflin & Company, 1899.

was then living. "I remember quite distinctly that first meeting," writes Miss Johnston. "The day was rainy. Standing at my window I watched Mr. Page—a characteristic figure, air and walk—approach the house. When a few minutes later I met him he was simplicity and kindliness itself. This was my first personal contact with publishers (my publishers) or with editors of anything so great as the *Atlantic*. My heart beat! But he was friendly and Southern. I told him what I had done upon a new story. He was going on that night. Might he take the manuscript with him and read it upon the train? It might—he couldn't say positively, of course—but it might have serial possibilities. I was only too glad for him to have the manuscript. I forget just how many chapters I had completed. But it was not quite in order. Could I get it so in a few hours? In that case he would send a messenger for it from the hotel. Yes, I could. Very good! A little further talk and he left with a strong handshake. Three or four hours later he had the manuscript and took it with him from Birmingham that night."

Page's enterprising visit had put into his hands the half-finished manuscript of a story, "To Have and to Hold," which, when printed in the *Atlantic*, more than doubled its circulation, and which, when made into a book, proved one of the biggest successes since "Uncle Tom's Cabin."

Page's most independent stroke in his *Atlantic* days came with the outbreak of the Spanish-American War. Boston was then the headquarters of a national mood which has almost passed out of popular remembrance. Its spokesmen called themselves anti-imperialists. The theory back of their protest was that the American declaration of war on Spain was not only the wanton attack of a great bully upon a feeble little country: it was something

that was bound to have deplorable consequences. The
United States was breaking with its past and engaging
in European quarrels; as a consequence of the war it
would acquire territories and embark on a career of
"imperialism." Page was impatient at this kind of
twaddle. He declared that the Spanish War was a
"necessary act of surgery for the health of civilization."
He did not believe that a nation, simply because it was
small, should be permitted to maintain indefinitely a
human slaughter house at the door of the United States.
The *Atlantic* for June, 1898, gave the so-called anti-
imperialists a thrill of horror. On the cover appeared
the defiantly flying American flag; the first article was a
vigorous and approving presentation of the American case
against Spain; though this was unsigned, its incisive style
at once betrayed the author. The *Atlantic* had printed
the American flag on its cover during the Civil War;
but certain New Englanders thought that this latest
struggle, in its motives and its proportions, was hardly
entitled to the distinction. Page declared, however, that
the Spanish War marked a new period in history; and he
endorsed the McKinley Administration, not only in the
war itself, but in its consequences, particularly the annexation of the Philippine Islands.

Page greatly enjoyed life in Boston and Cambridge.
The *Atlantic* was rapidly growing in circulation and in
influence, and the new friends that its editor was making
were especially to his taste. He now had a family of four
children, three boys and one girl—and their bringing up
and education, as he said at this time, constituted his
real occupation. So far as he could see, in the summer
of 1899, he was permanently established in life. But
larger events in the publishing world now again pulled him
back to New York.

CHAPTER III

"THE FORGOTTEN MAN"

I

IN JULY, 1899, the publishing community learned that financial difficulties were seriously embarrassing the great house of Harper. For nearly a century this establishment had maintained a position almost of prœminence among American publishers. Three generations of Harpers had successively presided over its destinies; its magazines and books had become almost a household necessity in all parts of the United States, and its authors included many of the names most celebrated in American letters. The average American could no more associate the idea of bankruptcy with this great business than with the federal Treasury itself. Yet this incredible disaster had virtually taken place. At this time the public knew nothing of the impending ruin; the fact was, however, that, in July, 1899, the banking house of J. P. Morgan & Company practically controlled this property. This was the situation which again called Page to New York.

In the preceding year Mr. S. S. McClure, whose recent success as editor and publisher had been little less than a sensation, had joined forces with Mr. Frank N. Doubleday, and organized the new firm of Doubleday & McClure. This business was making rapid progress; and that it would soon become one of the leading American publishing houses was already apparent. It was perhaps not unnatural, therefore, that Mr. J. Pierpont Morgan, scanning the horizon for the men who might rescue the

Harper concern from approaching disaster, should have had his attention drawn to Mr. McClure and Mr. Doubleday. "The failure of Harper & Brothers," Mr. Morgan said in a published statement, "would be a national calamity." One morning, therefore, a member of the Harper firm called upon Mr. McClure. Without the slightest hesitation he unfolded the Harper situation to his astonished contemporary. The solution proposed was more astonishing still. This was that Mr. Doubleday and Mr. McClure should amalgamate their young and vigorous business with the Harper enterprise and become the active managers of the new corporation. Both Mr. McClure and Mr. Doubleday were comparatively young men, and the magnitude of the proposed undertaking at first rather staggered them. It was as though a small independent steel maker should suddenly be invited to take over the United States Steel Corporation. Mr. McClure, characteristically impetuous and daring, wished to accept the invitation outright; Mr. Doubleday, however, suggested a period of probation. The outcome was that the two men offered to take charge of Harper & Brothers for a few months, and then decide whether they wished to make the association a permanent one. One thing was immediately apparent; Messrs. Doubleday and McClure, able as they were, would need the help of the best talent available in the work that lay ahead. The first man to whom they turned was Page, who presently left Boston and took up his business abode at Franklin Square. The rumble of the elevated road was somewhat distracting after the four quiet years in Park Street, but the new daily routine was not lacking in interest. The Harper experiment, however, did not end as Mr. Morgan had hoped. After a few months Messrs. Doubleday, Page and McClure withdrew, and left the work of rescue to be performed by Mr. George Harvey, who, curiously enough, succeeded Page, twenty-one years afterward, in an even more important post—that of ambassador to the Court of St. James's. The one important outcome of the Harper episode, so far as Page was concerned, was the forming of a close business and personal association with Mr. Frank N. Doubleday. As soon as the two men definitely decided not to assume the Harper responsibility, therefore, they joined forces and founded the firm of Doubleday, Page & Company. Page now had the opportunity which he had long wished for; the mere editing of magazines, even magazines of such an eminent character as the *Forum* and the *Atlantic Monthly*, could hardly satisfy his ambition; he yearned to possess something which he could call his own, at least in part.

The life of an editor has its unsatisfactory aspect, unless the editor himself has an influential ownership in his periodical. Page now found his opportunity to establish a monthly magazine which he could regard as his own in both senses. He was its untrammelled editor, and also, in part, its proprietor. All editors and writers will sympathize with the ideas expressed in a letter written about this time to Page's friend, Mr. William Roscoe Thayer, already distinguished as the historian of Italian unity and afterward to win fame as the biographer of Cavour and John Hay. When the first number of the *World's Work* appeared Mr. Thayer wrote, expressing a slight disappointment that its leading tendency was journalistic rather than literary and intellectual. "When you edited the *Forum*," wrote Mr. Thayer, "I perceived that no such talent for editing had been seen in America before, and when, a little later, you rejuvenated the *Atlantic*. making it for a couple of years the best periodical printed in English, I felt that you had a great mission before you as evoker and editor of the best literary work and weightiest thought on important topics of our foremost men." He had hoped to see a magnified *Atlantic*, and the new publication, splendid as it was, seemed to be of rather more popular character than the publications with which Page had previously been associated. Page met this challenge in his usual hearty fashion.

To William Roscoe Thayer

34 Union Square East, New York,
December 5, 1900.

MY DEAR THAYER:

The *World's Work* has brought me nothing so good as your letter of yesterday. When Mrs. Page read it, she shouted "Now that's it!" For "it" read "truth," and you will have her meaning and mine. My thanks you may be sure you have, in great and earnest abundance.

You surprise me in two ways—(1) that you think as well of the magazine as you do. If it have half the force and earnestness that you say it has, how happy I shall be, for then it will surely bring something to pass. The other way in which you surprise me is by the flattering things that you say about my conduct of the *Atlantic*. Alas! it was not what you in your kind way say—no, no.

Of course the *World's Work* is not yet by any means what I hope to make it. But it has this incalculable advantage (to me) over every other magazine in existence: it is mine (mine and my partners', i. e., partly mine), and I shall not work to build up a good piece of machinery and then be turned out to graze as an old horse is. This of course, is selfish and personal—not wholly selfish either, I think. I threw down the *Atlantic* for this reason: (Consider the history of its editors) Lowell[1] complained bitterly that he was never rewarded properly for the time and work he did; Fields was (in a way) one of its owners; it was sold out from under Howells, etc., etc.   I might (probably should) have been at the mercy completely of owners some day who would have dismissed me for a younger man.   Nearly all hired editors suffer this fate.   My good friends in Boston were sincere in thinking that my day of doom would never come; but they didn't offer me any guarantee—part ownership, for instance; and the years go swiftly.   I could afford, of my own volition, to leave the *Atlantic*.   I couldn't afford to take permanently the risks that a hired editor must take.   Nor should I ever again have turned my hand to such a task except on a magazine of my own. I should have sought other employment.   There are many easier and better and more influential things to do—yet; ten years hence I might have been too old.   Harry Houghton[2] has an old horse thirty years old.   I used to see him grazing sometimes and hear his master's self-congratulatory explanation of his own kindness to that faithful beast.   In the office of Houghton, Mifflin & Company there is an old man whom I used to see every day— pensioned, grazing.   Then I would go home and see four bright children.   Three of them are now away from home at school; and the four cost a pretty penny to educate. My income had been the same for ten years—or very nearly the same.   If I was a "magic" editor, I confess I didn't see the magic; and there is no power under Heaven or in it that can prove to me that I ought to keep on making magazines as a hired man—without the common

---

[1] A memorandum of an old *Atlantic* balance sheet discloses that James Russell Lowell's salary as editor was $1,500 a year.

[2] A member of the firm of Houghton, Mifflin & Company.

security of permanent service for lack of which nearly all my predecessors lost their chance.

But this is not all, nor half. A man ought to express himself, ought to live his own life, say his own little say, before silence comes. The "say" may be bad—a mere yawp, and silence might be more becoming. But the same argument would make a man dissatisfied with his own nose if it happened to be ugly. It's *his* nose, and he must content himself. So it's *his* yawp and he must let it go.

I'm not going to make the new magazine my own megaphone—you may be sure of that. It will nevertheless contain my general interpretation of things, in which I swear I do believe! The first thing, of course, is to establish it. Then it can be shaped more nearly into what I wish it to become. If it seem unmannerly, aggressive, I know no other way to make it heard. If it died, then the game would be up. Well, we seem to have established it at once. It promises not to cost us a penny of investment.

Now, the magazines need new topics. They have all threshed over old straw for many years. There is *one* new subject, to my thinking worth all the old ones: the new impulse in American life, the new feeling of nationality, our coming to realize ourselves. To my mind there is greater promise in democracy than men of any preceding period ever dared dream of—aggressive democracy— growth by action. Our writers (the few we have) are yet in the pre-democratic era. When men's imaginations lay hold on the things that already begin to appear above the horizon, we shall have something worth reading. At present I can do no more than bawl out, "See! here are new subjects." One of these days somebody will come along who can write about them. I have started out without a writer. Fiske is under contract, James would give nothing more to the *Atlantic*, you were ill (I thank Heaven you are no longer so) the second- and third-rate essayists have been bought by mere Wall Street publishers. Beyond these are the company of story tellers and beyond them only a dreary waste of dead-level unimaginative men and women. I can (soon) get all that I could ever have got in the *Atlantic* and new ones (I know they'll come) whom I could never have got there.

You'll see—within a year or two—by far a better magazine than I have ever made; and you and I will differ in nothing unless you feel despair about the breakdown of certain democratic theories, which I think were always mere theories. Let 'em go! The real thing, which is life and action, is better.

Heartily and always your grateful friend,

WALTER H. PAGE.

Thus the fact that Page's new magazine was intended for a popular audience was not the result of accident, but of design. It represented a periodical plan which had long been taking shape in Page's mind. The things that he had been doing for the *Forum* and the *Atlantic* he aspired to do for a larger audience than that to which publications of this character could appeal. Scholar though Page was, and lover of the finest things in literature that he had always been, yet this sympathy and interest had always lain with the masses. Perhaps it is impossible to make literature democratic, but Page believed that he would be genuinely serving the great cause that was nearest his heart if he could spread wide the facts of the modern world, especially the facts of America, and if he could clothe the expression in language which, while always dignified and even "literary," would still be sufficiently touched with the vital, the picturesque, and the "human," to make his new publication appeal to a wide audience of intelligent, everyday Americans. It was thus part of his general programme of improving the status of the average man, and it formed a logical part of his philosophy of human advancement. For the only acceptable measure of any civilization, Page believed, was the extent to which it improved the condition of the common citizen. A few cultured and university-trained men at the top; a few ancient families living in luxury; a few painters and poets and statesmen and generals; these things, in Page's view, did not constitute a satisfactory state of society; the real test was the extent to which the masses participated in education, in the necessities and comforts of existence, in the right of self-evolution and self-expression, in that "equality of opportunity," which, Page never wearied of repeating, "was the basis of social progress." The mere right to vote and to hold office was not democracy; parliamentary majorities and political caucuses were not democracy—at the best these things were only details and not the most important ones; democracy was the right of every man to enjoy, in accordance with his aptitudes of character and mentality, the material and spiritual opportunities that nature and science had placed at the disposition of mankind. This democratic creed had now become the dominating interest of Page's life. From this time on it consumed all his activities. His new magazine set itself first of all to interpret the American panorama from this point of view; to describe the progress that the several parts of the country were making in the several manifestations of democracy— education, agriculture, industry, social life, politics— and the importance that Page attached to them was practically in the order named. Above all it concerned itself with the men and women who were accomplishing most in the definite realization of this great end.

And now also Page began to carry his activities far beyond mere print.   In his early residence in New York, from 1885 to 1895, he had always taken his part in public movements; he had been a vital spirit in the New York Reform Club, which was engaged mainly in advocating the Cleveland tariff; he had always shown a willingness to experiment with new ideas; at one time he had mingled with Socialists and he had been quite captivated by the personal and literary charm of Henry George.   After 1900, however, Page became essentially a public man, though not in the political sense.   His work as editor and writer was merely one expression of the enthusiasms that occupied his mind.   From 1900 until 1913, when he left for England, life meant for him mainly an effort to spread the democratic ideal, as he conceived it; concretely it represented a constant campaign for improving the fundamental opportunities and the everyday social advantages of the masses.

II

Inevitably the condition of the people in his own homeland enlisted Page's sympathy, for he had learned of their necessities at first hand.   The need of education had powerfully impressed him even as a boy.   At twenty-three he began writing articles for the Raleigh *Observer*, and practically all of them were pleas for the education of the Southern child.   His subsequent activities of this kind, as editor of the *State Chronicle*, have already been described.   The American from other parts of the country is rather shocked when he first learns of the backwardness of education in the South a generation ago.   In any real sense there was no publicly supported system for training the child.   A few wretched hovels, scattered through a sparsely settled country, served as school houses; a few uninspiring and neglected women, earning perhaps $50 or $75 a year, did weary duty as teachers; a few groups of anemic and listless children, attending school for only forty days a year—such was the preparation for life which most Southern states gave the less fortunate of their citizens. The glaring fact that emphasized the outcome of this official carelessness was an illiteracy, among white men and women, of 26 per cent. Among the Negroes it was vastly larger.

The first exhortation to reform came from the Wautauga Club, which Page had organized in Raleigh in 1884. After Page had left his native state, other men began preaching the same crusade. Perhaps the greatest of those advocates whom the South loves to refer to as "educational statesmen" was Dr. Charles D. McIver, of Greensboro, N. C. McIver's personality and career had an heroic quality all their own. Back in the 'eighties McIver and Edwin A. Alderman, now President of the University of Virginia, endured all kinds of hardships and buffetings in the cause of popular education; they stumped the state, much like political campaigners, preaching the strange new gospel in mountain cabin, in village church, at the cart's tail—all in an attempt to arouse their lethargic countrymen to the duty of laying a small tax to save their children from illiteracy. Some day the story of McIver and Alderman will find its historian; when it does, he will learn that, in those dark ages, one of their greatest sources of inspiration was Walter Page. McIver, a great burly boy, physically and intellectually, so full of energy that existence for him was little less than an unending tornado, so full of zeal that any other oc-cupation than that of training the neglected seemed a trifling with life, so sleepless in his efforts that, at the age of forty-five, he one day dropped dead while travelling on a railroad train; Alderman, a man of finer culture, quieter in his methods, an orator of polish and restraint, but an advocate vigorous in the prosecution of the great end; and Page, living faraway in the North, but pumping his associates full of courage and enthusiasm—these were the three guardsmen of this new battle for the elevation of the white and black men of the South. McIver's great work was the State Normal College for Women, which, amid unparallelled difficulties, he founded for teaching the teachers of the new Southern generation. It was at this institution that Page, in 1897, delivered the address which gave the cause of Southern education that one thing which is worth armies to any struggling reform—a phrase; and it was a phrase that lived in the popular mind and heart and summed up, in a way that a thousand speeches could never have done, the great purpose for which the best people in the state were striving.

His editorial gift for title-making now served Page in good stead. "The Forgotten Man," which was the heading of his address, immediately passed into the common speech of the South and even at this day inevitably appears in all discussions of social progress. It was again Page's familiar message of democracy, of improving the condition of the everyday man, woman, and child; and the message, as is usually the case in all incitements to change, involved many unpleasant facts. Page had first of all to inform his fellow Southerners that it was only in the South that "The Forgotten Man" was really an outstanding feature. He did not exist in New England, in the Middle States, in the Mississippi Valley, or in the West, or existed in these regions to so slight an extent that he was not a grave menace to society. But in the South the situation was quite different. And for this fact the explanation was found in history. The South certainly could not fix the blame upon Nature. In natural wealth —in forests, mines, quarries, rich soil, in the unlimited power supplied by water courses—the Southern States formed perhaps the richest region in the country. These things North Carolina and her sister communities had not developed; more startling still, they had not developed a source of wealth that was infinitely greater than all these combined; they had not developed their men and their women. The Southern States represented the purest "Anglo-Saxon" strain in the United States; to-day in North Carolina only one person in four hundred is of "foreign stock," and a voting list of almost any town contains practically nothing except the English and Scotch names that were borne by the original settlers. Yet here democracy, in any real sense, had scarcely obtained a footing. The region which had given Thomas Jefferson and George Washington to the world was still, in the year 1897, organized upon an essentially aristocratic basis. The conception of education which prevailed in the most hidebound aristocracies of Europe still ruled south of the Potomac. There was no acceptance of that fundamental American doctrine that education was the function of the state. It was generally regarded as the luxury of the rich and the socially high placed; it was certainly not for the poor; and it was a generally accepted view that those who enjoyed this privilege must pay for it out of their own pockets. Again Page returned to the "mummy" theme —the fact that North Carolina, and the South generally, were too much ruled by "dead men's" hands. The state was controlled by a "little aristocracy, which, in its social and economic character, made a failure and left a stubborn crop of wrong social notions behind it—

especially about education." The chief backward influences were the stump and the pulpit. "From the days of King George to this day, the politicians of North Carolina have declaimed against taxes, thus laying the foundation of our poverty. It was a misfortune for us that the quarrel with King George happened to turn upon the question of taxation—so great was the dread of taxation that was instilled into us." What had the upper classes done for the education of the average man? The statistics of illiteracy, the deplorable economic and social conditions of the rural population—and most of the population of North Carolina was rural—furnished the answer.

Thus the North Carolina aristocracy had failed in education and the failure of the Church had been as complete and deplorable. The preachers had established preparatory schools for boys and girls, but these were under the control of sects; and so education was either a class or an ecclesiastical concern. "The forgotten man remained forgotten. The aristocratic scheme of education had passed him by. To a less extent, but still to the extent of hundreds of thousands, the ecclesiastical scheme had passed him by." But even the education which these institutions gave was inferior. Page told his North Carolina audience that the University of which they were so proud did not rank with Harvard, Yale, Princeton, and other universities of the North. The state had not produced great scholars nor established great libraries. In the estimation of publishers North Carolina was unimportant as a book market. "By any test that may be made, both these systems have failed even with the classes that they appealed to." The net result was that "One in every four was wholly forgotten"—that is, was unable to read and write. And the worst of it all was that the victim of this neglect was not disturbed over his situation. "The forgotten man was content to be forgotten. He became not only a dead weight, but a definite opponent of social progress. He faithfully heard the politician on the stump praise him for virtues that he did not have. The politicians told him that he lived in the best state in the Union; told him that the other politicians had some hare-brained plan to increase his taxes, told him as a consolation for his ignorance how many of his kinsmen had been killed in the war, told him to distrust any one who wished to change anything. What was good enough for his fathers was good enough for him. Thus the 'forgotten man' became a dupe, became thankful for being neglected. And the preacher told him that the ills and misfortunes of this life were blessings in disguise, that God meant his poverty as a means of grace, and that if he accepted the right creed all would be well with him. These influences encouraged inertia. There could not have been a better means to prevent the development of the people."

Even more tragic than these "forgotten men" were the "forgotten women." "Thin and wrinkled in youth from ill-prepared food, clad without warmth or grace, living in untidy houses, working from daylight till bedtime at the dull round of weary duties, the slaves of men of equal slovenliness, the mothers of joyless children—all uneducated if not illiterate." "This sight," Page told his hearers, "every one of you has seen, not in the countries whither we send missionaries, but in the borders of the State of North Carolina, in this year of grace."

"Our civilization," he declared, "has been a failure." Both the politicians and the preacher had failed to lift the masses. "It is a time for a wiser statesmanship and a more certain means of grace." He admitted that there had been recent progress in North Carolina, owing largely to the work of McIver and Alderman, but taxes for educational purposes were still low.   What was the solution? "A public school system generously supported by public sentiment and generously maintained by both state and local taxation, is the only effective means to develop the forgotten man and even more surely the only means to develop the forgotten woman. . . ." "If any beggar for a church school oppose a local tax for schools or a higher school tax, take him to the huts of the forgotten women and children, and in their hopeless presence remind him that the church system of education has not touched tens of thousands of these lives and ask him whether he thinks it wrong that the commonwealth should educate them.   If he think it wrong ask him and ask the people plainly, whether he be a worthy preacher of the gospel that declares one man equal to another in the sight of God? . . .   The most sacred thing in the commonwealth and to the commonwealth is the child, whether it be your child or the child of the dull-faced mother of the hovel.   The child of the dull-faced mother may, as you know, be the most capable child in the state. . . .   Several of the strongest personalities that were ever born in North Carolina were men whose very fathers were unknown.   We have all known two such, who held high places in Church and State.   President Eliot said a little while ago that the ablest man that he had known in his many years' connection with Harvard University was the son of a brick mason."

In place of the ecclesiastical creed that had guided North Carolina for so many generations Page proposed his creed of democracy.   He advised that North Carolina commit this to memory and teach it to its children.   It was as follows:

"I believe in the free public training of both the hands and the mind of every child born of woman.

"I believe that by the right training of men we add to the wealth of the world. All wealth is the creation of man, and he creates it only in proportion to the trained uses of the community; and the more men we train the more wealth everyone may create.

"I believe in the perpetual regeneration of society, and in the immortality of democracy and in growth everlasting."

Thus Page nailed his theses upon the door of his native state, and mighty was the reverberation. In a few weeks Page's Greensboro address had made its way all over the Southern States, and his melancholy figure, "the forgotten man" had become part of the indelible imagery of the Southern people. The portrait etched itself deeply into the popular consciousness for the very good reason that its truth was pretty generally recognized. The higher type of newspaper, though it winced somewhat at Page's strictures, manfully recognized that the best way of meeting his charge was by setting to work and improving conditions. The fact is that the better conscience of North Carolina welcomed this eloquent description of unquestioned evils; but the gentlemen whom Page used to stigmatize as "professional Southerners"— the men who commercialized class and sectional prejudice to their own political and financial or ecclesiastical profit —fell foul of this "renegade," this "Southern Yankee" this sacrilegious "intruder" who had dared to visit his old home and desecrate its traditions and its religion. This clerical wrath was kindled into fresh flame when Page, in an editorial in his magazine, declared that these same preachers, ignoring their real duties, were content "to herd their women and children around the stagnant pools of theology." For real religion Page had the deepest reverence, and he had great respect also for the robust evangelical preachers whose efforts had contributed so much to the opening up of the frontier. In his Greensboro address Page had given these men high praise. But for the assiduous idolaters of stratified dogma he entertained a contempt which he was seldom at pains to conceal. North Carolina had many clergymen of the more progressive type; these men chuckled at Page's vigorous characterization of the brethren, but those against whom it had been aimed raged with a fervour that was almost unchristian. This clerical excitement, however, did not greatly disturb the philosophic Page. The hubbub lasted for several years—for Page's Greensboro speech was only the first of many pronouncements of the same kind—but he never publicly referred to the attacks upon him. Occasionally in letters to his friends he would good-naturedly discuss them. "I have had several letters," he wrote to Professor Edwin Mims, of Trinity College, North Carolina, "about an 'excoriation' (Great Heavens! What a word!) that somebody in North Carolina has been giving me. I never read these things and I don't know what it's all about—nor do I care. But perhaps you'll be interested in a letter that I wrote an old friend (a lady) who is concerned about it. I enclose a copy of it. I shall never notice any 'excoriator.' But if you wish to add to the gaiety of nations, give this copy to some newspaper and let it loose in the state—if you care to do so. We must have patience with these puny and peevish brethren. They've been trained to a false view of life. Heaven knows I bear them no ill-will."

The letter to which Page referred follows:

MY DEAR FRIEND:

I have your letter saying that some of the papers in North Carolina are again "jumping on" me. I do not know which they are, and I am glad that you did not tell me. I had heard of it before. A preacher wrote me the other day that he approved of every word of an "excoriation" that some religious editor had given me. A kindly Christian act—wasn't it, to send a stranger word that you were glad that he had been abused by a religious editor? I wrote him a gentle letter, telling him that I hoped he'd have a long and happy life preaching a gospel of friendliness and neighbourliness and good-will, and that I cared nothing about "excoriations." Why should he, then, forsake his calling and take delight in disseminating personal abuse?

And why do you not write me about things that I really care for in the good old country—the budding trees, the pleasant weather, news of old friends, gossip of good people—cheerful things? I pray you, don't be concerned about what any poor whining soul may write about me. I don't care for myself: I care only for him; for the writer of personal abuse always suffers from it—never the man abused.

I haven't read what my kindly clerical correspondent calls an "excoriation" for ten years, and I never shall read one if I know what it is beforehand. Why should I or anybody read such stuff? I can't find time to do half the positive things that I should like to do for the broadening of my own character and for the encouragement of others. Why should I waste a single minute in such a negative and cheerless way as reading anybody's personal abuse of anybody else—least of all myself?

These silly outbursts never reach me and they never can; and they, therefore, utterly fail, and always will fail, of their aim; yet, my dear friend, there is nevertheless a serious side to such folly. For it shows the need of education, education, education. The religious editor and the preacher who took joy in his abuse of me have such a starved view of life that they cannot themselves, perhaps, ever be educated into kindliness and dignity of thought. But their children may be—must be. Think of beautiful children growing up in a home where "excoriating" people who differ with you is regarded as a manly Christian exercise! It is pitiful beyond words. There is no way to lift up life that is on so low a level except by the free education of all the people. Let us work for that and, when the growlers are done growling and forgotten, better men will remember us with gratitude.

I felt greatly complimented and pleased to receive an invitation the other day to attend the North Carolina Teachers' Assembly in June. I have many things to do in June, but I am going—going with great pleasure. I hope to see you there. I know of no other company of people that I should be so glad to meet. They are doing noble work—the most devoted and useful work in this whole wide world. They are the true leaders of the people. I often wish that I were one of them. They inspire me as nobody else does. They are the army of our salvation.

Write me what they are doing. Write me about the wonderful educational progress. And write me about the peach trees and the budding imminence of spring; and about the children who now live all day outdoors and grow brown and plump. And never mind that queer sect, "The Excoriators." They and their stage thunder will be forgotten to-morrow. Meantime let us live and work for things nobler than any controversies, for things that are larger than the poor mission of any sect; and let

us have charity and a patient pity for those that think
they serve God by abusing their fellow-men. I wish I
saw some way to help them to a broader and a higher life.

Faithfully yours,

WALTER H. PAGE.

III

That Page should have little interest in "excoriators"
at the time this letter was written—in April, 1902—was
not surprising, for his educational campaign and that of
his friends was now bearing fruit. "Write me about
the wonderful educational progress," he says to this
correspondent; and, indeed, the change that was coming
over North Carolina and the South generally seemed to
be tinged with the miraculous. The "Forgotten Man"
and the "Forgotten Woman" were rapidly coming into
their own. Two years after the delivery of Page's
Greensboro address, a small group of educational en-
thusiasts met at Capon Springs, West Virginia, to discuss the general situation in the South. The leader of
this little gathering was Robert C. Ogden, a great New
York merchant who for many years had been President
of the Board of Hampton Institute. Out of this meeting grew the Southern Educational Conference, which
was little more than an annual meeting for advertising broadcast the educational needs of the South. Each
year Mr. Ogden chartered a railroad train; a hundred
or so of the leading editors, lawyers, bankers, and the
like became his guests; the train moved through the
Southern States, pausing now and then to investigate
some particular institution or locality; and at some
Southern city, such as Birmingham or Atlanta or Winston-
Salem, a stop of several days would be made, a public
building engaged, and long meetings held. In all these

proceedings Page was an active figure, as he became in the Southern Education Board, which directly resulted from Mr. Ogden's public spirited excursions. Like the Conference, the Southern Education Board was a purely missionary organization, and its most active worker was Page himself. He was constantly speaking and writing on his favourite subject; he printed article after article, not only in his own magazine, but in the *Atlantic*, in the *Outlook*, and in a multitude of newspapers, such as the Boston *Transcript*, the New York *Times*, and the Kansas City *Star*. And always through his writings, and, indeed, through his life, there ran, like the motif of an opera, that same perpetual plea for "the forgotten man"—the need of uplifting the backward masses through training, both of the mind and of the hand.

The day came when this loyal group had other things to work with than their voices and their pens; their efforts had attracted the attention of Mr. John D. Rockefeller, who brought assistance of an extremely substantial character. In 1902 Mr. Rockefeller organized the General Education Board. Of the ten members six were taken from the Southern Education Board; other members represented general educational movements and especially the Baptist interests to which Mr. Rockefeller had been contributing for years. In a large sense, therefore, especially in its membership, the General Education Board was a development of the Ogden organization; but it was much broader in its sweep, taking under its view the entire nation and all forms of educational effort. It immediately began to concern itself with the needs of the South. In 1902 Mr. Rockefeller gave this new corporation $1,000,000; in 1905 he gave it $10,000,000; in 1907 he astonished the Nation by giving $32,000,000, and, in 1909, another $10,000,000; the whole making a total of $53,000,000, the largest sum ever given by a single man, up to that time, for social or philanthropic purposes. The General Education Board now became the chief outside interest of Page's life. He was made a member of the Executive Committee, faithfully attended all its sessions, and participated intimately in every important plan. All such bodies have their decorative members and their working members; Page belonged emphatically in the latter class. Not only was he fertile in suggestions, but his ready mind could give almost any proposal its proper emphasis and clearly set forth its essential details. Between Page and Dr. Buttrick, Secretary and now President of the Board, a close personal intimacy grew up. Dr. Buttrick moved to Teaneck Road, Englewood, where Page had his home, and many a long evening did the two men spend together, many a long walk did they take in the surrounding country, always discussing education, especially Southern education. A letter to the present writer from Dr. Abraham Flexner, the present Secretary of the Board, perhaps sums up the matter. "Page was one of the real educational statesmen of this country," says Dr. Flexner, "probably the greatest that we have had since the Civil War."

And this Rockefeller support came at a time when that movement known as the "educational awakening" had started in the South. In 1900 North Carolina elected its greatest governor since the Civil War—Charles B. Aycock. A much repeated anecdote attributes Lincoln's detestation of slavery to a slave auction that he witnessed as a small boy; Aycock's first zeal as an educational reformer had an origin that was even more pathetic, for he always carried in his mind his recollection of his own mother signing an important legal document with a cross. As a young man fresh from the university Aycock also

came under the influence of Page. An old letter, preserved among Page's papers, dated February 26, 1886,
discloses that he was a sympathizing reader of the
"mummy" controversy; when the brickbats began flying
in Page's direction Aycock wrote, telling Page that
"fully three fourths of the people are with you and wish
you Godspeed in your effort to awaken better work,
greater activity, and freer opinion in the state." And
now under Aycock's governorship North Carolina began
to tackle the educational problem with a purpose. School
houses started up all over the state at the rate of one a
day—many of them beautiful, commodious, modern structures, in every way the equals of any in the North or
West; high schools, normal schools, trade schools made
their appearance wherever the need was greatest; and
in other parts of the South the response was similarly
energetic. The reform is not yet complete, but the
description that Page gave of Southern education in
1897, accurate in all its details as it was then, has now
become ancient history.

IV

And in occupations of this kind Page passed his years
of maturity. His was not a spectacular life; his family
for the most part still remained his most immediate
interest; the daily round of an editor has its imaginative
quality, but in the main it was for Page a quiet, even a
cloistered existence; the work that an editor does, the
achievements that he can put to his credit, are usually
anonymous; and the American public little understood
the extent to which Page was influencing many of the
most vital forces of his time. The business association
that he had formed with Mr. Doubleday turned out
most happily. Their publishing house, in a short time,

attained a position of great influence and prosperity. The two men, on both the personal and the business side, were congenial and complementary; and the love that both felt for country life led to the establishment of a publishing and printing plant of unusual beauty. In Garden City, Long Island, a great brick structure was built, somewhat suggestive in its architecture of Hampton Court, surrounded by pools and fountains, Italian gardens, green walks and pergolas, gardens blooming in appropriate seasons with roses, peonies, rhododendrons, chrysanthemums, and the like, and parks of evergreen, fir, cedar, and more exotic trees and shrubs. Certainly fate could have designed no more fitting setting for Page's favourite activities than this. In assembling authors, in instigating the writing of books, in watching the achievements and the tendencies of American life, in the routine of editing his magazine—all this in association with partners whose daily companionship was a delight and a stimulation—Page spent his last years in America.

Page's independence as an editor, sufficiently indicated in the days of his vivacious youth, became even more emphatic in his maturer years. In his eyes, merely inking over so many pages of good white paper was not journalism; conviction, zeal, honesty—these were the important points. Almost on the very day that his appointment as Ambassador to Great Britain was announced his magazine published an editorial from his pen, which contained not especially complimentary references to his new chief, Mr. Bryan, the Secretary of State; naturally the newspapers found much amusement in these few sentences; but the thing was typical of Page's whole career as an editor. He held to the creed that an editor should divorce himself entirely from prejudices, animosities, and predilections; this seems an obvious, even a trite thing to say, yet there are so few men who can leave personal considerations aside in writing of men and events that it is worth while pointing out that Page was such a man. When his firm was planning to establish its magazine, his partner, Mr. Doubleday, was approached by a New York politician of large influence but shady reputation who wished to be assured that it would reflect correct political principles. "You should see Mr. Page about that," was the response. "No, this is a business matter," the insinuating gentleman went on, and then he proceeded to show that about twenty-five thousand subscribers could be obtained if the publication preached orthodox standpat doctrine. "I don't think you had better see Mr. Page," said Mr. Doubleday, dismissing his caller.

Many incidents which illustrate this independence could be given; one will suffice. In 1907 and 1908, Page's magazine published the "Random Reminiscences cf John D. Rockefeller." While the articles were appearing, the Hearst newspapers obtained a large number of letters that, some years before, had passed between Mr. John D. Archbold, President of the Standard Oil Company and one of Mr. Rockefeller's business associates from the earliest days, and Senator Joseph B. Foraker, of Ohio. These letters uncovered one of the gravest scandals that had ever involved an American public man; they instantaneously destroyed Senator Foraker's political career and hastened his death. They showed that this brilliant man had been obtaining large sums of money from the Standard Oil Company while he was filling the post of United States Senator and that at the same time he was receiving suggestions from Mr. Archbold about pending legislation. Mr. Rockefeller was not personally involved, for he had retired from active business many years before these things had been done; but the Standard Oil Company, with which his name was intimately associated, was involved and in a way that seemed to substantiate the worst charges that had been made against it. At this time Page, as a member of the General Education Board, was doing his part in helping to disperse the Rockefeller millions for public purposes; his magazine was publishing Mr. Rockefeller's reminiscences; there are editors who would have felt a certain embarrassment in commenting on the Archbold transaction. Page, however, did not hesitate. Mr. Archbold, hearing that he intended to treat the subject fully, asked him to come and see him. Page replied that he would be glad to have Mr. Archbold call upon him. The two men were brought together by friendly intermediaries in a neutral place; but the great oil magnate's explanation of his iniquities did not satisfy Page. The November, 1908, issue of the magazine contained, in one section, an interesting chapter by Mr. Rockefeller, describing the early days of the Standard Oil Company, and, in another, ten columns by Page, discussing the Archbold disclosures in language that was discriminating and well tempered, but not at all complimentary to Mr. Archbold or to the Standard Oil Company.

Occasionally Page was summoned for services of a public character. Thus President Roosevelt, whose friendship he had enjoyed for many years, asked him to serve upon his Country Life Commission—a group of men called by the President to study ways of improving the surroundings and extending the opportunities of American farmers. Page's interest in Negro education led to his appointment to the Jeanes Board. He early became an admirer of Booker Washington, and especially approved his plan for uplifting the Negro

by industrial training. One of the great services that
Page rendered literature was his persuasion of Washington to write that really great autobiography, "Up
from Slavery," and another biography in a different
field, for which he was responsible, was Miss Helen
Keller's "Story of My Life." And only once, amid these
fine but not showy activities, did Page's life assume anything in the nature of the sensational. This was in
1909, when he published his one effort at novel writing,
"The Southerner." To write novels had been an early
ambition with Page; indeed his papers disclose that he
had meditated several plans of this kind; but he never
seriously settled himself to the task until the year 1906.
In July of that year the *Atlantic Monthly* began publishing a serial entitled "The Autobiography of a Southerner Since the Civil War," by Nicholas Worth. The
literary matter that appeared under this title most
readers accepted as veracious though anonymous autobiography. It related the life adventures of a young man,
born in the South, of parents who had had little sympathy
with the Confederate cause, attempting to carve out his
career in the section of his birth and meeting opposition
and defeat from the prejudices with which he constantly
found himself in conflict. The story found its main
theme and background in the fact that the Southern
States were so exclusively living in the memories of the
Civil War that it was impossible for modern ideas to
obtain a foothold. "I have sometimes thought," said the
author, and this passage may be taken as embodying the
leading point of the narrative, "that many of the men
who survived that unnatural war unwittingly did us a
greater hurt than the war itself. It gave everyone of
them the intensest experience of his life and ever afterward he referred every other experience to this. Thus

it stopped the thought of most of them as an earthquake stops a clock. The fierce blow of battle paralyzed the mind. Their speech was a vocabulary of war, their loyalties were loyalties, not to living ideas or duties, but to old commanders and to distorted traditions. They were dead men, most of them, moving among the living as ghosts; and yet, as ghosts in a play, they held the stage." In another passage the writer names the "ghosts" which are chiefly responsible for preventing Southern progress. They are three: "The Ghost of the Confederate dead, the Ghost of religious orthodoxy, the Ghost of Negro domination." Everywhere the hero finds his progress blocked by these obstructive wraiths of the past. He seeks a livelihood in educational work—becomes a local superintendent of Public Instruction, and loses his place because his religious views are unorthodox, because he refuses to accept the popular estimate of Confederate statesmen, and because he hopes to educate the black child as well as the white one. He enters politics and runs for public office on the platform of the new day, is elected, and then finds himself counted out by political ringsters. Still he does not lose faith, and finally settles down in the management of a cotton mill, convinced that the real path of salvation lies in economic effort. This mere skeleton of a story furnishes an excuse for rehearsing again the ideas that Page had already made familiar in his writings and in his public addresses. This time the lesson is enlivened by the portrayal of certain typical characters of the post-bellum South. They are all there—the several types of Negro, ranging all the way from the faithful and philosophic plantation retainer to the lazy "'Publican" office-seeker; the political colonel, to whom the Confederate veterans and the "fair daughters of the South (God bless 'em)" are the mainstays of "civerlerzation" and indispensable in-strumentalities in the game of partisan politics; the evan-gelical clergymen who cared more for old-fashioned creeds than for the education of the masses; the disreputable edi-tor who specialized in Negro crime and constantly preached the doctrine of the "white man's country"; the Southern woman who, innocently and sincerely and even charm-ingly, upheld the ancient tradition and the ancient feud. On the other hand, Page's book portrays the buoyant enthusiast of the new day, the reformer who was seeking to establish a public school system and to strengthen the position of woman; and, above all, the quiet, hard-working industrialist who cared nothing for stump speak-ing but much for cotton mills, improved methods of farming, the introduction of diversified crops, the tidying up of cities and the country.

These chapters, extensively rewritten, were published as a book in 1909. Probably Page was under no illusion that he had created a real romance when he described his completed work as a "novel." The *Atlantic* auto-biography had attracted wide attention, and the identi-fication of the author had been immediate and accurate. Page's friends began calling his house on the telephone and asking for "Nicholas" and certain genial spirits addressed him in letters as "Marse Little Nick"—the name under which the hero was known to the old Negro family ser-vant, Uncle Ephraim—perhaps the best drawn character in the book. Page's real purpose in calling the book a "novel" therefore, was to inform the public that the story, so far as its incidents and most of its characters were concerned, was pure fiction. Certain episodes, such as those describing the hero's early days, were, in the main, veracious transcripts from Page's own life, but the rest of the book bears practically no relation to his career.

The fact that he spent his mature years in the North, editing magazines and publishing, whereas Nicholas Worth spends his in the South, engaged in educational work and in politics and industry, settles this point. The characters, too, are rather types than specific individuals, though one or two of them, particularly Professor Billy Bain, who is clearly Charles D. McIver, may be accepted as fairly accurate portraits. But as a work of fiction "The Southerner" can hardly be considered a success; the love story is too slight, the women not well done, most of the characters rather personified qualities than flesh and blood people. Its strength consists in the picture that it gives of the so-called "Southern problem," and especially of the devastating influence of slavery. From this standpoint the book is an autobiography, for the ideas and convictions it presents had formed the mental life of Page from his earliest days.

And these were the things that hurt. Yet the stories of the anger caused by "The Southerner" have been much exaggerated. It is said that a certain distinguished Southern senator declared that, had he known that Page was the author of "The Southerner," he would have blocked his nomination as Ambassador to Great Britain; certain Southern newspapers also severely denounced the volume; even some of Page's friends thought that it was a little unkind in spots; yet as a whole the Southern people accepted it as a fair, and certainly as an honest, treatment of a very difficult subject. Possibly Page was a little hard upon the Confederate veteran, and did not sufficiently portray the really pathetic aspects of his character; any shortcomings of this sort are due, not to any failing in sympathy, but to the fact that Page's zeal was absorbingly concentrated upon certain glaring abuses. And as to the accuracy of his vision in these respects there could be no question. The volume was a welcome antidote to the sentimental Southern novels that had contented themselves with glorifying a vanished society which, when the veil is stripped, was not heroic in all its phases, for it was based upon an institution so squalid as human slavery, and to those even more pernicious books which, by luridly portraying the unquestioned vices of reconstruction and the frightful consequences which resulted from giving the Negro the ballot, simply aroused useless passions and made the way out of the existing wilderness still more difficult. So the best public opinion, North and South, regarded "The Southerner," and decided that Page had performed a service to the section of his birth in writing it. Indeed the fair-minded and intelligent spirit with which the best elements in the South received "The Southerner" in itself demonstrated that this great region had entered upon a new day.

v

Nor was Page's work for the South yet ended. In the important five years from 1905 to 1910 he performed two services of an extremely practical kind. In 1906 the problem of Southern education assumed a new phase. Dr. Wallace Buttrick, the Secretary of the General Education Board, had now decided that the fundamental difficulty was economic. By that time the Southern people had revised their original conception that education was a private and not a public concern; there was now a general acceptance of the doctrine that the mental and physical training of every child, white and black, was the responsibility of the state; Aycock's campaign had worked such a popular revolution on this subject that no politician who aspired to public office would dare to take a contrary view. Yet the economic difficulty

still remained.   The South was poor; whatever might be
the general desire, the taxable resources were not sufficient to support such a comprehensive system of
popular instruction as existed in the North and West.
Any permanent improvement must therefore be based
upon the strengthening of the South's economic position.
Essentially the task was to build up Southern agriculture, which for generations had been wasteful, unintel-
ligent and consequently unproductive.   Such a far-reaching programme might well appall the most energetic
reformer, but Dr. Buttrick set to work.   He saw little
light until his attention was drawn to a quaint and
philosophic gentleman—a kind of bucolic Ben Franklin
—who was then obscurely working in the cotton lands of
Louisiana, making warfare on the boll weevil in a way
of his own.   At that time Dr. Seaman A. Knapp had
made no national reputation; yet he had evolved a plan
for redeeming country life and making American farms
more fruitful that has since worked marvellous results.
There was nothing especially sensational about its details.
Dr. Knapp had made the discovery in relation to farms
that the utilitarians had long since made with reference
to other human activities: that the only way to improve
agriculture was not to talk about it, but to go and do it.
During the preceding fifty years agricultural colleges had
sprung up all over the United States—Dr. Knapp had
been president of one himself; practically every Southern
state had one or more; agricultural lecturers covered
thousands of miles annually telling their yawning audiences how to farm; these efforts had scattered broadcast
much valuable information about the subject, but the difficulty lay in inducing the farmers to apply it.   Dr.
Knapp had a new method.   He selected a particular
farmer and persuaded him to work his fields for a period

according to methods which he prescribed.   He told his
pupil how to plough, what seed to plant, how to space his
rows, what fertilizers to use, and the like.   If a selected
acreage yielded a profitable crop which the farmer could
sell at an increased price Dr. Knapp had sufficient faith
in human nature to believe that that particular farmer
would continue to operate his farm on the new method
and that his neighbours, having this practical example of
growing prosperity, would imitate him.

Such was the famous "Demonstration Work" of Dr.
Seaman A. Knapp; this activity is now a regular branch
of the Department of Agriculture, employing thousands
of agents and spending not far from $18,000,000 a year.
Its application to the South has made practically a new
and rich country, and it has long since been extended to
other regions.   When Dr. Buttrick first met Knapp, however, there were few indications of this splendid future.
He brought Dr. Knapp North and exhibited him to
Page.   This was precisely the kind of man who appealed
to Page's sympathies.   His mind was always keenly on
the scent for the new man—the original thinker who had
some practical plan for uplifting humankind and making
life more worth while.   And Dr. Knapp's mission was
one that had filled most of his thoughts for many years;
its real purpose was the enrichment of country life.
Page therefore took to Dr. Knapp with a mighty zest.
He supported him on all occasions; he pled his cause with
great eloquence before the General Education Board,
whose purse strings were liberally unloosed in behalf of
the Knapp work; in his writings, in speeches, in letters,
in all forms of public advocacy, he insisted that Dr.
Knapp had found the solution of the agricultural problem.
The fact is that Page regarded Knapp as one of the greatest men of the time.   His feeling came out with character-

istic intensity on the occasion of the homely reformer's funeral. "The exercises," Page once told a friend, "were held in a rather dismal little church on the outskirts of Washington. The day was bleak and chill, the attendants were few—chiefly officials of the Department of Agriculture. The clergyman read the service in the most perfunctory way. Then James Wilson, the Secretary of Agriculture, spoke formally of Dr. Knapp as a faithful servant of the Department who always did well what he was told to do, commending his life in an altogether commonplace fashion. By that time my heart was pretty hot. No one seemed to divine that in the coffin before them was the body of a really great man, one who had hit upon a fruitful idea in American agriculture—an idea that was destined to cover the nation and enrich rural life immeasurably." Page was so moved by this lack of appreciation, so full of sorrow at the loss of one of his dearest friends, that, when he rose to speak, his appraisment took on a certain indignation. Their dead associate, Page declared, would outrank the generals and the politicians who received the world's plaudits, for he had devoted his life to a really great purpose; his inspiration had been the love of the common people, his faith, his sympathy had all been expended in an effort to brighten the life of the too frequently neglected masses. Page's address on this occasion was entirely extemporaneous; no record of it was ever made, but those who heard it still carry the memory of an eloquent and fiery outburst that placed Knapp's work in its proper relation to American history and gave an unforgettable picture of a patient, idealistic, achieving man whose name will loom large in the future.

During this same period Page, always on the outlook for the exceptional man, made another discovery

which has had world-wide consequences. As a member
of President Roosevelt's Country Life Commission Page
became one of the committee assigned to investigate conditions in the Southern States. The sanitarian of this
commission was Dr. Charles W. Stiles, a man who held
high rank as a zoölogist, and who, as such, had for many
years done important work with the Department of
Agriculture. Page had hardly formed Dr. Stiles's acquaintance before he discovered that, at that time, he
was a man of one idea. And this one idea had for years
brought upon his head much good-natured ridicule.
For Dr. Stiles had his own explanation for much of the
mental and physical sluggishness that prevailed in the
rural sections of the Southern States. Yet he could not
mention this without exciting uproarious laughter—
even in the presence of scientific men. Several years
previously Dr. Stiles had discovered that a hitherto unclas-
sified species of a parasite popularly known as the hookworm prevailed to an astonishing extent in all the Southern States. The pathological effects of this creature had
long been known; it localized in the intestines, there se-
creted a poison that destroyed the red blood corpuscles,
and reduced its victims to a deplorable state of anæmia,
making them constantly ill, listless, mentally dull—in
every sense of the word useless units of society. The
encouraging part of this discovery was that the patients
could quickly be cured and the hookworm eradicated by
a few simple improvements in sanitation. Dr. Stiles had
long been advocating such a campaign as an indispensable
preliminary to improving Southern life. But the humorous aspect of the hookworm always interfered with
his cause; the microbe of laziness had at last been found!

It was not until Dr. Stiles, in the course of this Southern
trip, cornered Page in a Pullman car, that he finally found

an attentive listener. Page, of course, had his preliminary laugh, but then the hookworm began to work on his
imagination. He quickly discovered that Dr. Stiles was
no fool; and before the expedition was finished, he had
become a convert and, like most converts, an extremely
zealous one. The hookworm now filled his thoughts as
completely as it did those of his friend; he studied it, he
talked about it; and characteristically he set to work to
see what could be done. How much Southern history
did the thing explain? Was it not forces like this, and
not statesmen and generals, that really controlled the destinies of mankind? Page's North Carolina country people
had for generations been denounced as "crackers," and as
"hill-billies," but here was the discovery that the great
mass of them were ill—as ill as the tuberculosis patients in
the Adirondacks. Free these masses from the enervating
parasite that consumed all their energies—for Dr. Stiles
had discovered that the disease afflicted the great majority of the rural classes—and a new generation would result. Naturally the cause strongly touched Page's sympathies. He laid the case before the ever sympathetic
Dr. Buttrick, but here again progress was slow. By
hard hammering, however, he half converted Dr. Buttrick, who, in turn, took the case of the hookworm to his
old associate, Dr. Frederick T. Gates. What Page was
determined to obtain was a million dollars or so from
Mr. John D. Rockefeller, for the purpose of engaging in
deadly warfare upon this pest. This was the proper way
to produce results: first persuade Dr. Buttrick, then
induce him to persuade Dr. Gates, who, if convinced,
had ready access to the great treasure house. But Dr.
Gates also began to smile; even the combined eloquence of Page and Dr. Buttrick could not move him.
So the reform marked time until one day Dr. Buttrick,

Dr. Gates, and Dr. Simon Flexner, the Director of the Rockefeller Institute, happened to be fellow travellers—again on a Pullman car.

"Dr. Flexner," said Dr. Buttrick—this for the benefit of his incredulous friend—"what is the scientific standing of Dr. Charles W. Stiles?"

"Very, very high," came the immediate response, and at this Dr. Gates pricked up his ears. Yet the subsequent conversation disclosed that Dr. Flexner was unfamiliar with the Stiles hookworm work. He, too, smiled at the idea, but, like Page his smile was not one of ridicule.

"If Dr. Stiles believes this," was his dictum, "it is something to be taken most seriously."

As Dr. Flexner is probably the leading medical scientist in the United States, his judgment at once lifted the hookworm issue to a new plane. Dr. Gates ceased laughing and events now moved rapidly. Mr. Rockefeller gave a million dollars to a sanitary commission for the eradication of the hookworm in the Southern States, and of this Page became a charter member. In this way an enterprise that is the greatest sanitary and health reform of modern times had its beginnings. So great was the success of the Hookworm Commission in the South, so many thousands were almost daily restored to health and usefulness, that Mr. Rockefeller extended its work all over the world—to India, Egypt, China, Australia, to all sections that fall within the now accurately located "hookworm belt." Out of it grew the great International Health Commission, also endowed with unlimited millions of Rockefeller money, which is engaged in stamping out disease and promoting medical education in all quarters of the globe. Dr. Stiles and Page's associates on the General Education Board attribute the origin of this work to the simple fact that Page,

Walter H. Page (1899), from a photograph taken when he was
editor of the *Atlantic Monthly*

Dr. Wallace Buttrick, President of the General Education Board

great humourist that he was, could temper his humour with intelligence, and could therefore perceive the point at which a joke ceased to be a joke and actually concealed a truth of the most far-reaching importance to mankind.

Page enjoyed the full results of this labour one night in the autumn of 1913, when Dr. Wickliffe Rose, the head of the International Health Board, came to London to discuss the possibility of beginning hookworm work in the British Empire, especially in Egypt and India. Page, as Ambassador, arranged a dinner at the Marlborough Club, attended by the leading medical scientists of the kingdom and several members of the Cabinet. Dr. Rose's description of his work made a deep impression. He was informed that the British Government was only too ready to coöperate with the Health Board. When the discussion was ended the Right Honourable Lewis Harcourt, the Secretary of State for the Colonies, concluded an eloquent address with these words:

"The time will come when we shall look back on this evening as the beginning of a new era in British colonial administration."

CHAPTER IV

THE WILSONIAN ERA BEGINS

I

IT WAS Page's interest in the material and spiritual elevation of the masses that first directed his attention to the Presidential aspirations of Woodrow Wilson. So much history has been made since 1912 that the public questions which then stirred the popular mind have largely passed out of recollection. Yet the great rallying cry of that era was democracy, spelled with a small "d." In the fifty years since the Civil War only one Democratic President had occupied the White House. The Republicans' long lease of power had produced certain symptoms which their political foes now proceeded to describe as great public abuses. The truth of the matter, of course, is that neither political virtue nor political depravity was the exclusive possession of either of the great national organizations. The Republican party, especially under the enlightened autocracy of Roosevelt, had started such reforms as conservation, the improvement of country life, the regulation of the railroads, and the warfare on the trusts, and had shown successful interest in such evidences of the new day as child labour laws, employer's liability laws, corrupt practice acts, direct primaries and the popular election of United States Senators—not all perhaps wise as methods, but all certainly inspired with a new conception of democratic government. Roosevelt also had led in the onslaught on that corporation influence which, after all, constituted the great problem of American politics. But Mr. Taft's administration had impressed many men, and especially Page, as a discouraging slump back into the ancient system. Page was never blind to the inadequacies of his own party; the three campaigns of Bryan and his extensive influence with the Democratic masses at times caused him deep despair; that even the corporations had extended their tentacles into the ranks of Jefferson was all too obvious a fact; yet the Democratic party at that time Page regarded as the most available instrument for embodying in legislation and practice the new things in which he most believed. Above all, the Democratic party in 1912 possessed one asset to which the Republicans could lay no claim—a new man, a new leader, the first statesman who had crossed its threshold since Grover Cleveland.

Like many scholarly Americans, Page had been charmed by the intellectual brilliancy of Woodrow Wilson. The utter commonplaceness of much of what passes for political thinking in this country had for years discouraged him. American political life may have possessed energy, character, even greatness; but it was certainly lacking in distinction. It was this new quality that Wilson brought, and it was this that attracted thousands of cultivated Americans to his standard, irrespective of party. The man was an original thinker; he exercised the priceless possession of literary style. He entertained; he did not weary; even his temperamental deficiencies, which were apparent to many observers in 1912, had at least the advantage that attaches to the interesting and the unusual.

What Page and thousands of other public-spirited men saw in Wilson was a leader of fine intellectual gifts who was prepared to devote his splendid energies to making life more attractive and profitable to the "Forgotten Man." Here was the opportunity then, to embody in one imaginative statesman all the interest which for a generation had been accumulating in favour of the democratic revival. At any rate, after thirty years of Republican half-success and half-failure, here was the chance for a new deal. Amid a mob of shopworn public men, here was one who had at least the charm of novelty.

Page had known Mr. Wilson for thirty years, and all this time the Princeton scholar had seemed to him to be one of the most helpful influences at work in the United States. As already noted Page had met the future President when he was serving a journalistic apprenticeship in Atlanta, Georgia. Wilson was then spending his days in a dingy law office and was putting to good use the time consumed in waiting for the clients who never came by writing that famous book on "Congressional Government" which first lifted his name out of obscurity. This work, the product of a man of twenty-nine, was perhaps the first searching examination to which the American Congressional system had ever been subjected. It brought Wilson a professorship at the newly established Bryn Mawr College and drew to him other growing minds like Page's. "Watch that man!" was Page's admonition to his friends. Wilson then went into academic work and Page plunged into the exactions of daily and periodical journalism, but Page's papers show that the two men had kept in touch with each other during the succeeding thirty years. These papers include a collection of letters from Woodrow Wilson, the earliest of which is dated October 30, 1885, when the future President was beginning his career at Bryn Mawr. He was eager to come to New York, Wilson said, and discuss with Page "half a hundred topics" suggested by "Congressional Government." The atmosphere at Bryn Mawr was evidently not stimulating. "Such a talk would give me a chance to let off some of the enthusiasm I am just now painfully stirring up in enforced silence." The *Forum* and the *Atlantic Monthly*, when Page was editor, showed many traces of his interest in Wilson, who was one of his most frequent contributors. When Wilson became President of Princeton, he occasionally called upon his old *Atlantic* friend for advice. He writes to Page on various matters—to ask for suggestions about filling a professorship or a lectureship; and there are also references to the difficulties Wilson is having with the Princeton trustees.

Page's letters also portray the new hopes with which Wilson inspired him. One of his best loved correspondents was Henry Wallace, editor of *Wallace's Farmer*, a homely and genial Rooseveltian. Page was one of those who immensely admired Roosevelt's career; but he regarded him as a man who had finished his work, at least in domestic affairs, and whose great claim upon posterity would be as the stimulator of the American conscience. "I see you are coming around to Wilson," Page writes, "and in pretty rapid fashion. I assure you that that is the solution of the problem. I have known him since we were boys, and I have been studying him lately with a great deal of care. I haven't any doubt but that is the way out. The old labels 'Democrat' and 'Republican' have ceased to have any meaning, not only in my mind and in yours, but I think in the minds of nearly all the people. Don't you feel that way?"

The campaign of 1912 was approaching its end when this letter was written; and no proceeding in American politics had so aroused Page's energies. He had himself played a part in Wilson's nomination. He was one of the first to urge the Princeton President to seize the great opportunity that was rising before him. These suggestions were coming from many sources in the summer of 1910; Mr. Wilson was about to retire from the Presidency of Princeton; the movement had started to make him Governor of New Jersey, and it was well understood that this was merely intended as the first step to the White House. But Mr. Wilson was himself undecided; to escape the excitement of the moment he had retired to a country house at Lyme, Connecticut. In this place, in response to a letter, Page now sought him out. His visit was a plea that Mr. Wilson should accept his proffered fate; the Governorship of New Jersey, then the Presidency, and the opportunity to promote the causes in which both men believed.

"But do you think I can do it, Page?" asked the hesitating Wilson.

"I am sure you can": and then Page again, with his customary gusto, launched into his persuasive argument. His host at one moment would assent; at another present the difficulties; it was apparent that he was having trouble in reaching a decision. To what extent Page's conversation converted him the record does not disclose; it is apparent, however, that when, in the next two years, difficulties came, his mind seemed naturally to turn in Page's direction. Especially noticeable is it that he appeals to Page for help against his fool friends. An indiscreet person in New Jersey is booming Mr. Wilson for the Presidency; the activity of such a man inevitably brings ridicule upon the object of his attention; cannot Page find some kindly way of calling him off? Mr. Wilson asks Page's advice about a campaign manager, and incidentally expresses his own aversion to a man of "large calibre" for this engagement. There were occasional conferences with Mr. Wilson on his Presidential prospects, one of which took place at Page's New York apartment. Page was also the man who brought Mr. Wilson and Colonel House together; this had the immediate result of placing the important state of Texas on the Wilson side, and, as its ultimate consequence, brought about one of the most important associations in the history of American politics. Page had known Colonel House for many years and was the advocate who convinced the sagacious Texan that Woodrow Wilson was the man. Wilson also acquired the habit of referring to Page men who offered themselves to him as volunteer workers in his cause. "Go and see Walter Page" was his usual answer to this kind of an approach. But Page was not a collector of delegates to nominating conventions; not his the art of manipulating these assemblages in the interest of a favoured man; yet his services to the Wilson cause, while less demonstrative, were almost as practical. His talent lay in exposition; and he now took upon himself the task of spreading Wilson's fame. In his own magazine and in books published by his firm, in letters to friends, in personal conferences, he set forth Wilson's achievements. Page also persuaded Wilson to make his famous speechmaking trip through the Western States in 1911 and this was perhaps his largest definite contribution to the Wilson campaign. It was in the course of this historic pilgrimage that the American masses obtained their first view of a previously too-much hidden figure.

On election day Page wrote the President-elect a letter of congratulation which contains one item of the greatest interest. When the time came for the new President to deliver his first message to Congress, he surprised the country by abandoning the usual practice of sending a long written communication to be droned out by a reading clerk to a yawning company of legislators. He appeared in person and read the document himself. As President Harding has followed his example it seems likely that this innovation, which certainly represents a great improvement over the old routine, has become the established custom. The origin of the idea therefore has historic value.

To Woodrow Wilson

Garden City, N. Y.
Election Day, 1912. [Nov. 5]

MY DEAR MR. PRESIDENT-ELECT:

Before going into town to hear the returns, I write you my congratulations. Even if you were defeated, I should still congratulate you on putting a Presidential campaign on a higher level than it has ever before reached since Washington's time. Your grip became firmer and your sweep wider every week. It was inspiring to watch the unfolding of the deep meaning of it and to see the people's grasp of the main idea. It was fairly, highly, freely, won, and now we enter the Era of Great Opportunity. It is hard to measure the extent or the thrill of the new interest in public affairs and the new hope that you have aroused in thousands of men who were becoming hopeless under the long-drawn-out reign of privilege.

To the big burden of suggestions that you are receiving, may I add these small ones?

1. Call Congress in extra session mainly to revise the tariff and incidentally to prepare the way for rural credit societies.

Mr. Taft set the stage admirably in 1909 when he promptly called an extra session; but then he let the villain run the play. To get the main job in hand at once will be both dramatic and effective and it will save time. Moreover, it will give you this great tactical advantage—you can the better keep in line those who have debts or doubts before you have answered their importunities for offices and for favours.

The time is come when the land must be developed by the new agriculture and farming made a business. This calls for money. Every acre will repay a reasonable loan on long time at a fair interest rate, and group-borrowing develops the men quite as much as the men will develop the soil. It saved the German Empire and is remaking Italy. And this is the proper use of much of the money that now flows into the reach of the credit barons. This building up of farm life will restore the equilibrium of our civilization and, besides, will prove to be one half the solution of our currency and credit problem. . . .

2. Set your trusted friends immediately to work, every man in the field he knows best, to prepare briefs for you on such great subjects and departments as the Currency, the Post Office, Conservation, Rural Credit, the Agricultural Department, which has the most direct power for good to the most people—to make our farmers as independent as Denmark's and to give our best country folk the dignity of the old-time English gentleman —this expert, independent information to compare with your own knowledge and with official reports.

3. The President reads (or speaks) his Inaugural to the people. Why not go back to the old custom of himself delivering his Messages to Congress? Would that not restore a feeling of comradeship in responsibility and make the Legislative branch feel nearer to the Executive? Every President of our time has sooner or later got away with Congress.

I cannot keep from saying what a new thrill of hope and tingle of expectancy I feel—as of a great event about to happen for our country and for the restoration of popular government; for you will keep your rudder true.

Most heartily yours,

WALTER H. PAGE.

To Governor Wilson,
  Princeton, N. J.

Page was one of the first of Mr. Wilson's friends to discuss with the President-elect the new legislative programme. The memorandum which he made of this interview shows how little any one, in 1912, appreciated the tremendous problems that Mr. Wilson would have to face. Only domestic matters then seemed to have the slightest importance. Especially significant is the fact that even at this early date, Page was chiefly impressed by Mr. Wilson's "loneliness."

Memorandum dated November 15, 1912

To use the Government, especially the Department of Agriculture and the Bureau of Education, to help actively in the restoration of country life—that's the great chance for Woodrow Wilson, ten days ago elected President. Precisely how well he understands this chance, how well, for example, he understands the grave difference between the Knapp Demonstration method of teaching farmers and the usual Agricultural College method of lecturing to them, and what he knows about the rising movement for country schools of the right sort, and agricultural credit societies—how all this great constructive problem of Country Life lies in his mind, who knows? I do not. If I do not know, who does know? The political managers who have surrounded him these six months have now done their task. *They* know nothing of this Big Chance and Great Outlook. And for the moment they have left him alone. In two days he will go to Bermuda for a month to rest and to meditate. He ought to meditate on this Constructive programme. It seemed my duty to go and tell him about it. I asked for an interview and he telegraphed to go to-day at five o'clock.

Arthur and I drove in the car and reached Princeton just before five—a beautiful drive of something less than four hours from New York. Presently we arrived at the Wilson house.

"The Governor is engaged," I was informed by the man who opened the door. "He can see nobody. He is going away to-morrow."

"I have an appointment with him," said I, and I gave him my card.

"I know he can't see anybody."

"Will you send my card in?"

We waited at the door till the maid took it in and returned to say the Governor would presently come down.

The reception room had a desk in the corner, and on a row of chairs across the whole side of the room were piles of unopened letters. It is a plain, modestly but decently furnished room, such as you would expect to find in the modest house of a professor at Princeton. During his presidency of the college, he had lived in the President's house in the college yard. This was his own house of his professorial days.

"Hello, Page, come out here: I am glad to see you." There he stood in a door at the back of the room, which led to his library and work room. "Come back here."

"In the best of all possible worlds the right thing does sometimes happen," said I.

"Yes."

"And a great opportunity."

He smiled and was cordial and said some pleasant words. But he was weary. "I have cobwebs in my head." He was not depressed but oppressed—rather shy, I thought, and I should say rather lonely. The campaign noise and the little campaigners were hushed and gone. There were no men of companionable size about him, and the Great Task lay before him. The Democratic party has not brought forward large men in public life during its long term of exclusion from the Government; and the newly elected President has had few opportunities and a very short time to make acquaintances of a continental kind. This little college town, this little hitherto corrupt state, are both small.

I went at my business without delay. The big country-life idea, the working of great economic forces to put its vitalization within sight, the coming equilibrium by the restoration of country life—all coincident with his coming into the Presidency. His Administration must fall in with it, guide it, further it. The chief instruments are the Agricultural Department, the Bureau of Education, and the power of the President himself to bring about Rural Credit Societies and similar organized helps. He quickly saw the difference between Demonstration Work by the Agricultural Department and the plan to vote large sums to agricultural colleges and to the states to build up schools.

"Who is the best man for Secretary of Agriculture?"

I ought to have known, but I didn't. For who is?

"May I look about and answer your question later?"

"Yes, I will thank you."

"I wish to find the very best men for my Cabinet, regardless of consequences. I do not forget the party as an instrument of government, and I do not wish to do violence to it. But I must have the best men in the

Nation"—with a very solemn tone as he sat bolt upright, with a stern look on his face, and a lonely look.

I told him my idea of the country school that must be and talked of the Bureau of Education. He saw quickly and assented to all my propositions.

And then we talked somewhat more conservatively of Conservation, about which he knows less.

I asked if he would care to have me make briefs about the Agricultural Department, the Bureau of Education, the Rural Credit Societies, and Conservation. "I shall be very grateful, if it be not too great a sacrifice."

I had gained that permission, which (if he respect my opinion) ought to guide him somewhat toward a real understanding of how the Government may help toward our Great Constructive Problem.

I gained also the impression that he has no sympathy with the idea of giving government grants to schools and agricultural colleges—a very distinct impression.

I had been with him an hour and had talked (I fear) too much. But he seemed hearty in his thanks. He came to the front door with me, insisted on helping me on with my coat, envied me the motor-car drive in the night back to New York, spoke to eight or ten reporters who had crowded into the hall for their interview—a most undignified method, it seemed to me, for a President-elect to reach the public; I stepped out on the muddy street, and, as I walked to the Inn, I had the feeling of the man's oppressive loneliness as he faced his great task. There is no pomp of circumstance, nor hardly dignity in this setting, except the dignity of his seriousness and his loneliness.

There was a general expectation that Page would become a member of President Wilson's Cabinet, and the place

for which he seemed particularly qualified was the Secretaryship of Agriculture. The smoke of battle had hardly
passed away, therefore, when Page's admirers began
bringing pressure to bear upon the President-elect.
There was probably no man in the United States who had
such completely developed views about this Department
as Page; and it is not improbable that, had circumstances
combined to offer him this position, he would have accepted it. But fate in matters of this sort is sometimes
kinder than a man's friends. Page had a great horror of
anything which suggested office-seeking, and the campaign which now was started in his interest greatly
embarrassed him. He wrote Mr. Wilson, disclaiming
all responsibility and begging him to ignore these
misguided efforts. As the best way of checking the
movement, Page now definitely answered Mr. Wilson's
question: Who was the best man for the Agricultural
Department? It is interesting to note that the candidate
whom Page nominated in this letter—a man who had
been his friend for many years and an associate on the
Southern Education Board—was the man whom Mr.
Wilson chose.

To Woodrow Wilson

Garden City, N. Y.
November 27, 1912.

MY DEAR WILSON:

I send you (wrongly, perhaps, when you are trying to
rest) the shortest statement that I could make about the
demonstration field-work of the Department of Agriculture. This is the best tool yet invented to shape country
life. Other (and shorter) briefs will be ready in a little
while.

You asked me who I thought was the best man for Secretary of Agriculture. Houston,[1] I should say, of the men that I know. You will find my estimate of him in the little packet of memoranda. Van Hise[2] may be as good or even better if he be young in mind and adaptable enough. But he seems to me a man who may already have done his big job.

I answer the other questions you asked at Princeton and I have taken the liberty to send some memoranda about a few other men—on the theory that every friend of yours ought now to tell you with the utmost frankness about the men he knows, of whom you may be thinking.

The building up of the countryman is the big constructive job of our time. When the countryman comes to his own, the town man will no longer be able to tax, and to concentrate power, and to bully the world.

Very heartily yours,
WALTER H. PAGE.

To Henry Wallace

Garden City, N. Y.
11 March, 1913.

MY DEAR UNCLE HENRY:

What a letter yours is! By George! we must get on the job, you and I, of steering the world— get on it a little more actively. Else it may run amuck. We have frightful responsibilities in this matter. The subject weighs the more deeply and heavily on me because I am just back from a month's vacation in North Carolina, where I am going to build me a winter and old-age bungalow. No; you would be disappointed if you went out of

---

[1]Mr. David F. Houston, ex-President of the University of Texas, and in 1912 Chancellor of the Washington University of St. Louis.

[2]Charles R. Van Hise, President of the University of Wisconsin.

your way to see my boys. Moreover, they are now
merely clearing land. They sold out the farm they put
in shape, after two years' work, for just ten times what
it had cost, and they are now starting another one *de
novo*. About a year hence, they'll have something to
show. And next winter, when my house is built down
there, I want you to come and see me and see that country. I'll show you one of the most remarkable farmers'
clubs you ever saw and many other interesting things as
well—many, very many. I'm getting into this farm
business in dead earnest. That's the dickens of it: how
can I do my share in our partnership to run the universe
if I give my time to cotton-growing problems? It's a
tangled world.

Well, bless your soul! You and the younger Wallaces
(my regards to every one of them) and Poe[1]—you are all
very kind to think of me for that difficult place—too difficult by far, for me. Besides, it would have cost me my
life. If I were to go into public life, I should have had
to sell my whole interest here. This would have meant
that I could never make another dollar. More than that,
I'd have thrown away a trade that I've learned and gone
at another one that I know little about—a bad change,
surely. So, you see, there never was anything serious
in this either in my mind or in the President's. Arthur
hit it off right one day when somebody asked him:

"Is your father going to take the Secretaryship of
Agriculture?"

He replied: "Not seriously."

Besides, the President didn't ask me! He knew too
much for that.

But he did ask me who would be a good man and I
said "Houston." You are not quite fair to him in your

---

[1]Clarence Poe, editor of *The Progressive Farmer*.

Charles D. McIver of Greensboro, North Carolina, a
leader in the cause of Southern Education

Woodrow Wilson in 1912

editorial. He does know—knows much and well and is the strongest man in the Cabinet—in promise. The farmers don't yet know him: that's the only trouble. Give him a chance.

I've "put it up" to the new President and to the new Secretary to get on the job immediately of *organizing country life.* I've drawn up a scheme (a darned good one, too) which they have. I have good hope that they'll get to it soon and to the thing that we have all been working toward. I'm very hopeful about this. I told them both last week to get their minds on this before the wolves devour them. Don't you think it better to work with the Government and to try to steer it right than to go off organizing other agencies?

God pity our new masters! The President is all right. He's sound, earnest, courageous. But his party! I still have some muscular strength. In certain remote regions they still break stones in the road by hand. Now I'll break stones before I'd have a job at Washington now. I spent four days with them last week—the new crowd. They'll try their best. I think they'll succeed. But, if they do succeed and survive, they'll come out of the scrimmage bleeding and torn. We've got to stand off and run 'em, Uncle Henry. That's the only hope I see for the country. Don't damn Houston, then, beforehand. He's a real man. Let's get on the job and tell 'em how.

Now, when you come East, come before you need to get any of your meetings and strike a bee-line for Garden City; and don't be in a hurry when you get here. If a Presbyterian meeting be necessary for your happiness, I'll drum up one on the Island for you. And, of course, you must come to my house and pack up right and get your legs steady sometime before you sail—you and Mrs. Wallace: will she not go with you?

In the meantime, don't be disgruntled.   We can steer
the old world right, if you'll just keep your shoulder to
the wheel.   We'll work it all out here in the summer and
verify it all (including your job of setting the effete
kingdoms of Europe all right)—we'll verify it all next
winter down in North Carolina.   I think things have
got such a start that they'll keep going in some fashion,
till we check up the several items, political, ethical, agricultural, journalistic, and international.   God bless us
all!

Most heartily always yours,

WALTER H. PAGE.

Though Mr. Wilson did not offer Page the Agricultural
Department, he much desired to have him in his Cabinet,
and had already decided upon him for a post which the
new President probably regarded as more important—
the Interior.   The narrow margin with which Page
escaped this responsibility illustrates again the slender
threads upon which history is constructed.   The episode
is also not without its humorous side.   For there was
only one reason why Page did not enter the Cabinet as
Secretary of the Interior; and that is revealed in the above
letter to "Uncle Henry"; he was so busy planning his
new house in the sandhills of North Carolina that, while
cabinets were being formed and great decisions taken,
he was absent from New York.   A short time before the
inauguration, Mr. Wilson asked Colonel House to arrange a meeting with Page in the latter's apartment.
Mr. Wilson wished to see him on a Saturday; the purpose was to offer him the Secretaryship of the Interior.
Colonel House called up Page's office at Garden City and
was informed that he was in North Carolina.   Colonel
House then telegraphed asking Page to start north im-

mediately, and suggesting the succeeding Monday as a good time for the interview. A reply was at once received from Page that he was on his way.

Meanwhile certain of Mr. Wilson's advisers had heard of the plan and were raising objections. Page was a Southerner; the Interior Department has supervision over the pension bureau, with its hundreds of thousands of Civil War veterans as pensioners; moreover, Page was an outspoken enemy of the whole pension system and had led several "campaigns" against it. The appointment would never do! Mr. Wilson himself was persuaded that it would be a mistake.

"But what are we going to do about Page?" asked Colonel House. "I have summoned him from North Carolina on important business. What excuse shall I give for bringing him way up here?"

But the President-elect was equal to the emergency.

"Here's the cabinet list," he drily replied. "Show it to Page. Tell him these are the people I have about decided to appoint and ask him what he thinks of them. Then he will assume that we summoned him to get his advice."

When Page made his appearance, therefore, Colonel House gave him the list of names and solemnly asked him what he thought of them. The first name that attracted Page's attention was that of Josephus Daniels, as Secretary of the Navy. Page at once expressed his energetic dissent.

"Why, don't you think he is Cabinet timber?" asked Colonel House.

"Timber!" Page fairly shouted. "He isn't a splinter! Have you got a time table? When does the next train leave for Princeton?"

In a couple of hours Page was sitting with Mr. Wilson,

earnestly protesting against Mr. Daniels's appointment. But Mr. Wilson said that he had already offered Mr. Daniels the place.

II

About the time of Wilson's election a great calamity befell one of Page's dearest friends.   Dr. Edwin A. Alderman, the President of the University of Virginia, one of the pioneer educational forces in the Southern States, and for years an associate of Page on the General Education Board, was stricken with tuberculosis.   He was taken to Saranac, and here a patient course of treatment happily restored him to health.   One of the dreariest aspects of such an experience is its tediousness and loneliness.   Yet the maintenance of one's good spirits and optimism is an essential part of the treatment.   And it was in this work that Page now proved an indispensable aid to the medical men.   As soon as Dr. Alderman found himself stretched out, a weak and isolated figure, cut off from those activities and interests which had been his inspiration for forty years, with no companions except his own thoughts and a few sufferers like himself, letters began to arrive with weekly regularity from the man whom he always refers to as "dear old Page."   The gayety and optimism of these letters, the lively comments which they passed upon men and things, and their wholesome and genial philosophy, were largely instrumental, Dr. Alderman has always believed, in his recovery.   Their effect was so instant and beneficial that the physicians asked to have them read to the other patients, who also derived abounding comfort and joy from them.   The whole episode was one of the most beautiful in Page's life, and brings out again that gift for friendship which was perhaps his finest quality.   For this reason it is a calamity that most of these letters have not been preserved. The few that have survived are interesting not only in themselves; they reveal Page's innermost thoughts on the subject of Woodrow Wilson. That he admired the new President is evident, yet these letters make it clear that, even in 1912 and 1913, there was something about Mr. Wilson that caused him to hesitate, to entertain doubts, to wonder how, after all, the experiment was to end.

To Edwin A. Alderman

Garden City, L. I.
December 31, 1912.

MY DEAR ED ALDERMAN:

I have a new amusement, a new excitement, a new study, as you have and as we all have who really believe in democracy—a new study, a new hope, and sometimes a new fear; and its name is Wilson. I have for many years regarded myself as an interested, but always a somewhat detached, outsider, believing that the democratic idea was real and safe and lifting, if we could ever get it put into action, contenting myself ever with such patches of it as time and accident and occasion now and then sewed on our gilded or tattered garments. But now it is come—the real thing; at any rate a man somewhat like us, whose thought and aim and dream are our thought and aim and dream. That's enormously exciting! I didn't suppose I'd ever become so interested in a general proposition or in a governmental hope.

Will he do it? Can he do it? Can anybody do it? How can we help him do it? Now that the task is on him, does he really understand? Do I understand him and he me? There's a certain unreality about it.

The man himself—I find that nobody quite knows him

now. Alas! I wonder if he quite knows himself. Temperamentally very shy, having lived too much alone and far too much with women (how I wish two of his daughters were sons!) this Big Thing having descended on him before he knew or was quite prepared for it, thrust into a whirl of self-seeking men even while he is trying to think out the theory of the duties that press, knowing the necessity of silence, surrounded by small people—well, I made up my mind that his real friends owed it to him and to what we all hope for, to break over his reserve and to volunteer help. He asks for conferences with official folk —only, I think. So I began to write memoranda about those subjects of government about which I know something and have opinions and about men who are or who may be related to them. It has been great sport to set down in words without any reserve precisely what you think. It is imprudent, of course, as most things worth doing are. But what have I to lose, I who have my life now planned and laid out and have got far beyond the reach of gratitude or hatred or praise or blame or fear of any man? I sent him some such memoranda. Here came forthwith a note of almost abject thanks. I sent more. Again, such a note—written in his own hand. Yet not a word of what he thinks. The Sphinx was garrulous in comparison. Then here comes a mob of my good friends crying for office for me. So I sent a ten-line note, by the hand of my secretary, saying that this should not disturb my perfect frankness nor (I knew it would not) his confidence. Again, a note in his own hand, of perfect understanding and with the very glow of gratitude. And he talks—generalities to the public. Perhaps that's all he can talk now. Wise? Yes. But does he know the men about him? Does he really know men? Nobody knows. Thus 'twixt fear and hope I see—suspense. I'll swear I can't doubt, I can't believe. Whether it is going to work out or not—whether he or anybody can work it out of the haze of theory—nobody knows; and nobody's speculation is better than mine and mine is worthless.

This is the game, this is the excitement, this is the doubthope and the hopedoubt. I send this word about it to you (I could and would to nobody else: you're snow-bound, you see, and don't write much and don't see many people: restrain your natural loquacity!) But for the love of heaven tell me if you see any way *very clearly.* It's a kind of misty dream to me.

I ask myself why should I concern myself about it? Of course the answer's easy and I think creditable: I do profoundly hold this democratic faith and believe that it can be worked into action among men; and it may be I shall yet see it done. That's the secret of my interest. But when this awful office descends on a man, it oppresses him, changes him, you are not quite so sure of him, you doubt whether he knows himself or you in the old way.

And I find among men the very crudest ideas of government or of democracy. They have not thought the thing out. They hold no ordered creed of human organization or advancement. They leave all to chance and think, when they think at all, that chance determines it. And yet the Great Hope persists, and I think I have grown an inch by it.

I wonder how it seems, looked at from the cold mountains of Lake Saranac?

It's the end of the year. Mrs. Page and I (alone!) have been talking of democracy, of these very things I've written. The bell-ringing and the dancing and the feasting are not, on this particular year, to our liking.

We see all our children gone—half of them to nests of their own building, the rest on errands of their own pleasure, and we are left, young yet, but the main job of life behind us! We're going down to a cottage in southern North Carolina (with our own cook and motor car, praise God!) for February, still further to think this thing out and incidentally to build us a library, in which we'll live when we can. That, for convention's sake, we call a Vacation.

Your brave note came to-day. Of course, you'll "get" 'em—those small enemies. The gain of twelve pounds tells the story. The danger is, your season of philosophy and reverie will be too soon ended. Don't fret; the work and the friends will be here when you come down. There's many a long day ahead; and there may not be so many seasons of rest and meditation. You are the only man I know who has time enough to think out a clear answer to this: "What ought to be done with Bryan?" What *can* be done with Bryan? When you find the answer, telegraph it to me.

I've a book or two more to send you. If they interest you, praise the gods. If they bore you, fling 'em in the snow and think no worse of me. You can't tell what a given book may be worth to a given man in an unknown mood. They've become such a commodity to me that I thank my stars for a month away from them when I may come at 'em at a different angle and really need a few old ones—Wordsworth, for instance. When you get old enough, you'll wake up some day with the feeling that the world is much more beautiful than it was when you were young, that a landscape has a closer meaning, that the sky is more companionable, that outdoor colour and motion are more splendidly audacious and beautifully rhythmical than you had ever thought. That's true. The gently snow-clad little pines out my window are more to me than the whole Taft Administration. They'll soon be better than the year's dividends. And the few great craftsmen in words who can confirm this feeling—they are the masters you become grateful for. Then the sordidness of the world lies far beneath you and your great democracy is truly come—the democracy of Nature. To be akin to a tree, in this sense, is as good as to be akin to a man. I have a grove of little long-leaf pines down in the old country and I know they'll have some consciousness of me after all men have forgotten me: I've saved 'em, and they'll sing a century of gratitude if I can keep 'em saved. Joe Holmes gave me a dissertation on them the other day. He was down there "on a little Sunday jaunt" of forty miles—the best legs and the best brain that ever worked together in one anatomy.

A conquering New Year—that's what you'll find, begun before this reaches you, carrying all good wishes from

Yours affectionately,

W. H. P.

To Edwin A. Alderman

Garden City, New York,
January 26, 1913.

MY DEAR ED ALDERMAN:

This has been "Board"[1] week, as you know. The men came from all quarters of the land, and we had a good time. New work is opening; old work is going well; the fellowship ran in good tide—except that everybody asked everybody else: "What do you know about Alderman?" Everybody who had late news of you gave

---

[1]The reference is to the meeting of the Southern and the General Education Boards.

a good report. The Southern Board formally passed a resolution to send affectionate greetings to you and high hope and expectation, and I was commissioned to frame the message. This is it. I shall write no formal resolution, for that wasn't the spirit of it. The fellows all asked me, singly and collectively, to send their love. And we don't put that sort of a message under *whereases* and *wherefores*. There they were, every one of them, except Peabody and Bowie. Mr. Ogden in particular was anxious for his emphatic remembrance and good wishes to go. The dear old man is fast passing into the last stage of his illness and he knows it and he soon expects the end, in a mood as brave and as game as he ever was. I am sorry to tell you he suffers a good deal of pain.

What a fine thing to look back over—this Southern Board's work! Here was a fine, zealous merchant twenty years ago, then fifty-seven years old, who saw this big job as a modest layman. If he had known more about "Education" or more about "the South, bygawd, sir!" he'd never have had the courage to tackle the job. But with the bravery of ignorance, he turned out to be the wisest man on that task in our generation. He has united every real, good force, and he showed what can be done in a democracy even by one zealous man. I've sometimes thought that this is possibly the wisest single piece of work that I have ever seen done—*wisest*, not smartest. I don't know what can be done when he's gone. His phase of it is really done. But, if another real leader arise, there will doubtless be another phase.

The General Board doesn't find much more college-endowing to do. We made only one or two gifts. But we are trying to get the country school task rightly focussed. We haven't done it yet; but we will. Buttrick and Rose will work it out. I wish to God I could throw down my practical job and go at it with 'em. Darned if I couldn't get it going! though *I* say it, as shouldn't. And we are going pretty soon to begin with the medical colleges; that, I think, is good—very.

But the most efficient workmanlike piece of organization that my mortal eyes have ever seen is Rose's hookworm work. We're going soon to organize country life in a sanitary way, the county health officer being the biggest man on the horizon. Stiles has moved his marine hospital and his staff to Wilmington, North Carolina, and he and the local health men are quietly going to make New Hanover the model county for sanitary condition and efficiency. You'll know what a vast revolution that denotes!—And Congress seems likely to charter the big Rockefeller Foundation, which will at once make five millions available for chasing the hookworm off the face of the earth. Rose will spread himself over Honduras, etc., etc., and China, and India! This does literally beat the devil; for, if the hookworm isn't the devil, what is?

I'm going to farming. I've two brothers and two sons, all young and strong, who believe in the game. We have land without end, thousands of acres; engines to pull stumps, to plough, to plant, to reap. The nigger go hang! A white boy with an engine can outdo a dozen of 'em. Cotton and corn for staple crops; peaches, figs, scuppernongs, vegetables, melons for incidental crops; God's good air in North Carolina; good roads, too—why, man, Moore County has authorized the laying out of a strip of land along all highways to be planted in shrubbery and fruit trees and kept as a park, so that you will motor for 100 miles through odorous bloom in spring!—I mean I am going down there to-morrow for a month, one day for golf at Pinehurst, the next day for clearing land with an oil locomotive, ripping up stumps! Every day for life out-of-doors and every night, too. I'm going to grow dasheens. You know what a dasheen is? It's a Trinidad potato, which keeps and tastes like a sweet potato stuffed with chestnuts. There are lots of things to learn in this world.

God bless us all, old man. It's a pretty good world, whether seen from the petty excitements of reforming the world and dreaming of a diseaseless earth in New York, or from the stump-pulling recreation of a North Carolina wilderness.

Health be with you!

W. H. P.

To Edwin A. Alderman

Garden City, L. I.
March 10, 1913.

My dear Ed Alderman:

I'm home from a month of perfect climate in the sandhills of North Carolina, where I am preparing a farm and building a home at least for winter use; and I had the most instructive and interesting month of my life there. I believe I see, even in my life-time, the coming of a kind of man and a kind of life that shall come pretty near to being the model American citizen and the model American way to live. Half of it is climate; a fourth of it occupation; the other fourth, companionship. And the climate (with what it does) is three fourths companionship.

Then I came to Washington and saw Wilson made President—a very impressive experience indeed. The future —God knows; but I believe in Wilson very thoroughly. Men fool him yet. Men fool us all. He has already made some mistakes. But he's sound. And, if we have moral courage enough to beat back the grafters, little and big—I mean if we, the people, will vote two years and four years hence, to keep them back, I think that we shall now really work toward a democratic government. I have a stronger confidence in government now as an instrument of human progress than I have ever had before. And I find it an exhilarating and exciting experience.

I have seen many of your good friends in North Carolina, Virginia, and Washington. How we all do love you, old man! Don't forget that, in your successful fight. And, with my affectionate greetings to Mrs. Alderman, ask her to send me the news of your progress.

Always affectionately yours,
WALTER H. PAGE.

To Edwin A. Alderman

On the *Baltic*, New York to Liverpool,
May 19, 1913.

MY DEAR ED ALDERMAN:

It was the best kind of news I heard of you during my last weeks at home—every day of which I wished to go to Briarcliff to see you. At a distance, it seems absurd to say that it was impossible to go. But it was. I set down five different days in my calendar for this use; and somehow every one of them was taken. Two were taken by unexpected calls to Washington. Another was taken by my partners who arranged a little good-bye dinner. Another was taken by the British Ambassador—and so on. Absurd—of course it was absurd, and I feel now as if it approached the criminal. But every stolen day I said, "Well, I'll find another." But another never came.

But good news of you came by many hands and mouths. My congratulations, my cheers, my love, old man. Now when you do take up work again, don't take up all the work. Show the fine virtue called self-restraint. We work too much and too hard and do too many things even when we are well. There are three titled Englishmen who sit at the table with me on this ship—one a former Lord Mayor of London, another a peer, and the third an M. P. Damn their self-sufficiencies! They do excite my envy. *They* don't shoulder the work of the world: they shoulder the world and leave the work to be done by somebody else. Three days' stories and political discussion with them have made me wonder why the devil I've been so industrious all my life. They know more than I know; they are richer than I am; they have been about the world more than I have; they are far more influential than I am; and yet one of them asked me to-day if George Washington was a born American! I said to him, "Where the devil do you suppose he came from—Hades?" And he laughed at himself as heartily as the rest of us laughed at him, and didn't care a hang!

If that's British, I've a mind to become British; and, the point is, you must, too. Work is a curse. There was some truth in that old doctrine. At any rate a little of it must henceforth go a long way with you.

A sermon? Yes. But, since it's a good one, I know you'll forgive me; for it is preached in love, my dear boy, and accompanied with the hearty and insistent hope that you'll write to me.

Affectionately,

WALTER PAGE.

This last letter apparently anticipates the story. A few weeks before it was written President Wilson had succeeded in carrying out his determination to make Page an important part of his Administration. One morning Page's telephone rang and Colonel House's well-known and well-modulated voice came over the wire.

"Good morning, Your Excellency," was his greeting.

"What the devil are you talking about?" asked Page.

Then Colonel House explained himself. The night before, he said, he had dined at the White House. In a pause of the conversation the President had quietly remarked:

"I've about made up my mind to send Walter Page to England. What do you think of that?"

Colonel House thought very well of it indeed and the result of his conversation was this telephone call, in which he was authorized to offer Page the Ambassadorship to Great Britain.

CHAPTER V

THE London Embassy is the greatest diplomatic gift at the disposal of the President, and, in the minds of the American people, it possesses a glamour and an historic importance all its own. Page came to the position, as his predecessors had come, with a sense of awe; the great traditions of the office; the long line of distinguished men, from Thomas Pinckney to Whitelaw Reid, who had filled it; the peculiar delicacy of the problems that then existed between the two countries; the reverent respect which Page had always entertained for English history, English literature, and English public men—all these considerations naturally quickened the new ambassador's imagination and, at the same time, made his arrival in England a rather solemn event. Yet his first days in London had their grotesque side as well. He himself has recorded his impressions, and, since they contain an important lesson for the citizens of the world's richest and most powerful Republic, they should be preserved. When the ambassador of practically any other country reaches London, he finds waiting for him a spacious and beautiful embassy, filled with a large corps of secretaries and servants—everything ready, to the minutest detail, for the beginning of his labours. He simply enters these elaborate state-owned and state-supported quarters and starts work. How differently the mighty United States welcomes its ambassadors let Page's memorandum tell:

132

The boat touched at Queenstown, and a mass of Irish reporters came aboard and wished to know what I thought of Ireland. Some of them printed the important announcement that I was quite friendly to Ireland! At Liverpool was Mr. Laughlin,[1] Chargé d' Affaires in London since Mr. Reid's death, to meet me, and of course the consul, Mr. Washington. . . . On our arrival in London, Laughlin explained that he had taken quarters for me at the Coburg Hotel, whither we drove, after having fought my way through a mob of reporters at the station. One fellow told me that since I left New York the papers had published a declaration by me that I meant to be very "democratic" and would under no conditions wear "knee breeches"; and he asked me about that report. I was foolish enough to reply that the existence of an ass in the United States ought not necessarily to require the existence of a corresponding ass in London. He printed that! I never knew the origin of this "knee breeches" story.

That residence at the Coburg Hotel for three months was a crowded and uncomfortable nightmare. The indignity and inconvenience—even the humiliation—of an ambassador beginning his career in an hotel, especially during the Court season, and a green ambassador at that! I hope I may not die before our Government does the conventional duty to provide ambassadors' residences.

The next morning I went to the Chancery (123, Victoria Street) and my heart sank. I had never in my life been in an American Embassy. I had had no business with them in Paris or in London on my previous visits. In fact I had never been in any embassy except the British Embassy at Washington. But the moment I

---

[1]Mr. Irwin Laughlin, first secretary of the American Embassy in London.

entered that dark and dingy hall at 123, Victoria Street, between two cheap stores—the same entrance that the dwellers in the cheap flats above used—I knew that Uncle Sam had no fit dwelling there. And the Ambassador's room greatly depressed me—dingy with twenty-nine years of dirt and darkness, and utterly undignified. And the rooms for the secretaries and attachés were the little bedrooms, kitchen, etc., of that cheap flat; that's all it was. For the place we paid $1,500 a year. I did not understand then and I do not understand yet how Lowell, Bayard, Phelps, Hay, Choate, and Reid endured that cheap hole. Of course they stayed there only about an hour a day; but they sometimes saw important people there. And, whether they ever saw anybody there or not, the offices of the United States Government in London ought at least to be as good as a common lawyer's office in a country town in a rural state of our Union. Nobody asked for anything for an embassy: nobody got anything for an embassy. I made up my mind in ten minutes that I'd get out of this place.[1]

At the Coburg Hotel, we were very well situated; but the hotel became intolerably tiresome. Harold Fowler and Frank and I were there until W. A. W. P.[2] and Kitty[3] came (and Frances Clark came with them). Then we were just a little too big a hotel party. Every morning I drove down to the old hole of a Chancery and remained about two hours. There wasn't very much work to do; and my main business was to become acquainted with the work and with people—to find myself with reference to

---

[1]In about a year Page moved the Chancery to the present satisfactory quarters at No. 4 Grosvenor Gardens.

[2]Mrs. Walter H. Page.

[3]Miss Katharine A. Page, the Ambassador's daughter.

this task, with reference to official life and to London life in general.

Every afternoon people came to the hotel to see me— some to pay their respects and to make life pleasant, some out of mere curiosity, and many for ends of their own. I confess that on many days nightfall found me completely worn out. But the evenings seldom brought a chance to rest. The social season was going at its full gait; and the new ambassador (any new ambassador) would have been invited to many functions. A very few days after my arrival, the Duchess of X invited Frank and me to dinner. The powdered footmen were the chief novelty of the occasion for us. But I was much confused because nobody introduced anybody to anybody else. If a juxtaposition, as at the dinner table, made an introduction imperative, the name of the lady next you was so slurred that you couldn't possibly understand it.

Party succeeded party. I went to them because they gave me a chance to become acquainted with people.

But very early after my arrival, I was of course summoned by the King. I had presented a copy of my credentials to the Foreign Secretary (Sir Edward Grey) and the real credentials—the original in a sealed envelope— I must present to His Majesty. One morning the King's Master of the Ceremonies, Sir Arthur Walsh, came to the hotel with the royal coaches, four or five of them, and the richly caparisoned grooms. The whole staff of the Embassy must go with me. We drove to Buckingham Palace, and, after waiting a few moments, I was ushered into the King's presence. He stood in one of the drawing rooms on the ground floor looking out on the garden. There stood with him in uniform Sir Edward Grey. I entered and bowed. He shook my hand, and I spoke my little piece of three or four sentences.

He replied, welcoming me and immediately proceeded to express his surprise and regret that a great and rich country like the United States had not provided a residence for its ambassadors. "It is not fair to an ambassador," said he; and he spoke most earnestly.

I reminded him that, although the lack of a home was an inconvenience, the trouble or discomfort that fell on an ambassador was not so bad as the wrong impression which I feared was produced about the United States and its Government, and I explained that we had had so many absorbing domestic tasks and, in general, so few absorbing foreign relations, that we had only begun to develop what might be called an international consciousness.

Sir Edward was kind enough the next time I saw him to remark that I did that very well and made a good impression on the King.

I could now begin my ambassadorial career proper— call on the other ambassadors and accept invitations to dinners and the like.

I was told after I came from the King's presence that the Queen would receive me in a few minutes. I was shown upstairs, the door opened, and there in a small drawing room, stood the Queen alone—a pleasant woman, very royal in appearance. The one thing that sticks in my memory out of this first conversation with her Majesty was her remark that she had seen only one man who had been President of the United States—Mr. Roosevelt. She hoped he was well. I felt moved to remark that she was not likely to see many former Presidents because the office was so hard a task that most of them did not long survive.

"I'm hoping that office will not soon kill the King," she said.

In time Page obtained an entirely adequate and dignified house at 6 Grosvenor Square, and soon found that the American Ambassadorship had compensations which were hardly suggested by his first glimpse of the lugubrious Chancery. He brought to this new existence his plastic and inquisitive mind, and his mighty gusto for the interesting and the unusual; he immensely enjoyed his meetings with the most important representatives of all types of British life. The period of his arrival marked a crisis in British history; Mr. Lloyd George was supposed to be taxing the aristocracy out of existence; Mr. Asquith was accused of plotting the destruction of the House of Lords; the tide of liberalism, even of radicalism, was running high, and, in the judgment of the conservative forces, England was tottering to its fall; the gathering mob was about to submerge everything that had made it great. And the Irish question had reached another crisis with the passage of the Home Rule Bill, which Sir Edward Carson was preparing to resist with his Irish "volunteers."

All these matters formed the staple of talk at dinner tables, at country houses and at the clubs; and Page found constant entertainment in the variegated pageant. There were important American matters to discuss with the Foreign Office—more important than any that had arisen in recent years—particularly Mexico and the Panama Tolls. Before these questions are considered, however, it may be profitable to print a selection from the many letters which Page wrote during his first year, giving his impressions of this England which he had always loved and which a closer view made him love and admire still more. These letters have the advantage of presenting a frank and yet sympathetic picture of British society and British life as it was just before the war.

To Frank N. Doubleday

The Coburg Hotel,
Carlos Place, Grosvenor Square,
London, W.

DEAR EFFENDI:[1]

You can't imagine the intensity of the party feeling here.   I dined to-night in an old Tory family.   They had just had a "division" an hour or two before in the House of Lords on the Home Rule Bill.   Six Lords were at the dinner and their wives.   One was a Duke, two were Bishops, and the other three were Earls.   They expect a general "bust-up."   If the King does so and so, off with the King!   That's what they fear the Liberals will do. It sounds very silly to me; but you can't exaggerate their fear.   The Great Lady, who was our hostess, told me, with tears in her voice, that she had suspended all social relations with the Liberal leaders.

At lunch—just five or six hours before—we were at the Prime Minister's, where the talk was precisely on the other side.   Gladstone's granddaughter was there and several members of the Cabinet.

Somehow it reminds me of the tense days of the slavery controversy just before the Civil War.

Yet in the everyday life of the people, you hear nothing about it.   It is impossible to believe that the ordinary man cares a fig!

Good-night.   You don't care a fig for this.   But I'll get time to write you something interesting in a little while.

Yours,

W. H. P.

---

[1] "Effendi" is the name by which Mr. F. N. Doubleday, Page's partner, is known to his intimates.   It is obviously suggested by the initials of his name.

To Herbert S. Houston

American Embassy
London
Sunday, 24 Aug., 1913.

DEAR H. S. H.:

. . . You know there's been much discussion of the decadence of the English people. I don't believe a word of it. They have an awful slum, I hear, as everybody knows, and they have an idle class. Worse, from an equal-opportunity point-of-view, they have a very large servant-class, and a large class that depends on the no-bility and the rich. All these are economic and social drawbacks. But they have always had all these—except that the slum has become larger in modern years. And I don't see or find any reason to believe in the theory of decadence. The world never saw a finer lot of men than the best of their ruling class. You may search the world and you may search history for finer men than Lord Morley, Sir Edward Grey, Mr. Harcourt, and other members of the present Cabinet. And I meet such men everywhere—gently bred, high-minded, physically fit, intellectually cultivated, patriotic. If the devotion to old forms and the inertia which makes any change al-most impossible strike an American as out-of-date, you must remember that in the grand old times of England, they had all these things and had them worse than they are now. I can't see that the race is breaking down or giving out. Consider how their political morals have been pulled up since the days of the rotten boroughs; consider how their court-life is now high and decent, and think what it once was. British trade is larger this year than it ever was, Englishmen are richer then they ever were and more of them are rich. They write and speak and play cricket, and govern, and fight as well as they have ever done—excepting, of course, the writing of Shakespeare.

Another conclusion that is confirmed the more you see of English life is their high art of living. When they make their money, they stop money-making and cultivate their minds and their gardens and entertain their friends and do all the high arts of living—to perfection. Three days ago a retired soldier gave a garden-party in my honour, twenty-five miles out of London. There was his historic house, a part of it 500 years old; there were his ten acres of garden, his lawn, his trees; and they walk with you over it all; they sit out-of-doors; they serve tea; they take life rationally; they talk pleasantly (not jocularly, nor story-telling); they abhor the smart in talk or in conduct; they have gentleness, cultivation, the best manners in the world; and they are genuine. The hostess has me take a basket and go with her while she cuts it full of flowers for us to bring home; and, as we walk, she tells the story of the place. She is a tenant-for-life; it is entailed. Her husband was wounded in South Africa. Her heir is her nephew. The home, of course, will remain in the family forever. No, they don't go to London much in recent years: why should they? But they travel a month or more. They give three big tea-parties—one when the rhododendrons bloom and the others at stated times. They have friends to stay with them half the time, perhaps—sometimes parties of a dozen. England never had a finer lot of folk than these. And you see them everywhere. The art of living sanely they have developed to as high a level, I think, as you will find at any time in any land.

The present political battle is fiercer than you would ever guess. The Lords feel that they are sure to be robbed: they see the end of the ordered world. Chaos and confiscation lie before them. Yet that, too, has nearly always been so. It was so in the Reform Bill days. Lord Morley said to me the other day that when all the abolitions had been done, there would be fewer things abolished than anybody hopes or fears, and that there would be the same problems in some form for many generations. I'm beginning to believe that the Englishman has always been afraid of the future—that's what's keeps him so alert. They say to me: "You have frightful things happen in the United States—your Governor of New York,[1] your Thaw case, your corruption, etc., etc.; and yet you seem sure and tell us that your countrymen feel sure of the safety of your government." In the newspaper comments on my Southampton[2] speech the other day, this same feeling cropped up; the American Ambassador assures us that the note of hope is the dominant note of the Republic—etc., etc. Yes, they are dull, *in a way*—not dull, so much as steady; and yet they have more solid sense than any other people.

It's an interesting study—the most interesting in the world. The genuineness of the courtesy, the real kindness and the hospitality of the English are beyond praise and without limit. In this they show a strange contradiction to their dickering habits in trade and their "unctuous rectitude" in stealing continents. I know a place in the world now where they are steadily moving their boundary line into other people's territory. I guess they really believe that the earth belongs to them.

Sincerely,

W. H. P.

---

[1] A reference to William Sulzer, Governor of New York, who at this time was undergoing impeachment.

[2] See Chapter VIII, page 258.

To Arthur W. Page[1]

Gordon Arms Hotel, Elgin, Scotland.
September 6, 1913.

DEAR ARTHUR:

Your mother and Kitty[2] and I are on our way to see Andy.[3] Had you any idea that to motor from London to Skibo means driving more than eight hundred miles? Our speedometer now shows more than seven hundred and we've another day to go—at least one hundred and thirty miles. And we haven't even had a tire accident. We're having a delightful journey—only this country yields neither vegetables nor fruits, and I have to live on oatmeal. They spell it p-o-r-r-i-d-g-e, and they call it pŭruge. But they beat all creation as carnivorous folk. We stayed last night at a beautiful mountain hotel at Braemar (the same town whereat Stevenson wrote "Treasure Island") and they had nine kinds of meat for dinner and eggs in three ways, and no vegetables but potatoes. But this morning we struck the same thin oatbread that you ate at Grandfather Mountain.

I've never understood the Scotch. I think they are, without doubt, the most capable race in the world— away from home. But how they came to be so and how they keep up their character and supremacy and keep breeding true needs explanation. As you come through the country, you see the most monotonous and dingy little houses and thousands of robust children, all dirtier than niggers. In the fertile parts of the country, the fields are beautifully cultivated—for Lord This-and-T'Other who lives in London and comes up here in sum-

---

[1]The Ambassador's son.

[2]Miss Katharine A. Page.

[3]Mr. Andrew Carnegie.

mer to collect his rents and to shoot. The country people seem desperately poor. But they don't lose their robustness. In the solid cities—the solidest you ever saw, all being of granite—such as Edinburgh and Aberdeen, where you see the prosperous class, they look the sturdiest and most independent fellows you ever saw. As they grow old they all look like blue-bellied Presbyterian elders. Scotch to the marrow—everybody and everything seem—bare knees alike on the street and in the hotel with dress coats on, bagpipes—there's no sense in these things, yet being Scotch they live forever. The first men I saw early this morning on the street in front of the hotel were two weather-beaten old chaps, with gray beards under their chins. "Guddddd Murrrrninggggg, Andy," said one. "Guddddd murrninggggg, Sandy," said the other; and they trudged on. They'd dethrone kings before they'd shave differently or drop their burrs and gutturals or cover their knees or cease lying about the bagpipe. And you can't get it out of the blood. Your mother[1] becomes provoked when I say these things, and I shouldn't wonder if you yourself resent them and break out quoting Burns. Now the Highlands can't support a population larger than the mountain counties of Kentucky. Now your Kentucky feud is a mere disgrace to civilization. But your Highland feud is celebrated in song and story. Every clan keeps itself together to this day by its history and by its plaid. At a turn in the road in the mountains yesterday, there stood a statue of Rob Roy painted every stripe to life. We saw his sword and purse in Sir Walter's house at Abbotsford. The King himself wore the kilt and one of the plaids at the last court ball at Buckingham Palace, and there is a man who writes his name and is called

---

[1]Mrs. Walter H. Page is the daughter of a Scotchman from Ayrshire.

"The Macintosh of Macintosh," and that's a prouder title than the King's.   A little handful of sheep-stealing bandits got themselves immortalized and heroized, and they are now all Presbyterian elders.   They got *their* church "established" in Scotland, and when the King comes to Scotland, by Jehoshaphat! he is obliged to become a Presbyterian.   Yet your Kentucky feudist— poor devil—he comes too late.   The Scotchman has pre-empted that particular field of glory.   And all such comparisons make your mother fighting mad.   .   .   .

Affectionately,   W. H. P.

To the President

American Embassy, London.
October 25, 1913.

DEAR MR. PRESIDENT:

I am moved once in a while to write you privately, not about any specific piece of public business, but only, if I can, to transmit something of the atmosphere of the work here.   And, since this is meant quite as much for your amusement as for any information it may carry, don't read it "in office hours."

The future of the world belongs to us.   A man needs to live here, with two economic eyes in his head, a very little time to become very sure of this.   Everybody will see it presently.   These English are spending their capital, and it is their capital that continues to give them their vast power.   Now what are we going to do with the leadership of the world presently when it clearly falls into our hands?[1]   And how can we use the English for the highest uses of democracy?

---

[1] The astonishing thing about Page's comment on the leadership of the United States—if it would only take this leadership—is that these letters were written in 1913, a year before the outbreak of the war, and eight years before the Washington Disarmament Conference of 1921–22.

You see their fear of an on-sweeping democracy in their social treatment of party opponents. A Tory lady told me with tears that she could no longer invite her Liberal friends to her house: "I have lost them—they are robbing us, you know." I made the mistake of saying a word in praise of Sir Edward Grey to a duke. "Yes, yes, no doubt an able man; but you must understand, sir, that I don't train with that gang." A bishop explained to me at elaborate length why the very monarchy is doomed unless something befalls Lloyd George and his programme. Every dinner party is made up with strict reference to the party politics of the guests. Sometimes you imagine you see something like civil war; and money is flowing out of the Kingdom into Canada in the greatest volume ever known and I am told that a number of old families are investing their fortunes in African lands.

These and such things are, of course, mere chips which show the direction the slow stream runs. The great economic tide of the century flows our way. *We* shall have the big world questions to decide presently. Then we shall need world policies; and it will be these old-time world leaders that we shall then have to work with, more closely than now.

The English make a sharp distinction between the American people and the American Government—a distinction that they are conscious of and that they themselves talk about. They do not think of our *people* as foreigners. I have a club book on my table wherein the members are classified as British, Colonial, American, and Foreign—quite unconsciously. But they do think of our Government as foreign, and as a frontier sort of thing without good manners or good faith. This distinction presents the big task of implanting here a real respect for our Government. People often think to compliment the American Ambassador by assuming that he is better than his Government and must at times be ashamed of it. Of course the Government never does this—never—but persons in unofficial life; and I have sometimes hit some hard blows under this condescending provocation. This is the one experience that I have found irritating. They commiserate me on having a Government that will not provide an Ambassador's residence—from the King to my servants. They talk about American lynchings. Even the *Spectator*, in an early editorial about you, said that we should now see what stuff there is in the new President by watching whether you would stop lynchings. They forever quote Bryce on the badness of our municipal government. They pretend to think that the impeachment of governors is common and ought to be commoner. One delicious M. P. asked me: "Now, since the Governor of New York is impeached, who becomes Vice-President?"[1] Ignorance, unfathomable ignorance, is at the bottom of much of it; if the Town Treasurer of Yuba Dam gets a $100 "rake off" on a paving contract, our city government is a failure.

I am about to conclude that our yellow press does us more harm abroad than at home, and many of the American correspondents of the English papers send exactly the wrong news. The whole governing class of England has a possibly exaggerated admiration for the American people and something very like contempt for the American Government.

---

[1]Just what this critical Briton had in mind, in thinking that the removal of a New York governor created a vacancy in the Vice-Presidency, is not clear. Possibly, however, he had a cloudy recollection of the fact that Theodore Roosevelt, after serving as Governor of New York State, became Vice-President, and may have concluded from this that the two offices were held by the same man.

If I make it out right two causes (in addition to their ignorance) of their dislike of our Government are (1) its lack of manners in the past, and (2) its indiscretions of publicity about foreign affairs. We ostentatiously stand aloof from their polite ways and courteous manners in many of the every-day, ordinary, unimportant dealings with them—aloof from the common amenities of long-organized political life. . . .

Not one of these things is worth mentioning or remembering. But generations of them have caused our Government to be regarded as thoughtless of the fine little acts of life—as rude. The more I find out about diplomatic customs and the more I hear of the little-big troubles of others, the more need I find to be careful about details of courtesy.

Thus we are making as brave a show as becomes us. I no longer dismiss a princess after supper or keep the whole diplomatic corps waiting while I talk to an interesting man till the Master of Ceremonies comes up and whispers: "Your Excellency, I think they are waiting for you to move." But I am both young and green, and even these folk forgive much to green youth, if it show a willingness to learn.

But our Government, though green, isn't young enough to plead its youth. It is time that it, too, were learning Old World manners in dealing with Old World peoples. I do not know whether we need a Bureau, or a Major-Domo, or a Master of Ceremonies at Washington, but we need somebody to prompt us to act as polite as we really are, somebody to think of those gentler touches that we naturally forget. Some other governments have such officers—perhaps all. The Japanese, for instance, are newcomers in world politics. But this Japanese Ambassador and his wife here never miss a trick; and they come across the square and ask us how to do it! All the other governments, too, play the game of small courtesies to perfection—the French, of course, and the Spanish and—even the old Turk.

Another reason for the English distrust of our Government is its indiscretions in the past of this sort: one of our Ministers to Germany, you will recall, was obliged to resign because the Government at Washington inadvertently published one of his confidential despatches; Griscom saved his neck only by the skin, when he was in Japan, for a similar reason. These things travel all round the world from one chancery to another and all governments know them. Yesterday somebody in Washington talked about my despatch summarizing my talk with Sir Edward Grey about Mexico, and it appeared in the papers here this morning that Sir Edward had told me that the big business interests were pushing him hard. This I sent as only *my* inference. I had at once to disclaim it. This leaves in his mind a doubt about our care for secrecy. They have monstrous big doors and silent men in Downing Street; and, I am told, a stenographer sits behind a big screen in Sir Edward's room while an Ambassador talks![1] I wonder if my comments on certain poets, which I have poured forth there to provoke his, are preserved in the archives of the British Empire. The British Empire is surely very welcome to them. I have twice found it useful, by the way, to bring up Wordsworth

---

[1]For years this idea of the stenographer back of a screen in the Foreign Office has been abroad, but it is entirely unfounded. Several years ago a Foreign Secretary, perhaps Lord Salisbury, put a screen behind his desk to keep off the draughts and from this precaution the myth arose that it shielded a stenographer who took a complete record of ambassadorial conversations. After an ambassador leaves, the Foreign Secretary, however, does write out the important points in the conversation. Copies are made and printed, and sent to the King, the Prime Minister, the British Ambassador in the country to which the interview relates, and occasionally to others. All these records are, of course, carefully preserved in the archives of the Foreign Office.

when he has begun to talk about Panama tolls. Then your friend Canon Rawnsley[1] has, without suspecting it, done good service in diplomacy.

The newspaper men here, by the way, both English and American, are disposed to treat us fairly and to be helpful. The London *Times*, on most subjects, is very friendly, and I find its editors worth cultivating for their own sakes and because of their position. It is still the greatest English newspaper. Its general friendliness to the United States, by the way, has started a rumour that I hear once in a while—that it is really owned by Americans—nonsense yet awhile. To the fairness and helpfulness of the newspaper men there are one or two exceptions, for instance, a certain sneaking whelp who writes for several papers. He went to the Navy League dinner last night at which I made a little speech. When I sat down, he remarked to his neighbour, with a yawn, "Well, nothing in it for me. The Ambassador, I am afraid, said nothing for which I can demand his recall." They, of course, don't care thrippence about me; it's you they hope to annoy.

Then after beating them at their own game of daily little courtesies, we want a fight with them—a good stiff fight about something wherein we are dead right, to remind them sharply that we have sand in our craw.[2] I pray every night for such a fight; for they like fighting men. Then they'll respect our Government as they already respect us—if we are dead right.

But I've little hope for a fight of the right kind with Sir Edward Grey. He is the very reverse of insolent—

[1] The Rev. Hardwicke Drummond Rawnsley, the well-known Vicar of Crosthwaite, Keswick, poet and student of Wordsworth. President Wilson, who used occasionally to spend his vacation in the Lake region, was one of his friends.

[2] It is perhaps unnecessary to say that the Ambassador was thinking only of a diplomatic "fight."

fair, frank, sympathetic, and he has so clear an understanding of our real character that he'd yield anything
that his party and Parliament would permit.   He'd make
a good American with the use of very little sandpaper.
Of course I know him better than I know any other
member of the Cabinet, but he seems to me the best-
balanced man of them all.

I can assure you emphatically that the tariff act[1] does
command their respect and is already having an amazing
influence on their opinion of our Government.   Lord
Mersey, a distinguished law lord and a fine old fellow of
the very best type of Englishman, said to me last Sunday,
"I wish to thank you for stopping half-way in reducing
your tariff; that will only half ruin us."   A lady of a
political family (Liberal) next whom I sat at dinner the
other night (and these women know their politics as no
class of women among us do) said: "Tell me something
about your great President.   We hadn't heard much
about him nor felt his hand till your tariff bill passed.
He seems to have real power in the Government.   You
know we do not always know who has power in your
Government."   Lord Grey, the one-time Governor-
General of Canada, stopped looking at the royal wedding
presents the other evening long enough to say: "The
United States Government is waking up—waking up."

I sum up these atmospheric conditions—I do not presume to call them by so definite a name as recommenda-
tions:

We are in the international game—not in its Old World
intrigues and burdens and sorrows and melancholy, but
in the inevitable way to leadership and to cheerful mastery

---

[1]The Underwood Bill revising the tariff "downward" became a law October,
1913.   It was one of the first important measures of the new Wilson Administration.

in the future; and everybody knows that we are in it but us. It is a sheer blind habit that causes us to continue to try to think of ourselves as aloof. They think in terms of races here, and we are of their race, and we shall become the strongest and the happiest branch of it.

While we play the game with them, we shall play it better by playing it under their long-wrought-out rules of courtesy in everyday affairs.

We shall play it better, too, if our Government play it quietly—except when the subject demands publicity. I have heard that in past years the foreign representatives of our Government have reported too few things and much too meagrely. I have heard since I have been here that these representatives become timid because Washington has for many a year conducted its foreign business too much in the newspapers; and the foreign governments themselves are always afraid of this.

Meantime I hardly need tell you of my appreciation of such a chance to make so interesting a study and to enjoy so greatly the most interesting experience, I really believe, in the whole world. I only hope that in time I may see how to shape the constant progression of incidents into a constructive course of events; for we are soon coming into a time of big changes.

Most heartily yours,
WALTER H. PAGE.

To David F. Houston[1]

American Embassy, London [undated].

DEAR HOUSTON:

You're doing the bigger job: as the world now is, there is no other job so big as yours or so well worth doing; but I'm having more fun. I'm having more fun than any-

[1]Secretary of Agriculture in President Wilson's Cabinet.

body else anywhere. It's a large window you look through on the big world—here in London; and, while I am for the moment missing many of the things that I've most cared about hitherto (such as working for the countryman, guessing at American public opinion, coffee that's fit to drink, corn bread, sunshine, and old faces) big new things come on the horizon. Yet a man's personal experiences are nothing in comparison with the large job that our Government has to do in its Foreign Relations. I'm beginning to begin to see what it is. The American people are taken most seriously here. I'm sometimes almost afraid of the respect and even awe in which they hold us. But the American Government is a mere joke to them. They don't even believe that we ourselves believe in it. We've had no foreign policy, no continuity of plan, no matured scheme, no settled way of doing things and we seem afraid of Irishmen or Germans or some "element" when a chance for real action comes. I'm writing to the President about this and telling him stories to show how it works.

We needn't talk any longer about keeping aloof. If Cecil Spring Rice would tell you the complaints he has already presented and if you saw the work that goes on here—more than in all the other posts in Europe—you'd see that all the old talk about keeping aloof is Missouri buncombe. We're very much "in," but not frankly in.

I wish you'd keep your eye on these things in cabinet meetings. The English and the whole English world are ours, if we have the courtesy to take them—fleet and trade and all; and we go on pretending we are afraid of "entangling alliances." What about disentangling alliances?

We're in the game. There's no use in letting a few wild Irish or cocky Germans scare us. We need courtesy and frankness, and the destinies of the world will be in our hands. They'll fall there anyhow after we are dead; but I wish to see them come, while my own eyes last. Don't you?

Heartily yours,

W. H. P.

To Robert N. Page[1]

London, December 22, 1913.

MY DEAR BOB:

. . . We have a splendid, big old house—not in any way pretentious—a commonplace house in fact for fashionable London and the least showy and costly of the Embassies. But it does very well—it's big and elegantly plain and dignified. We have fifteen servants in the house. They do just about what seven good ones would do in the United States, but they do it a great deal better. They pretty nearly run themselves and the place. The servant question is admirably solved here. They divide the work according to a fixed and unchangeable system and they do it remarkably well—in their own slow English way. We simply let them alone, unless something important happens to go wrong. Katharine simply tells the butler that we'll have twenty-four people to dinner to-morrow night and gives him a list of them. As they come in, the men at the door address every one correctly—Your Lordship or Your Grace, or what not. When they are all in, the butler comes to the reception room and announces dinner. We do the rest. As every man goes out, the butler asks him if he'll have a glass of water or of grog or a cigar; he calls his car, puts him in it, and that's the end of it. Bully good plan. But in the United States that butler, whose wages are less than the ramshackle nigger I had at Garden City to keep the place

[1] Of Aberdeen, North Carolina, the Ambassador's brother.

neat, would have a business of his own.   But here he is a
sort of duke downstairs.   He sits at the head of the servants' table and orders them around and that's worth
more than money to an Old World servile mind.

The "season" doesn't begin till the King comes back
and Parliament opens, in February.   But every kind of
club and patriotic and educational organization is giving
its annual dinner now.   I've been going to them and
making after-dinner speeches to get acquainted and also
to preach into them some little knowledge of American
ways and ideals.   They are very nice—very.   You could
not suggest or imagine any improvement in their kindness
and courtesy.   They do all these things in some ways
better than we.   They have more courtesy.   They make
far shorter speeches.   But they do them all too much
alike.   Still they do get much pleasure out of them and
much instruction too.

Then we are invited to twice as many private dinners
and luncheons as we can attend.   At these, these people are
at their best.   But it is yet quite confusing.   A sea of
friendly faces greets you—you can't remember the names.
Nobody ever introduces anybody to anybody; and if by
accident anybody ever tries, he simply says—"Uh-o-oh-
Lord Xzwwxkmpt."   You couldn't understand it if you
had to be hanged.

But we are untangling some of this confusion and coming to make very real and very charming friends.

About December 20, everybody who is anybody leaves
London.   They go to their country places for about a
fortnight or they go to the continent.   Almost everything
stops.   It has been the only dull time at the Embassy that
I've had.   Nothing is going on now.   But up to two days
ago, it kept a furious gait.   I'm glad of a little rest.

Dealing with the Government doesn't present the

difficulties that I feared. Sir Edward Grey is in the main responsible for the ease with which it is done. He is a frank and fair and truthful man. You will find him the day after to-morrow precisely where you left him the day before yesterday. We get along very well indeed. I think we should get along if we had harder tasks one with the other. And the English people are even more friendly than the Government. You have no idea of their respect for the American Nation. Of course there is much ignorance, sometimes of a surprising sort. Very many people, for instance, think that all the Americans are rich. A lady told me the other night how poor she is—she is worth only $1,250,000—"nothing like all you Americans." She was quite sincere. In fact the wealth of the world (and the poverty, too) is centred here in an amazing way. You can't easily take it in—how rich or how many rich English families there are. They have had wealth for generation after generation, and the surprising thing is, they take care of it. They spend enormously—seldom ostentatiously—but they are more than likely to add some of their income every year to their principal. They have better houses in town and in the country than I had imagined. They spend vast fortunes in making homes in which they expect to live forever—generation after generation.

To an American democrat the sad thing is the servile class. Before the law the chimney sweep and the peer have exactly the same standing. They have worked that out with absolute justice. But there it stops. The serving class is what we should call abject. It does not occur to them that they might ever become—or that their descendants might ever become—ladies and gentlemen.

The "courts" are a very fine sight. The diplomatic

ladies sit on a row of seats on one side the throne room, the Duchesses on a row opposite. The King and Queen sit on a raised platform with the royal family. The Ambassadors come in first and bow and the King shakes hands with them. Then come the forty or more Ministers—no shake for them. In front of the King are a few officers in gaudy uniform, some Indians of high rank (from India) and the court officials are all round about, with pages who hold up the Queen's train. Whenever the Queen and King move, two court officials back before them, one carrying a gold stick and the other a silver stick.

The ladies to be presented come along. They curtsy to the King, then to the Queen, and disappear in the rooms farther on. The Ambassadors (all in gaudy uniforms but me) stand near the throne—stand through the whole performance. One night after an hour or two of ladies coming along and curtsying and disappearing, I whispered to the Spanish Ambassador, "There must be five hundred of these ladies." "U-m," said he, as he shifted his weight to the other foot, "I'm sure there are five thousand!" When they've all been presented, the King and Queen go into a room where a stand-up supper is served. The royalty and the diplomatic folks go into that room, too; and their Majesties walk around and talk with whom they please. Into another and bigger room everybody else goes and gets supper. Then we all flock back to the throne room; and preceded by the backing courtiers, their Majesties come out into the floor and bow to the Ambassadors, then to the Duchesses, then to the general diplomatic group and they go out. The show is ended. We come downstairs and wait an hour for our car and come home about midnight. The uniforms on the men and the jewels on the ladies (by the ton) and their trains—all this makes a very brilliant spectacle. The American Ambassador and his Secretaries and the Swiss and the Portuguese are the only ones dressed in citizens' clothes.

At a levee, the King receives only gentlemen. Here they come in all kinds of uniforms. If you are not entitled to wear a uniform, you have a dark suit, knee breeches, and a funny little tin sword. I'm going to adopt the knee breeches part of it for good when I go home—golf breeches in the day time and knee breeches at night. You've no idea how nice and comfortable they are—though it is a devil of a lot of trouble to put 'em on. Of course every sort of man here but the Americans wears some sort of decorations around his neck or on his stomach, at these functions. For my part, I like it—here. The women sparkle with diamonds, the men strut; the King is a fine man with a big bass voice and he talks very well and is most agreeable; the Queen is very gracious; the royal ladies (Queen Victoria's daughters, chiefly) are nice; you see all the big Generals and all the big Admirals and the great folk of every sort—fine show.

You've no idea how much time and money they spend on shooting. The King has been shooting most of the time for three months. He's said to be a very good shot. He has sent me, on different occasions, grouse, a haunch of venison, and pheasants.

But except on these occasions, you never think about the King. The people go about their business as if he didn't exist, of course. They begin work much later than we do. You'll not find any of the shops open till about ten o'clock. The sun doesn't shine except once in a while and you don't know it's daylight till about ten. You know the House of Commons has night sessions always. Nobody is in the Government offices, except clerks and secretaries, till the afternoon. We dine at eight, and, when we have a big dinner, at eight thirty.

I like these people (most of 'em) immensely. They are very genuine and frank, good fighters and folk of our own sort—after you come to know them. At first they have no manners and don't know what to do. But they warm up to you later. They have abundant wit, but much less humour than we. And they know how to live.

Except that part of life which is ministered to in mechanical ways, they resist conveniences. They don't really like bathrooms yet. They prefer great tin tubs, and they use bowls and pitchers when a bathroom is next door. The telephone—Lord deliver us!—I've given it up. They know nothing about it. (It is a government concern, but so is the telegraph and the post-office, and they are remarkably good and swift.) You can't buy a newspaper on the street, except in the afternoon. Cigar-stores are as scarce as hen's teeth. Barber-shops are all "hairdressers"—dirty and wretched beyond description. You can't get a decent pen; their newspapers are as big as tablecloths. In this aquarium in which we live (it rains every day) they have only three vegetables and two of them are cabbages. They grow all kinds of fruit in hothouses, and (I can't explain this) good land in admirable cultivation thirty miles from London sells for about half what good corn land in Iowa brings. Lloyd George has scared the land-owners to death.

Party politics runs so high that many Tories will not invite Liberals to dinner. They are almost at the point of civil war. I asked the Prime Minister the other day how he was going to prevent war. He didn't give any clear answer. During this recess of Parliament, though there's no election pending, all the Cabinet are all the

time going about making speeches on Ireland.   They talk
to me about it.

"What would you do?"

"Send 'em all to the United States," say I.

"No, no."

They have had the Irish question three hundred years
and they wouldn't be happy without it.   One old Tory
talked me deaf abusing the Liberal Government.

"You do this way in the United States—hate cne another, don't you?"

"No," said I, "we live like angels in perfect harmony
except a few weeks before election."

"The devil you do!   You don't hate one another?
What do you do for enemies?   I couldn't get along without enemies to swear at."

If you think it's all play, you fool yourself; I mean this
job.   There's no end of the work.   It consists of these
parts: Receiving people for two hours every day, some on
some sort of business, some merely "to pay respects,"
attending to a large (and exceedingly miscellaneous)
mail; going to the Foreign Office on all sorts of errands;
looking up the oddest assortment of information that
you ever heard of; making reports to Washington on all
sorts of things; then the so-called social duties—giving
dinners, receptions, etc., and attending them.   I hear the
most important news I get at so-called social functions.
Then the court functions; and the meetings and speeches!
The American Ambassador must go all over England and
explain every American thing.   You'd never recover from
the shock if you could hear me speaking about Education,
Agriculture, the observance of Christmas, the Navy, the
Anglo-Saxon, Mexico, the Monroe Doctrine, Co-educa-
tion, Woman Suffrage, Medicine, Law, Radio-Activity,
Flying, the Supreme Court, the President as a Man of

letters, Hookworm, the Negro—just get down the Encyclopædia and continue the list. I've done this every week-night for a month, hand running, with a few afternoon performances thrown in! I have missed only one engagement in these seven months; and that was merely a private luncheon. I have been late only once. I have the best chauffeur in the world—he deserves credit for much of that. Of course, I don't get time to read a book. In fact, I can't keep up with what goes on at home. To read a newspaper eight or ten days old, when they come in bundles of three or four—is impossible. What isn't telegraphed here, I miss; and that means I miss most things.

I forgot, there are a dozen other kinds of activities, such as American marriages, which they always want the Ambassador to attend; getting them out of jail, when they are jugged (I have an American woman on my hands now, whose four children come to see me every day); looking after the American insane; helping Americans move the bones of their ancestors; interpreting the income-tax law; receiving medals for Americans; hearing American fiddlers, pianists, players; sitting for American sculptors and photographers; sending telegrams for property owners in Mexico; reading letters from thousands of people who have shares in estates here; writing letters of introduction; getting tickets to the House Gallery; getting seats in the Abbey; going with people to this and that and t'other; getting tickets to the races, the art-galleries, the House of Lords; answering fool questions about the United States put by Englishmen. With a military attaché, a naval attaché, three secretaries, a private secretary, two automobiles, Alice's private secretary, a veterinarian, an immigration agent, consuls everywhere, a despatch agent, lawyers, doctors, messengers—they keep us all busy. A woman turned up dying the other day. I sent for a big doctor. She got well. As if that wasn't enough, both the woman and the doctor had to come and thank me (fifteen minutes each). Then each wrote a letter! Then there are people who are going to have a Fair here; others who have a Fair coming on at San Francisco; others at San Diego; secretaries and returning and outgoing diplomats come and go (lunch for 'em all); niggers come up from Liberia; Rhodes Scholars from Oxford; Presidential candidates to succeed Huerta; people who present books; women who wish to go to court; Jews who are excited about Rumania; passports, passports to sign; peace committees about the hundred years of peace; opera singers going to the United States; artists who have painted some American's portrait—don't you see? I haven't said a word about reporters and editors: the city's full of them.

A Happy New Year.

Affectionately,

WAT.

To Ralph W. Page[1]

London, December 23, 1913.

DEAR RALPH:

. . . The game is pretty much as it has been. I can't think of any new kinds of things to write you. The old kinds simply multiply and repeat themselves. But we are beginning now really to become acquainted, and some life friendships will grow out of our experience. And there's no doubt about its being instructive. I get glimpses of the way in which great governments deal with one another, in ways that our isolated, and, therefore, safe government seldom has any experience of. For instance, one of the Lords of the Admiralty told me the other night that he never gets out of telephone reach of

---

[1] Of Pinehurst, North Carolina, the Ambassador's eldest son.

the office—not even half an hour. "The Admiralty," said he, "never sleeps." He has a telephone by his bed which he can hear at any moment in the night. I don't believe that they really expect the German fleet to attack them any day or night. But they would not be at all surprised if it did so to-night. They talk all the time of the danger and of the probability of war; they don't expect it; but most wars have come without warning, and they are all the time prepared to begin a fight in an hour.

They talk about how much Germany must do to strengthen her frontier against Russia and her new frontier on the Balkan States. They now have these problems in hand and therefore they are for the moment not likely to provoke a fight. But they might.

It is all pitiful to see them thinking forever about danger and defense. The controversy about training boys for the army never ends. We don't know in the United States what we owe to the Atlantic Ocean—safe separation from all these troubles. . . .

But I've often asked both Englishmen and Americans in a dining room where there were many men of each country, whether they could look over the company and say which were English and which were Americans. Nobody can tell till—they begin to talk.

The ignorance of the two countries, each of the other, is beyond all belief. A friend of Kitty's—an American— received a letter from the United States yesterday. The maid noticed the stamp, which had the head of George Washington on it. Every stamp in this kingdom bears the image of King George. She asked if the American stamp had on it the head of the American Ambassador! I've known far wiser people to ask far more foolish questions.

Affectionately,

W. H. P.

To Mrs. Ralph W. Page

London, Christmas-is-coming, 1913.

MY DEAR LEILA:

. . . Her work [Mrs. Walter H. Page's] is all the work of going and receiving and—of reading. She reads incessantly and enormously; and, when she gets tired, she goes to bed. That's all there is about it. Lord! I wish I could. But, when I get tired, I have to go and make another speech. They think the American Ambassador has omniscience for a foible and oratory as a pastime.

In some ways my duties are very instructive. We get different points of view on many things, some better than we had before had, some worse. For instance, life is pretty well laid out here in water-tight compartments; and you can't let a stream in from one to another without danger of sinking the ship. Four reporters have been here to-day because Mr. and Mrs. Sayre[1] arrived this morning. Every one of 'em asked the same question, "Who met them at the station?" That's the chief thing they wished to know. When I said "I did"—that fixed the whole thing on the highest peg of dignity. They could classify the whole proceeding properly, and they went off happy. Again: You've got to go in to dinner in the exact order prescribed by the constitution; and, if you avoid that or confuse that, you'll never be able to live it down. And so about Government, Literature, Art—everything. Don't you forget your water-tight compartments. If you do, you are gone! They have the same toasts at every public dinner. One is to "the guests." Now you needn't say a word about the guests

---

[1]Mr. and Mrs. Francis B. Sayre, son-in-law and daughter of President Wilson, at that time on their honeymoon trip in Europe.

when you respond. But they've been having toasts to the guests since the time of James I and they can't change it. They had me speak to "the guests" at a club last night, when they wanted me to talk about Mexico! The winter has come—the winter months at least. But they have had no cold weather—not so cold as you have in Pinehurst. But the sun has gone out to sea—clean gone. We never see it. A damp darkness (semi-darkness at least) hangs over us all the time. But we manage to feel our way about.

A poor photograph goes to you for Xmas—a poor thing enough surely. But you get Uncle Bob[1] busy on the job of paying for an Ambassador's house. Then we'll bring Christmas presents home for you. What a game we are playing, we poor folks here, along with Ambassadors whose governments pay them four times what ours pays. But we don't give the game away, you bet! We throw the bluff with a fine, straight poker face.

Affectionately,

W. H. P.

To Frank N. Doubleday and Others

London, Sunday, December 28, 1913.

MY DEAR COMRADES:

I was never one of those abnormal creatures who got Christmas all ready by the Fourth of July. The true spirit of the celebration has just now begun to work on me —three days late. In this respect the spirit is very like Christmas plum-pudding. Moreover, we've just got the patriotic fervour flowing at high tide this morning. This is the President's birthday. We've put up the Stars and

---

[1]Mr. Robert N. Page, the Ambassador's brother, was at this time a Congressman from North Carolina.

Stripes on the roof; and half an hour ago the King's Master of Ceremonies drove up in a huge motor car and, being shown into my presence in the state drawing room, held his hat in his hand and (said he):

"Your Excellency: I am commanded by the King to express to you His Majesty's congratulations on the birthday of the President, to wish him a successful administration and good health and long life and to convey His Majesty's greetings to Your Excellency: and His Majesty commands me to express the hope that you will acquaint the President with His Majesty's good wishes."

Whereto I made just as pretty a little speech as your 'umble sarvant could. Then we sat down, I called in Mrs. Page and my secretary and we talked like human beings.

Having worked like the devil, upon whom, I imagine, at this bibulous season many heavy duties fall—having thus toiled for two months—the international docket is clean, I've got done a round of twenty-five speeches (O Lord!) I've slept three whole nights, I've made my dinner-calls— you see I'm feeling pretty well, in this first period of quiet life I've yet found in this Babylon. Praise Heaven! they go off for Christmas. Everything's shut up tight. The streets of London are as lonely and as quiet as the road to Oyster Bay while the Oyster is in South America. It's about as mild here as with you in October and as damp as Sheepshead's Bay in an autumn storm. But such people as you meet complain of the c-o-l-d—the c-o-l-d; and they run into their heatless houses and put on extra waistcoats and furs and throw shawls over their knees and curse Lloyd George and enjoy themselves. They are a great people—even without mint juleps in summer or eggnog in winter; and I like them. The old gouty Lords curse the Americans for the decline of drinking.   And you can't live among them without laughing yourself to death and admiring them, too.   It's a fine race to be sprung from.

All this field of international relations—you fellows regard it as a bore.   So it used to be before my entrance into the game!   But it's everlastingly interesting.   Just to give him a shock, I asked the Foreign Secretary the other day what difference it would make if the Foreign Offices were all to go out of business and all the Ambassadors were to be hanged.   He thought a minute and said: "Suppose war kept on in the Balkans, the Russians killed all their Jews, Germany took Holland and sent an air-fleet over London, the Japanese landed in California, the English took all the oil-wells in Central and South America and——"

"Good Lord!" said I, "do you and I prevent all these calamities?   If so, we don't get half the credit that is due us—do we?"

You could ask the same question about any group or profession of men in the world; and on a scratch, I imagine that any of them would be missed less than they think. But the realness and the bigness of the job here in London is simply oppressive.   We don't even know what it is in the United States and, of course, we don't go about doing it right.   If we did, we shouldn't pick up a green fellow on the plain of Long Island and send him here: we'd train the most capable male babies we have from the cradle.   But this leads a long way.

As I look back over these six or seven months, from the pause that has come this week, I'm bound to say (being frank, not to say vain) that I had the good fortune to do one piece of work that was worth the effort and worth coming to do—about that infernal Mexican situation.   An abler man would have done it better; but, as it was, I did it; and I have a most appreciative letter about it from the President.

By thunder, he's doing *his* job, isn't he? Whether you like the job or not, you've got to grant that. When I first came over here, I found a mild curiosity about Wilson—only mild. But now they sit up and listen and ask most eager questions. He has pressed his personality most strongly on the governing class here.

Yours heartily,

W. H. P.

To the President

American Embassy, London

[May 11, 1914.]

DEAR MR. PRESIDENT:

The King of Denmark (I always think of Hamlet) having come to make his royal kinsman of these Isles a visit, his royal kinsman to-night gave a state dinner at the palace whereto the Ambassadors of the eight Great Powers were, of course, invited. Now I don't know how other kings do, but I'm willing to swear by King George for a job of this sort. The splendour of the thing is truly regal and the friendliness of it very real and human; and the company most uncommon. Of course the Ambassadors and their wives were there, the chief rulers of the Empire and men and women of distinction and most of the royal family. The dinner and the music and the plate and the decorations and the jewels and the uniforms—all these were regal; but there is a human touch about it that seems almost democratic.

All for His Majesty of Denmark, a country with fewer people and less wealth than New Jersey. This whole royal game is most interesting. Lloyd George and H. H. Asquith and John Morley were there, all in white knee breeches of silk, and swords and most gaudy coats—these that are the radicals of the Kingdom, in literature and in action. Veterans of Indian and South African wars stood on either side of every door and of every stairway, dressed as Sir Walter Raleigh dressed, like so many statues, never blinking an eye. Every person in the company is printed, in all the papers, with every title he bears. Crowds lined the streets in front of the palace to see the carriages go in and to guess who was in each. To-morrow the Diplomatic Corps calls on King Christian and to-morrow night King George commands us to attend the opera as his guests.

Whether it's the court, or the honours and the orders and all the social and imperial spoils, that keep the illusion up, or whether it is the Old World inability to change anything, you can't ever quite decide. In Defoe's time they put pots of herbs on the desks of every court in London to keep the plague off. The pots of herbs are yet put on every desk in every court room in London. Several centuries ago somebody tried to break into the Bank of England. A special guard was detached—a little company of soldiers—to stand watch at night. The bank has twice been moved and is now housed in a building that would stand a siege; but that guard, in the same uniform goes on duty every night. Nothing is ever abolished, nothing ever changed. On the anniversary of King Charles's execution, his statue in Trafalgar Square is covered with flowers. Every month, too, new books appear about the mistresses of old kings—as if they, too, were of more than usual interest: I mean serious, historical books. From the King's palace to the humblest house I've been in, there are pictures of kings and queens. In every house, too (to show how nothing ever changes), the towels are folded in the same peculiar way. In every grate in the kingdom the coal fire is laid in precisely the same way.   There is not a salesman in any shop on Piccadilly who does not, in the season, wear a long-tail coat. Everywhere they say a second grace at dinner—not at the end—but before the dessert, because two hundred years ago they dared not wait longer lest the parson be under the table: the grace is said to-day *before* dessert!   I tried three months to persuade my "Boots" to leave off blacking the soles of my shoes under the instep.   He simply couldn't do it.   Every "Boots" in the Kingdom does it.   A man of learning had an article in an afternoon paper a few weeks ago which began thus: "It is now universally conceded by the French and the Americans that the decimal system is a failure," and he went on to concoct a scheme for our money that would be more "rational" and "historical."   In this hot debate about Ulster a frequent phrase used is, "Let us see if we can't find the right formula to solve the difficulty"; their whole lives are formulas.   Now may not all the honours and garters and thistles and O. M.'s and K. C. B.'s and all manner of gaudy sinecures be secure, only because they can't abolish anything?   My servants sit at table in a certain order, and Mrs. Page's maid wouldn't yield her precedence to a mere housemaid for any mortal consideration—any more than a royal person of a certain rank would yield to one of a lower rank.   A real democracy is as far off as doomsday. So you argue, till you remember that it is these same people who made human liberty possible—to a degree— and till you sit day after day and hear them in the House of Commons, mercilessly pounding one another.   Then you are puzzled.   Do they keep all these outworn things because they are incapable of changing anything, or do these outworn burdens keep them from becoming able to change anything?   I daresay it works both ways.   Every venerable ruin, every outworn custom, makes the King more secure; and the King gives veneration to every ruin and keeps respect for every outworn custom.

Praise God for the Atlantic Ocean!   It is the geographical foundation of our liberties.   Yet, as I've often written, there are men here, real men, ruling men, mighty men, and a vigorous stock.

A civilization, especially an old civilization, isn't an easy nut to crack.   But I notice that the men of vision keep their thought on us.   They never forget that we are 100 million strong and that we dare do new things; and they dearly love to ask questions about—Rockefeller! Our power, our adaptability, our potential wealth they never forget.   They'll hold fast to our favour for reasons of prudence as well as for reasons of kinship.   And, whenever we choose to assume the leadership of the world, they'll grant it—gradually—and follow loyally.   They cannot become French, and they dislike the Germans. They must keep in our boat for safety as well as for comfort.

Yours heartily,

WALTER H. PAGE.

The following extracts are made from other letters written at this time:

. . . To-night I had a long talk with the Duchess of X, a kindly woman who spends much time and money in the most helpful "uplift" work; that's the kind of woman she is.

Now she and the Duke are invited to dine at the French Ambassador's to-morrow night.   "If the Duke went into any house where there was any member of this Government," said she, "he'd turn and walk out again.   We thought we'd better find out who the French Ambassador's guests are. We didn't wish to ask him nor to have correspondence about it. Therefore the Duke sent his Secretary quietly to ask the Ambassador's Secretary—before we accepted."

This is now a common occurrence. We had Sir Edward Grey to dinner a little while ago and we had to make sure we had no Tory guests that night.

This same Duchess of X sat in the Peeresses' gallery of the House of Lords to-night till 7 o'clock. "I had to sit in plain sight of the wives of two members of the Cabinet and of the wife and daughter of the Prime Minister. I used to know them," she said, "and it was embarrassing."

Thus the revolution proceeds. For that's what it is.

. . . On the other hand the existing order is the most skilfully devised machinery for perpetuating itself that has ever grown up among civilized men. Did you ever see a London directory? It hasn't names alphabetically; but one section is "Tradesmen," another "The City," etc., etc., and another "The Court." Any one who has ever been presented at Court is in the "Court" section, and you must sometimes look in several sections to find a man. Yet everybody so values these distinctions that nobody complains of the inconvenience. When the Liberal party makes Liberals Peers in order to have Liberals in the House of Lords, lo! they soon turn Conservative after they get there. The system perpetuates itself and stifles the natural desire for change that most men in a state of nature instinctively desire in order to assert their own personalities. . . .

. . . All this social life which engages us at this particular season, sets a man to thinking. The mass of the people are very slow—almost dull; and the privileged are most firmly entrenched. The really alert people are the aristocracy. They see the drift of events. "What is the pleasantest part of your country to live in?" Dowager Lady X asked me on Sunday, more than half in earnest. "My husband's ancestors sat in the House of Lords for six hundred years. My son sits there now—a dummy. They have taken all power from the Lords; they are taxing us out of our lands; they are saving the monarchy for destruction last. England is of the past—all is going. God knows what is coming.". . .

. . . And presently the presentations come. Lord! how sensible American women scramble for this privilege! It royally fits a few of them. Well, I've made some rules about presentations myself, since it's really a sort of personal perquisite of the Ambassador. One rule is, I don't present any but handsome women. Pretty girls: that's what you want when you are getting up a show. Far too many of ours come here and marry Englishmen. I think I shall make another rule and exact a promise that after presentation they shall go home. But the American women do enliven London. . . .

That triumph with the tariff is historic. I wrote to the President: "Score one!" And I have been telling the London writers on big subjects, notably the editor of the *Economist*, that this event, so quiet and undramatic, will mark a new epoch in the trade history of the world.
. . . This island is a good breeding place for men whose children find themselves and develop into real men in freer lands. All that is needed to show the whole world that the future is ours is just this sort of an act of self-confidence. You know the old story of the Negro who

saw a ghost—"Git outen de way, Mr. Rabbit, and let somebody come who *kin* run!" Score one! We're making History, and these people here know it. The trade of the world, or as much of it as is profitable, we may take as we will. The over-taxed, under-productive, army-burdened men of the Old World—alas! I read a settled melancholy in much of their statesmanship and in more of their literature. The most cheerful men in official life here are the High Commissioners of Canada, Australia, New Zealand, and such fellows who know what the English race is doing and can do freed from uniforms and heavy taxes and class feeling and such like. . . .

. . . The two things that this island has of eternal value are its gardens and its men. Nature sprinkles it almost every day and holds its moisture down so that every inch of it is forever green; and somehow men thrive as the   lawns do—the most excellent of all races for progenitors. You and I[1] can never be thankful enough that our ancestors came of this stock. Even those that have stayed have cut a wide swath, and they wield good scythes yet. But I have moods when I pity them—for their dependence, for instance, on a navy (2 keels to 1) for their very bread and meat. They frantically resent conveniences. They build their great law court building (the architecture ecclesiastical) so as to provide an entrance hall of imposing proportions which they use once a year; and to get this fine hall they have to make their court rooms, which they must use all the time, dark and small and inaccessible. They think as much of that once-a-year ceremony of opening their courts as they think of the even justice that they dispense; somehow they feel that the justice depends on the ceremony.

[1] This is from a letter to President Wilson.

This moss that has grown all over their lives (some of it very pretty and most of it very comfortable—it's soft and warm) is of no great consequence—except that they think they'd die if it were removed. And this state of mind gives us a good key to their character and habits.

What are we going to do with this England and this Empire, presently, when economic forces unmistakably put the leadership of the race in our hands? How can we lead it and use it for the highest purposes of the world and of democracy? We can do what we like if we go about it heartily and with good manners (any man prefers to yield to a gentleman rather than to a rustic) and throw away—gradually—our isolating fears and alternate boasting and bashfulness. "What do we most need to learn from you?" I asked a gentle and bejewelled nobleman the other Sunday, in a country garden that invited confidences. "If I may speak without offence, modesty." A commoner in the company, who had seen the Rocky Mountains, laughed, and said: "No; see your chance and take it: that's what we did in the years when we made the world's history." . . .

CHAPTER VI
"POLICY" AND "PRINCIPLE" IN MEXICO

I

THE last days of February, 1913, witnessed one of those sanguinary scenes in Mexico which for generations had accompanied changes in the government of that distracted country. A group of revolutionists assailed the feeble power of Francisco Madero and virtually imprisoned that executive and his forces in the Presidential Palace. The Mexican army, whose most influential officers were General Blanquet and General Victoriano Huerta, was hastily summoned to the rescue of the Government; instead of relieving the besieged officials, however, these generals turned their guns upon them, and so assured the success of the uprising. The speedy outcome of these transactions was the assassination of President Madero and the seizure of the Presidency by General Huerta. Another outcome was the presentation to Page of one of the most delicate problems in the history of Anglo-American relations.

At almost any other time this change in the Mexican succession would have caused only a momentary disturbance. There was nothing new in the violent overthrow of government in Latin-America; in Mexico itself no president had ever risen to power except by revolution. The career of Porfirio Diaz, who had maintained his authority for a third of a century, had somewhat obscured this fundamental fact in Mexican politics, but Diaz had dominated Mexico for seven presidential terms, not because his

175

methods differed from the accepted methods of his country, but because he was himself an executive of great force and a statesman of genius, and could successfully hold his own against any aspiring antagonist. The civilized world, including the United States, had long since become reconciled to this situation as almost a normal one. In recognizing momentarily successful adventurers, Great Britain and the United States had never considered such details as justice or constitutionalism: the legality of the presidential title had never been the point at issue; the only question involved was whether the successful aspirant actually controlled the country, whether he had established a state of affairs that approximately represented order, and whether he could be depended upon to protect life and property. During the long dictatorship of Porfirio Diaz, however, certain events had taken place which had awakened the minds of Americans to the possibility of a new international relationship with all backward peoples. The consequences of the Spanish War had profoundly impressed Page. This conflict had left the United States a new problem in Cuba and the Philippines. Under the principles that for generations had governed the Old World there would have been no particular difficulty in meeting this problem. The United States would have candidly annexed the islands, and exploited their resources and their peoples; we should have concerned ourselves little about any duties that might be owed to the several millions of human beings who inhabited them. Indeed, what other alternatives were there?

One was to hand the possessions back to Spain, who in a four hundred years' experiment had demonstrated her unfitness to govern them; another was to give the islands their independence, which would have meant

merely an indefinite continuance of anarchy.   It is one
of the greatest triumphs of American statesmanship that
it discovered a more satisfactory solution.   Essentially,
the new plan was to establish in these undeveloped
and politically undisciplined regions the fundamental
conditions that may make possible the ultimate creation of
democratic, self-governing states.   It was recognized that
constitutions and election ballots in themselves did not
necessarily imply a democratic order.   Before these there
must come other things that were far more important, such
as popular education, scientific agriculture, sanitation, public highways, railroads, and the development of the resources of nature.   If the backward peoples of the world
could be schooled in such a preliminary apprenticeship,
the time might come when the intelligence and the conscience of the masses would be so enlightened that they
could be trusted with independence.   The labour of
Leonard Wood in Cuba, and of other Americans in the
Philippines, had apparently pointed the way to the only
treatment of such peoples that was just to them and
safe for mankind.

With the experience of Cuba and the Philippines as
a guide, it is not surprising that the situation in Mexico
appealed to many Americans as opening a similar opportunity to the United States.   The two facts that out-
stood all others were that Mexico, in her existing condition
of popular ignorance, could not govern herself, and that
the twentieth century could not accept indefinitely a
condition of disorder and bloodshed that had apparently
satisfied the nineteenth.   The basic difficulty in this
American republic was one of race and of national
character.   The fact that was constantly overlooked was
that Mexico was not a Caucasian country: it was a great
shambling Indian Republic.   Of its 15,000,000 people less

than 3,000,000 were of unmixed white blood, about 35 per cent. were pure Indian, and the rest represented varying mixtures of white and aboriginal stock. The masses had advanced little in civilization since the days of Cortez. Eighty per cent. were illiterate; their lives for the most part were a dull and squalid routine; protection against disease was unknown; the agricultural methods were most primitive; the larger number still spoke the native dialects which had been used in the days of Montezuma; and over good stretches of the country the old tribal régime still represented the only form of political organization. The one encouraging feature was that these Mexican Indians, backward as they might be, were far superior to the other native tribes of the North American Continent; in ancient times, they had developed a state of society far superior to that of the traditional Redskin. Nevertheless, it was true that the progress of Mexico in the preceding fifty years had been due almost entirely to foreign enterprise. By 1913, about 75,000 Americans were living in Mexico as miners, engineers, merchants, and agriculturists; American investments amounted to about $1,200,000,000—a larger sum than that of all the other foreigners combined. Though the work of European countries, particularly Great Britain, was important, yet Mexico was practically an economic colony of the United States. Most observers agree that these foreign activities had not only profited the foreigners, but that they had greatly benefited the Mexicans themselves. The enterprise of Americans had disclosed enormous riches, had given hundreds of thousands employment at very high wages, had built up new Mexican towns on modern American lines, had extended the American railway system over a large part of the land, and had developed street railways, electric lighting, and other modern necessities in all sections of the Republic. The opening up of Mexican oil resources was perhaps the most typical of these achievements, as it was certainly the most adventurous. Americans had created this, perhaps the greatest of Mexican industries, and in 1913, these Americans owned nearly 80 per cent. of Mexican oil. Their success had persuaded several Englishmen, the best known of whom was Lord Cowdray, to enter this same field. The activities of the Americans and the British in oil had an historic significance which was not foreseen in 1913, but which assumed the greatest importance in the World War; for the oil drawn from these Mexican fields largely supplied the Allied fleets and thus became an important element in the defeat of the Central Powers. In 1913, however, American and British oil operators were objects of general suspicion in both continents. They were accused of participating too actively in Mexican politics and there were those who even held them responsible for the revolutionary condition of the country. One picturesque legend insisted that the American oil interests looked with jealous hostility upon the great favours shown by the Diaz Administration to Lord Cowdray's company, and that they had instigated the Madero revolution in order to put in power politicians who would be more friendly to themselves. The inevitable complement to this interpretation of events was a prevailing suspicion that the Cowdray interests had promoted the Huerta revolt in order to turn the tables on "Standard Oil," to make safe the "concessions" already obtained from Diaz and to obtain still more from the new Mexican dictator.

To determine the truth in all these allegations, which were freely printed in the American press of the time, would demand more facts than are at present available; yet it is clear that these oil and other "concessions" presented the perpetual Mexican problem in a new and difficult light. The Wilson Administration came into power a few days after Huerta had seized the Mexican Government. The first difficulty presented to the State Department was to determine its attitude toward this usurper.

A few days after President Wilson's inauguration Mr. Irwin Laughlin, then Chargé d'Affaires in London—this was several weeks before Page's arrival—was instructed to ask the British Foreign Office what its attitude would be in regard to the recognition of President Huerta. Mr. Laughlin informed the Foreign Office that he was not instructed that the United States had decided on any policy, but that he felt sure it would be to the advantage of both countries to follow the same line. The query was not an informal one; it was made in definite obedience to instructions and was intended to elicit a formal commitment. The unequivocal answer that Mr. Laughlin received was that the British Government would not recognize Huerta, either formally or tacitly.

Mr. Laughlin sent his message immediately to Washington, where it apparently made a favourable impression. The Administration then let it be known that the United States would not recognize the new Mexican régime. Whether Mr. Wilson would at this time have taken such a position, irrespective of the British attitude, is not known, but at this stage of the proceedings Great Britain and the United States were standing side by side.

About three weeks afterward Mr. Laughlin heard that the British Foreign Office was about to recognize Huerta. Naturally the report astonished him; he at once called again on the Foreign Office, taking with him the despatch that he had recently sent to Washington. Why had the British Government recognized Huerta when it had given definite assurances to Washington that it had no intention of doing so? The outcome of the affair was that Sir Cecil Spring Rice, British Ambassador in Washington, was instructed to inform the State Department that Great Britain had changed its mind. France, Germany, Spain, and most other governments followed the British example in recognizing the new President of Mexico.

It is thus apparent that the initial mistake in the Huerta affair was made by Great Britain. Its action produced the most unpleasant impression upon the new Administration. Mr. Wilson, Mr. Bryan, and their associates in the cabinet easily found an explanation that was satisfactory to themselves and to the political enthusiasms upon which they had come into power. They believed that the sudden change in the British attitude was the result of pressure from British commercial interests which hoped to profit from the Huerta influence. Lord Cowdray was a rich and powerful Liberal; he had great concessions in Mexico which had been obtained from President Diaz; it was known that Huerta aimed to make his dictatorship a continuation of that of Diaz, to rule Mexico as Diaz had ruled it, that is, by force, and to extend a welcoming hand to foreign capitalists. An important consideration was that the British Navy had a contract with the Cowdray Company for oil, which was rapidly becoming indispensable as a fuel for warships, and this fact necessarily made the British Government almost a champion of the Cowdray interests. It was not necessary to believe all the rumours that were then afloat in the American press to conclude that a Huerta administration would be far more acceptable to the Cowdray Company than any headed by one of the military chieftains who were then disputing the control of Mexico. Mr. Wilson and Mr. Bryan believed that these events proved that certain "interests," similar to the "interests" which, in their view, had exercised so baleful an influence on American politics, were also active in Great Britain. The Wilson election in 1912 had been a protest against the dominance of "Wall Street" in American politics; Mr. Bryan's political stock-in-trade for a generation had consisted of little except a campaign against these forces; naturally, therefore, the suspicion that Great Britain was giving way to a British "Standard Oil" was enough to arm these statesmen against the Huerta policy, and to intensify that profound dislike of Huerta himself that was soon to become almost an obsession.

With this as a starting point President Wilson presently formulated an entirely new principle for dealing with Latin-American republics. There could be no permanent order in these turbulent countries and nothing approaching a democratic system until the habit of revolution should be checked. One of the greatest encouragements to revolution, said the President, was the willingness of foreign governments to recognize any politician who succeeded in seizing the executive power. He therefore believed that a refusal to recognize any government "founded upon violence" would exercise a wholesome influence in checking this national habit; if Great Britain and the United States and the other powers would set the example by refusing to have any diplomatic dealings with General Huerta, such an unfriendly attitude would discourage other forceful intriguers from attempting to repeat his experiment. The result would be that the decent elements in Mexico and other Latin-American countries would at last assert themselves, establish a constitutional system, and select their governments by constitutional means. At the bottom of the whole business were, in the President's and Mr. Bryan's opinion, the "concession" seekers, the "exploiters," who were constantly obtaining advantages at the hands of these corrupt governments and constantly stirring up revolutions for their financial profit. The time had now come to end the whole miserable business. "We are closing one chapter in the history of the world," said Mr. Wilson, "and opening another of unimaginable significance. . . . It is a very perilous thing to determine the foreign policy of a nation in the terms of material interests. . . . We have seen such material interests threaten constitutional freedom in the United States. Therefore we will now know how to sympathize with those in the rest of America who have to contend with such powers, not only within their borders, but from outside their borders."

In this way General Huerta, who, in his own eyes, was merely another in the long succession of Mexican revolutionary chieftains, was translated into an epochal figure in the history of American foreign policy; he became a symbol in Mr. Wilson's new scheme of things—the representative of the order which was to come to an end, the man who, all unwittingly, was to point the new way not only in Mexico, but in all Latin-American countries. The first diplomatic task imposed upon Page therefore was one that would have dismayed a more experienced ambassador. This was to persuade Great Britain to retrace its steps, to withdraw its recognition of Huerta, and to join hands with the United States in bringing about his downfall. The new ambassador sympathized with Mr. Wilson's ideas to a certain extent; the point at which he parted company with the President's Mexican policy will appear in due course. He therefore began zealously to preach the new Latin-American doctrine to the British Foreign Office, with results that appear in his letters of this period.

To the President

6 Grosvenor Square, London,
Friday night, October 24, 1913.

DEAR MR. PRESIDENT:

In this wretched Mexican business, about which I have read columns and columns and columns of comment these two days and turned every conceivable proposition back and forth in my mind—in this whole wretched waste of comment, I have not seen even an allusion to any moral principle involved nor a word of concern about the Mexican people. It is all about who is the stronger, Huerta or some other bandit, and about the necessity of order for the sake of financial interests. Nobody recalls our action in giving Cuba to the Cubans or our pledge to the people of the Philippine Islands. But there is reference to the influence of Standard Oil in the American policy. This illustrates the complete divorce of European politics from fundamental morals, and it shocks even a man who before knew of this divorce.

In my last talk with Sir Edward Grey I drove this home by emphasizing strongly the impossibility of your playing primary heed to any American business interest in Mexico —even the immorality of your doing so; there are many things that come before business and there are some things that come before order. I used American business interests because I couldn't speak openly of British business interests and his Government. I am sure he saw the obvious inference. But not even from him came a word about the moral foundation of government or about the welfare of the Mexican people. These are not in the European governing vocabulary.

I have been trying to find a way to help this Government to wake up to the effect of its pro-Huerta position

and to give them a chance to refrain from repeating that
mistake—and to save their faces; and I have telegraphed
one plan to Mr. Bryan to-day. I think they ought now
to be forced to show their hand without the possibility of
evasion. They will not risk losing our good-will—if it
seem wise to you to put them to a square test.

It's a wretched business, and the sordid level of European statecraft is sad.

I ran across the Prime Minister at the royal wedding
reception[1] the other day.

"What do you infer from the latest news from Mexico?"
he asked.

"Several things."

"Tell me the most important inference you draw."

"Well, the danger of prematurely making up one's
mind about a Mexican adventurer."

"Ah!" and he moved on.

Very heartily yours,
WALTER H. PAGE.

To the President

London, Sunday, Nov. 16, 1913.

. . . About the obligations and inferences of democracy, they are dense. They don't really believe in it;
and they are slow to see what good will come of ousting
Huerta unless we know beforehand who will succeed
him. Sir Edward Grey is not dense, but in this matter
even he is slow fully to understand. The Lord knows
I've told him plainly over and over again and, I fear, even
preached to him. At first he couldn't see the practical
nature of so "idealistic" a programme. I explained to
him how the immemorial "policy" that we all followed of

---

[1]Prince Arthur of Connaught and the Duchess of Fife were married in the Chapel
Royal, October 16, 1913.

recognizing momentarily successful adventurers in Latin-America had put a premium on revolution; that you had found something better than a policy, namely, a principle; that policies change, but principles do not; that he need not be greatly concerned about the successor to Huerta; that this is primarily and ultimately an American problem; that Great Britain's interest being only commercial is far less than the interest of the United States, which is commercial and also ethical; and so on and so on.   His sympathies and his friendliness are all right.   But Egypt and India were in his mind.   He confessed to me that he was much impressed—"if you can carry it through."   Many men are seeing the new idea (I wonder if you are conscious how new it is and how incredible to the Old World mind?) and they express the greatest and sincerest admiration for "your brave new President"; and a wave of friendliness to the United States swept over the Kingdom when the Government took its open stand. At the annual dinner of the oldest and richest of the merchants' guilds at which they invited me to respond to a toast the other night they proposed your health most heartily and, when I arose, they cheered longer and louder than I had before heard men cheer in this kingdom. There is, I am sure, more enthusiasm for the United States here, by far, than for England in the United States.   They are simply dense about any sort of government but their own—particularly dense about the application of democracy to "dependencies" and inferior peoples.   I have a neighbour who spent many years as an administrator in India.   He has talked me deaf about the inevitable failure of this "idealistic" Mexican programme.   He is wholly friendly and wholly incredulous. And for old-time Toryism gone to seed commend me to the *Spectator*.   Not a glimmering of the idea has entered

Strachey's head. The *Times*, however, now sees it pretty clearly. I spent Sunday a few weeks ago with two of its editors in the country, and they have come to see me several times since and written fairly good "leaders" out of my conversation with them. So much for this head. For the moment at least that is satisfactory. You must not forget that they can't all at once take it in, for they do not really know what democracy is or whither it leads and at bottom they do not really believe in it as a scheme of government—not even this Liberal Cabinet.

The British concern for commercial interests, which never sleeps, will, I fear, come up continuously. But we shall simply do justice and stand firm, when this phase of the subject comes forward.

It's amusing, when you forget its sadness, that their first impulse is to regard an unselfish international act as what Cecil Rhodes called the English "unctuous rectitude." But this experience that we are having with them will be worth much in future dealings. They already feel very clearly that a different hand has the helm in Washington; and we can drive them hard, if need be, for they will not forfeit our friendship.

It is worth something to discover that Downing Street makes many mistakes. Infallibility dwells a long way from them. In this matter they have made two terrible blunders—the recognition of Huerta (they know that now) and the sending of Carden (they may already suspect that: they'll know it presently).

Yours always faithfully,
WALTER H. PAGE.

P. S. By Jove, I didn't know that I'd ever have to put the British Government through an elementary course in Democracy!

To the President.

Occasionally Page discussed with Sir Edward Grey an alternative American policy which was in the minds of most people at that time:

To the President

. . . The foregoing I wrote before this Mexican business took its present place. I can't get away from the feeling that the English simply do not and will not believe in any unselfish public action—further than the keeping of order. They have a mania for order, sheer order, order for the sake of order. They can't see how anything can come in any one's thought before order or how anything need come afterward. Even Sir Edward Grey jocularly ran me across our history with questions like this:

"Suppose you have to intervene, what then?"

"Make 'em vote and live by their decisions."

"But suppose they will not so live?"

"We'll go in again and make 'em vote again."

"And keep this up 200 years?" asked he.

"Yes," said I. "The United States will be here two hundred years and it can continue to shoot men for that little space till they learn to vote and to rule themselves."

I have never seen him laugh so heartily. Shooting men into self-government! Shooting them into orderliness—he comprehends that; and that's all right. But that's as far as his habit of mind goes. At Sheffield last night, when I had to make a speech, I explained "idealism" (they always quote it) in Government. They listened attentively and even eagerly. Then they came up and asked if I really meant that Government should concern itself with idealistic things—beyond keeping order. Ought they to do so in India?—I assure you they don't think beyond order. A nigger lynched in Mississippi offends them more than a tyrant in Mexico.

To Edward M. House

London, November 2, 1913.

DEAR HOUSE:

I've been writing to the President that the Englishman has a mania for order, order for order's sake, and for—trade. He has reduced a large part of the world to order. He is the best policeman in creation; and—he has the policeman's ethics! Talk to him about character as a basis of government or about a moral basis of government in any outlying country, he'll think you daft. Bah! what matter who governs or how he governs or where he got his authority or how, so long as he keeps order. He won't see anything else. The lesson of our dealing with Cuba is lost on him. He doesn't believe *that*. We may bring this Government in line with us on Mexico. But in this case and in general, the moral uplift of government must be forced by us—I mean government in outlying countries.

Mexico is only part of Central America, and the only way we can ever forge a Central and South American policy that will endure is *this* way, precisely, by saying that your momentarily successful adventurer can't count on us anywhere; the man that rules must govern for the governed. Then we have a policy; and nobody else has that policy. This Mexican business is worth worlds to us—to establish this.

We may have a diplomatic fight here; and I'm ready! Very ready on this, for its own sake and for reasons that follow, to wit:

Extraordinary and sincere and profound as is the respect of the English for the American people, they hold the American Government in contempt. It shifts and doesn't keep its treaty, etc., etc.—They are right, too. But they need to feel the hand that now has the helm.

But one or two things have first to be got out of the way. That Panama tolls is the worst. We are dead wrong in that, as we are dead right on the Mexican matter. If it were possible (I don't know that it is) for the President to say (quietly, not openly) that he agrees with us—if he do—then the field would be open for a fight on Mexico; and the reënforcement of our position would be incalculable.

Then we need in Washington some sort of Bureau or Master of Courtesies for the Government, to do and to permit us to do those little courtesies that the English spend half their time in doing—this in the course of our everyday life and intercourse. For example: When I was instructed to inform this Government that our fleet would go to the Mediterranean, I was instructed also to say that they mustn't trouble to welcome us—don't pay no 'tention to us! Well, that's what they live for in times of peace—ceremonies. We come along and say, "We're comin' but, hell! don't kick up no fuss over us, we're from Missouri, we are!" And the Briton shrugs his shoulders and says, "Boor!" These things are happening all the time. Of course no one nor a dozen nor a hundred count; but generations of 'em have counted badly. A Government without manners.

If I could outdo these folk at their game of courtesy, and could keep our treaty faith with 'em, then I could lick 'em into the next century on the moral aspects of the Mexican Government, and make 'em look up and salute every time the American Government is mentioned. See?—Is there any hope?—Such is the job exactly. And you know what it would lead to—even in our lifetime—

to the leadership of the world: and we should presently be considering how we may best use the British fleet, the British Empire, and the English race for the betterment of mankind.

Yours eagerly,

W. H. P.

A word of caution is necessary to understand Page's references to the British democracy. That the parliamentary system is democratic in the sense that it is responsive to public opinion he would have been the first to admit. That Great Britain is a democracy in the sense that the suffrage is general is also apparent. But, in these reflections on the British commonwealth, the Ambassador was thinking of his old familiar figure, the "Forgotten Man"—the neglected man, woman, and child of the masses. In an address delivered, in June, 1914, before the Royal Institution of Great Britain, Page gave what he regarded as the definition of the American ideal. "The fundamental article in the creed of the American democracy—you may call it the fundamental dogma if you like—is the unchanging and unchangeable resolve that every human being shall have his opportunity for his utmost development—his chance to become and to do the best that he can." Democracy is not only a system of government—"it is a scheme of society." Every citizen must have not only the suffrage, he must likewise enjoy the same advantages as his neighbour for education, for social opportunity, for good health, for success in agriculture, manufacture, finance, and business and professional life. The country that most successfully opened all these avenues to every boy or girl, exclusively on individual merit, was in Page's view the most democratic. He believed that the United States did this more completely than Great Britain or any other country; and therefore he believed that we were far more democratic. He had not found in other countries the splendid phenomenon presented by America's great agricultural region. "The most striking single fact about the United States is, I think, this spectacle, which, so far as I know, is new in the world: On that great agricultural area are about seven million farms of an average size of about 140 acres, most of which are tilled by the owners themselves, a population that varies greatly, of course, in its thrift and efficiency, but most of which is well housed, in houses they themselves own, well clad, well fed, and a population that trains practically all its children in schools maintained by public taxation." It was some such vision as this that Page hoped to see realized ultimately in Mexico. And some such development as this would make Mexico a democracy. It was his difficulty in making the British see the Mexican problem in this light that persuaded him that, in this comprehensive meaning of the word, the democratic ideal had made an inappreciable progress in Europe—and even in Great Britain itself.

II

These letters are printed somewhat out of their chronological order because they picture definitely the two opposing viewpoints of Great Britain and the United States on Mexico and Latin-America generally. Here, then, was the sharp issue drawn between the Old World and the New—on one side the dreary conception of outlying countries as fields to be exploited for the benefit of "investors," successful revolutionists to be recognized in so far as they promoted such ends, and no consideration to be shown to the victims of their rapacity; and the new American idea, the idea which had been made reality in Cuba and the Philippines, that the enlightened and successful nations stood something in the position of trustees to such unfortunate lands and that it was their duty to lead them along the slow pathway of progress and democracy.   So far the Wilsonian principle could be joyfully supported by the Ambassador.   Page disagreed with the President, however, in that he accepted the logical consequences of this programme.   His formula of "shooting people into self-government," which had so entertained the British Foreign Secretary, was a characteristically breezy description of the alternative that Page, in the last resort, was ready to adopt, but which President Wilson and Secretary Bryan persistently refused to consider.   Page was just as insistent as the Washington Administration that Huerta should resign and that Great Britain should assist the United States in accomplishing his dethronement, and that the Mexican people should have a real opportunity of setting up for themselves.   He was not enough of an "idealist," however, to believe that the Mexicans, without the assistance of their powerful neighbours, could succeed in establishing a constitutional government.   In early August, 1913, President Wilson sent Mr. John Lind, ex-Governor of Minnesota, to Mexico as his personal representative. His mission was to invite Huerta to remove himself from Mexican politics, and to permit the Mexican people to hold a presidential election at which Huerta would himself agree not to be a candidate.   Mr. Lind presented these proposals on August 15th, and President Huerta rejected every one of them with a somewhat disconcerting promptitude.

That Page was prepared to accept the consequences of this failure appears in the following letter.   The lack of confidence which it discloses in Secretary Bryan was a

feeling that became stronger as the Mexican drama unfolded.

To Edward M. House

London, August 25, 1913.

MY DEAR HOUSE:

. . . If you find a chance, get the substance of this
memorandum into the hands of two men: the President
and the Secretary of Agriculture.   Get 'em in Houston's
at once—into the President's whenever the time is ripe.
I send the substance to Washington and I send many
other such things.   But I never feel sure that they reach
the President.   The most confidential letter I have
written was lost in Washington, and there is pretty good
testimony that it reached the Secretary's desk.   He does
not acknowledge the important things, but writes me
confidentially to inquire if the office of the man who
attends to the mail pouches (the diplomatic and naval
despatches in London)[1] is not an office into which he
might put a Democrat.—But I keep at it.   It would be
a pleasure to know that the President knows what I
am trying to do.   . . .

Yours heartily,

WALTER H. PAGE.

Following is the memorandum:

In October the provisional recognition of Huerta by
England will end.   Then this Government will be free.
Then is the time for the United States to propose to
England joint intervention merely to reduce this turbu-
lent scandal of a country to order—on an agreement, of
course, to preserve the territorial integrity of Mexico.
It's a mere police duty that all great nations have to do—
as they did in the case of the Boxer riots in China.   Of

---

[1] See the Appendix (at end of Vol. II) for this episode in detail.

course Germany and France, etc., ought to be invited—
on the same pledge: the preservation of territorial integrity. If Germany should come in, she will thereby
practically acknowledge the Monroe Doctrine, as England
has already done. If Germany stay out, then she can't
complain. England and the United States would have
only to announce their intention: there'd be no need to
fire a gun. Besides settling the Mexican trouble, we'd
gain much—having had England by our side in a praise-
worthy enterprise. That, and the President's visit[1]
would give the world notice to whom it belongs, and
cause it to be quiet and to go about its proper business of
peaceful industry.

Moreover, it would show all the Central and South
American States that we don't want any of their territory,
that we will not let anybody else have any, but that they,
too, must keep orderly government or the great Nations
of the earth, will, at our bidding, forcibly demand quiet in
their borders. I believe a new era of security would come
in all Spanish America. Investments would be safer,
governments more careful and orderly. And—we would
not have made any entangling alliance with anybody. All
this would prevent perhaps dozens of little wars. It's
merely using the English fleet and ours to make the world
understand that the time has come for orderliness and
peace and for the honest development of backward, turbulent lands and peoples.

If you don't put this through, tell me what's the
matter with it. I've sent it to Washington after talking
and being talked to for a month and after the hardest
kind of thinking. Isn't this constructive? Isn't it using

---

[1]There was a suggestion, which the Ambassador endorsed, that President Wilson
should visit England to accept, in the name of the United States, Sulgrave Manor,
the ancestral home of the Washingtons. See Chapter IX, page 274.

the great power lying idle about the world, to do the thing that most needs to be done?

Colonel House presented this memorandum to the President, but events sufficiently disclosed that it had no influence upon his Mexican policy. Two days after it was written Mr. Wilson went before Congress, announced that the Lind Mission had failed, and that conditions in Mexico had grown worse. He advised all Americans to leave the country, and declared that he would lay an embargo on the shipment of munitions—an embargo that would affect both the Huerta forces and the revolutionary groups that were fighting them.

Meanwhile Great Britain had taken another step that made as unpleasant an impression on Washington as had the recognition of Huerta. Sir Lionel Edward Gresley Carden had for several years been occupying British diplomatic posts in Central America, in all of which he had had disagreeable social and diplomatic relations with Americans. Sir Lionel had always shown great zeal in promoting British commercial interests, and, justly or unjustly, had acquired the fame of being intensely anti-American. From 1911 to 1913 Carden had served as British Minister to Cuba; here his anti-Americanism had shown itself in such obnoxious ways that Mr. Knox, Secretary of State under President Taft, had instructed Ambassador Reid to bring his behaviour to the attention of the British Foreign Office. These representations took practically the form of requesting Carden's removal from Cuba. Perhaps the unusual relations that the United States bore toward Cuba warranted Mr. Knox in making such an approach; yet the British refused to see the matter in that light; not only did they fail to displace Carden, but they knighted him—the traditional British way of defending a faithful public servant who has been attacked. Sir Lionel Carden refused to mend his ways; he continued to indulge in what Washington regarded as anti-American propaganda; and a second time Secretary Knox intimated that his removal would be acceptable to this country, and a second time this request was refused. With this preliminary history of Carden as a background, and with the British-American misunderstanding over Huerta at its most serious stage, the emotions of Washington may well be imagined when the news came, in July, 1913, that this same gentleman had been appointed British Minister to Mexico. If the British Government had ransacked its diplomatic force to find the one man who would have been most objectionable to the United States, it could have made no better selection. The President and Mr. Bryan were pretty well persuaded that the "oil concessionaires" were dictating British-Mexican policy, and this appointment translated their suspicion into a conviction. Carden had seen much service in Mexico; he had been on the friendliest terms with Diaz; and the newspapers openly charged that the British oil capitalists had dictated his selection. All these assertions Carden and the oil interests denied; yet Carden's behaviour from the day of his appointment showed great hostility to the United States. A few days after he had reached New York, on his way to his new post, the New York *World* published an interview with Carden in which he was reported as declaring that President Wilson knew nothing about the Mexican situation and in which he took the stand that Huerta was the man to handle Mexico at this crisis. His appearance in the Mexican capital was accompanied by other highly undiplomatic publications. In late October President Huerta arrested all his enemies in the Mexican Congress, threw them into jail, and proclaimed himself dictator. Washington was much displeased that Sir Lionel Carden should have selected the day of these high-handed proceedings to present to Huerta his credentials as minister; in its sensitive condition, the State Department interpreted this act as a reaffirmation of that recognition that had already caused so much confusion in Mexican affairs.

Carden made things worse by giving out more newspaper interviews, a tendency that had apparently grown into a habit. "I do not believe that the United States recognizes the seriousness of the situation here. . . . I see no reason why Huerta should be displaced by another man whose abilities are yet to be tried. . . . Safety in Mexico can be secured only by punitive and remedial methods, and a strong man;"—such were a few of the reflections that the reporters attributed to this astonishing diplomat. Meanwhile, the newspapers were filled with reports that the British Minister was daily consorting with Huerta, that he was constantly strengthening that chieftain's backbone in opposition to the United States and that he was obtaining concessions in return for this support. To what extent these press accounts rested on fact cannot be ascertained definitely at this time; yet it is a truth that Carden's general behaviour gave great encouragement to Huerta and that it had the deplorable effect of placing Great Britain and the United States in opposition. The interpretation of the casual reader was that Great Britain was determined to seat Huerta in the Presidency against the determination of the United States to keep him out. The attitude of the Washington cabinet was almost bitter at this time against the British Government. "There is a feeling here," wrote Secretary Lane to Page, "that England is playing a game unworthy of her."

The British Government promptly denied the authenticity of the Carden interview, but that helped matters little, for the American public insisted on regarding such denials as purely diplomatic. Something of a storm against Carden arose in England itself, where it was believed that his conception of his duties was estranging two friendly countries. Probably the chief difficulty was that the British Foreign Office could see no logical sequence in the Washington policy. Put Huerta out—yes, by all means: but what then? Page's notes of his visit to Sir Edward Grey a few days after the latest Carden interview confirm this:

I have just come from an hour's talk with Grey about Mexico. He showed me his telegram to Carden, asking about Carden's reported **interview** criticizing the United States, and Carden's flat denial. He showed me another telegram to Carden about Huerta's reported boast that he would have the backing of London, Paris, and Berlin against the United States, in which Grey advised Carden that British policy should be to keep aloof from Huerta's boasts and plans. Carden denied that Huerta made such a boast in his statement to the Diplomatic Corps. Grey wishes the President to know of these telegrams.

Talk then became personal and informal. I went over the whole subject again, telling how the Press and people of the United States were becoming critical of the British Government; that they regarded the problem as wholly American; that they resented aid to Huerta, whom they regarded as a mere tyrant; that they suspected British interests of giving financial help to Huerta; that many newspapers and persons refused to believe Carden's denial; that the President's policy was not academic but was the only policy that would square with American ideals and that it was unchangeable. I cited our treatment of Cuba. I explained again that I was talking unofficially and giving him only my own interpretation of the people's mood. He asked, if the British Government should withdraw the recognition of Huerta, what would happen.

"In my opinion," I replied, "he would collapse."

"What would happen then—worse chaos?"

"That is impossible," I said. "There is no worse chaos than deputies in jail, the dictatorial doubling of the tariff, the suppression of opinion, and the practical banishment of independent men. If Huerta should fall, there is hope that suppressed men and opinion will set up a successful government."

"Suppose that fail," he asked—"what then?"

I replied that, in case of continued and utter failure, the United States might feel obliged to repeat its dealings with Cuba and that the continued excitement of opinion in the United States might precipitate this.

Grey protested that he knew nothing of what British interests had done or were doing, that he wished time to think the matter out and that he was glad to await the President's communication. He thanked me cordially for my frank statements and declared that he understood perfectly their personal nature. I impressed him with the seriousness of American public opinion.

The last thing that the British Government desired at this time was a serious misunderstanding with the United States, on Mexico or any other matter. Yet the Mexican situation, in early November, 1913, clearly demanded a complete cleaning up. The occasion soon presented itself. Sir William Tyrrell, the private secretary of Sir Edward Grey sailed, in late October, for the United

States.   The purpose of his visit was not diplomatic, but Page evidently believed that his presence in the United States offered too good an opportunity to be lost.

To Edward M. House

Newton Hall, Newton, Cambridge.
Sunday, October 26, 1913.

DEAR HOUSE:

Sir William Tyrrell, the secretary of Sir Edward Grey—himself, I think, an M. P.—has gone to the United States to visit his friend, Sir Cecil Spring Rice.   He sailed yesterday, going first to Dublin, N. H., thence with the Ambassador to Washington.   He has never before been to the United States, and he went off in high glee, alone, to see it.   He's a good fellow, a thoroughly good fellow, and he's an important man.   He of course has Sir Edward's complete confidence, but he's also a man on his own account.   I have come to reckon it worth while to get ideas that I want driven home into his head.   It's a good head and a good place to put good ideas.

The Lord knows you have far too much to do; but in this juncture I should count it worth your while to pay him some attention.   I want him to get the President's ideas about Mexico, good and firm and hard.   They are so far from altruistic in their politics here that it would be a good piece of work to get our ideas and aims into this man's head.   His going gives you and the President and everybody a capital chance to help me keep our good American-English understanding.

Whatever happen in Mexico, I'm afraid there will be a disturbance of the very friendly feeling between the American people and the English.   I am delivering a series of well-thought-out discourses to Sir Edward—

with what effect, I don't know. If the American press could be held in a little, that would be as good as it is impossible.

I'm now giving the Foreign Office the chance to refrain from more premature recognizing.

Very hastily yours,

WALTER H. PAGE.

Sir William Tyrrell, to whom Page refers so pleasantly, was one of the most engaging men personally in the British Foreign Office, as well as one of the most influential. Though he came to America on no official mission to our Government, he was exceptionally qualified to discuss Mexico and other pending questions with the Washington Administration. He had an excellent background, and a keen insight into the human aspects of all problems, but perhaps his most impressive physical trait was a twinkling eye, as his most conspicuous mental quality was certainly a sense of humour. Constant association with Sir Edward Grey had given his mind a cast not dissimilar to that of his chief—a belief in ordinary decency in international relations, an enthusiasm for the better ordering of the world, a sincere admiration for the United States and a desire to maintain British-American friendship. In his first encounter with official Washington Sir William needed all that sense of the ludicrous with which he is abundantly endowed. This took the form of a long interview with Secretary Bryan on the foreign policy of Great Britain. The Secretary harangued Sir William on the wickedness of the British Empire, particularly in Egypt and India and in Mexico. The British oil men, Mr. Bryan declared, was nothing but the "paymasters" of the British Cabinet.

"You are wrong," replied the Englishman, who saw

that the only thing to do on an occasion of this kind was to refuse to take the Secretary seriously. "Lord Cowdray hasn't money enough. Through a long experience with corruption the Cabinet has grown so greedy that Cowdray hasn't the money necessary to reach their price."

"Ah," said Mr. Bryan, triumphantly, accepting Sir William's bantering answer as made in all seriousness. "Then you admit the charge."

From this he proceeded to denounce Great Britain in still more unmeasured terms. The British, he declared, had only one interest in Mexico, and that was oil. The Foreign Office had simply handed its Mexican policy over to the "oil barons" for predatory purposes.

"That's just what the Standard Oil people told me in New York," the British diplomat replied. "Mr. Secretary, you are talking just like a Standard Oil man. The ideas that you hold are the ones which the Standard Oil is disseminating. You are pursuing the policy which they have decided on. Without knowing it you are promoting the interest of Standard Oil."

Sir William saw that it was useless to discuss Mexico with Mr. Bryan—that the Secretary was not a thinker but an emotionalist. However, despite their differences, the two men liked each other and had a good time. As Sir William was leaving, he bowed deferentially to the Secretary of State and said:

"You have stripped me naked, Mr. Secretary, but I am unashamed."

With President Wilson, however, the Englishman had a more satisfactory experience. He was delighted by the President's courtesy, charm, intelligence, and conversational powers. The impression which Sir William obtained of the American President on this occasion remained with him for several years and was itself an important element in British-American relations after the outbreak of the World War. And the visit was a profitable one for Mr. Wilson, since he obtained a clear understanding of the British policy toward Mexico. Sir William succeeded in persuading the President that the so-called oil interests were not dictating the policy of Sir Edward Grey. That British oil men were active in Mexico was apparent; but they were not using a statesman of so high a character as Sir Edward Grey for their purposes and would not be able to do so. The British Government entertained no ambitions in Mexico that meant unfriendliness to the United States. In no way was the policy of Great Britain hostile to our own. In fact, the British recognized the predominant character of the American interest in Mexico and were willing to accept any policy in which Washington would take the lead. All it asked was that British property and British lives be protected; once these were safeguarded Great Britain was ready to stand aside and let the United States deal with Mexico in its own way.

The one disappointment of this visit was that Sir William Tyrrell was unable to obtain from President Wilson any satisfactory statement of his Mexican policy.

"When I go back to England," said the Englishman, as the interview was approaching an end, "I shall be asked to explain your Mexican policy. Can you tell me what it is?"

President Wilson looked at him earnestly and said, in his most decisive manner:

"I am going to teach the South American Republics to elect good men!"

This was excellent as a purpose, but it could hardly be regarded as a programme.

"Yes," replied Sir William, "but, Mr. President, I shall have to explain this to Englishmen, who, as you know, lack imagination. They cannot see what is the difference between Huerta, Carranza, and Villa."

The only answer he could obtain was that Carranza was the best of the three and that Villa was not so bad as he had been painted. But the phrase that remained with the British diplomat was that one so characteristically Wilsonian: "I propose to teach the South American Republics to elect good men." In its attitude, its phrasing, it held the key to much Wilson history.

Additional details of this historic interview are given in Colonel House's letters:

From Edward M. House

145 East 35th Street,
New York City.
November 4, 1913.

DEAR PAGE:

Your cablegram, telling me of the arrival of Sir William Tyrrell on the *Imperator*, was handed me on my way to the train as I left for Washington.

The President talked with me about the Mexican situation and it looks as if something positive will be done in a few days unless Huerta abdicates.

It is to be the policy of this Administration henceforth not to recognize any Central American government that is not formed along constitutional lines. Anything else would be a makeshift policy. As you know, revolutions and assassinations in order to obtain control of governments are instituted almost wholly for the purpose of loot and when it is found that these methods will not bring the desired results, they will cease.

The President also feels strongly in regard to foreign financial interests seeking to control those unstable governments through concessions and otherwise. This, too, he is determined to discourage as far as it is possible to do so.

This was a great opportunity for England and America to get together. You know how strongly we both feel upon this subject and I do not believe that the President differed greatly from us, but the recent actions of the British Government have produced a decided irritation, which to say the least is unfortunate.

Faithfully yours,

E. M. HOUSE.

145 East 35th Street,
New York City.
November 14, 1913.

DEAR PAGE:

Things have happened quickly since I last wrote to you.

I went to Washington Monday night as the guest of the Bryans. They have been wanting me to come to them and I thought this a good opportunity.

I talked the Mexican situation out thoroughly with him and one of your dispatches came while I was there. I found that he was becoming prejudiced against the British Government, believing that their Mexican policy was based purely upon commercialism, that they were backing Huerta quietly at the instance of Lord Cowdray, and that Cowdray had not only already obtained concessions from the Huerta Government, but expected to obtain others. Sir Lionel Carden was also all to the bad.

I saw the President and his views were not very different from those of Mr. Bryan. I asked the President to permit me to see Sir William Tyrrell and talk to him frankly and to attempt to straighten the tangle out. He gave me a free hand.

I lunched with Sir William at the British Embassy although Sir Cecil Spring Rice was not well enough to be present.   I had a long talk with Sir William after lunch and found that our suspicions were unwarranted and that we could get together without any difficulty whatever.

I told him very frankly what our purpose was in Mexico and that we were determined to carry it through if it was within our power to do so.   That being so I suggested that he get his government to coöperate cordially with ours rather than to accept our policy reluctantly.

I told him that you and I had dreamed of a sympathetic alliance between the two countries and that it seemed to me that this dream might come true very quickly because of the President and Sir Edward Grey.   He expressed a willingness to coöperate freely and I told him I would arrange an early meeting with the President.   I thought it better to bring the President into the game rather than Mr. Bryan.   I told him of the President's attitude upon the Panama toll question but I touched upon that lightly and in confidence, preferring for the President himself to make his own statement.

I left the Bryans in the morning of the luncheon with Sir William, intending to take an afternoon train for New York, but the President wanted me to stay with him at the White House over night and meet Sir William with him at half past nine the following morning.   He was so tired that I did not have the heart to urge a meeting that night.

From half past nine until half past ten the President and Sir William repeated to each other what they had said separately to me, and which I had given to each, and then the President elaborated upon the toll question much to the satisfaction of Sir William.

He explained the matter in detail and assured him of his entire sympathy and purpose to carry out our treaty obligations, both in the letter and the spirit.

Sir William was very happy after the interview and when the President left us he remained to talk to me and to express his gratification. He cleared up in the President's mind all suspicion, I think, in regard to concessions and as to the intentions and purposes of the British Government. He assured the President that his government would work cordially with ours and that they would do all that they could to bring about joint pressure through Germany and France for the elimination of Huerta.

We are going to give them a chance to see what they can do with Huerta before moving any further. Sir William thinks that if we are willing to let Huerta save his face he can be got out without force of arms.

Sir William said that if foreign diplomats could have heard our conversation they would have fallen in a faint; it was so frankly indiscreet and undiplomatic. I did not tell him so, but I had it in the back of my mind that where people wanted to do right and had the power to carry out their intentions there was no need to cloak their thoughts in diplomatic language.

All this makes me very happy for it looks as if we are in sight of the promised land.

I am pleased to tell you of the compliments that have been thrown at you by the President, Mr. Bryan, and Sir William. They were all enthusiastic over your work in London and expressed the keenest appreciation of the way in which you have handled matters. Sir William told me that he did not remember an American Ambassador that was your equal.

Faithfully yours,

E. M. House.

So far as a meeting between a British diplomat and the President of the United States could solve the Mexican problem, that problem was apparently solved. The dearest wish of Mr. Wilson, the elimination of Huerta, seemed to be approaching realization, now that he had persuaded Great Britain to support him in this enterprise. Whether Sir William Tyrrell, or Sir Edward Grey, had really become converted to the President's "idealistic" plans for Mexico is an entirely different question. At this time there was another matter in which Great Britain's interest was even greater than in Mexico. These letters have already contained reference to tolls on the Panama Canal. Colonel House's letter shows that the President discussed this topic with Sir William Tyrrell and gave him assurances that this would be settled on terms satisfactory to Great Britain. It cannot be maintained that that assurance was really the consideration which paved the way to an understanding on Huerta. The conversation was entirely informal; indeed, it could not be otherwise, for Sir William Tyrrell brought no credentials; there could be no definite bargain or agreement, but there is little question that Mr. Wilson's friendly disposition toward British shipping through the Panama Canal made it easy for Great Britain to give him a free hand in Mexico.

A few days after this White House interview Sir Lionel Carden performed what must have been for him an uncongenial duty. This loquacious minister led a procession of European diplomats to General Huerta, formally advised that warrior to yield to the American demands and withdraw from the Presidency of Mexico. The delegation informed the grim dictator that their governments were supporting the American policy and Sir Lionel brought him the unwelcome news that he could not depend upon British support. About the same time Premier Asquith made conciliatory remarks on Mexico at the Guildhall banquet. He denied that the British Government had undertaken any policy "deliberately opposed to that of the United States. There is no vestige of foundation for such a rumour." These events changed the atmosphere at Washington, which now became almost as cordial to Great Britain as it had for several months been suspicious.

To Edward M. House

London, November 15, 1913.

DEAR HOUSE:

All's well here. The whole trouble was caused not here but in Mexico City; and that is to be remedied yet. And it will be! For the moment it is nullified. But you need give yourself no concern about the English Government or people, in the long run. It is taking them some time to see the vast difference between acting by a principle and acting by what they call a "policy." They and we ourselves too have from immemorial time been recognizing successful adventurers, and they didn't instantly understand this new "idealistic" move; they didn't know the man at the helm! I preached many sermons to our friend, I explained the difference to many private groups, I made after-dinner speeches leading right up to the point—as far as I dared, I inspired many newspaper articles; and they see it now and have said it and have made it public; and the British people are enthusiastic as far as they understand it.

And anybody concerned here understands the language that the President speaks now. You mustn't forget that in all previous experiences in Latin America we ourselves have been as much to blame as anybody else. Now we have a clear road to travel, a policy based on character to follow forever—a new era. Our dealing with Cuba was

a new chapter in the history of the world. Our dealing
with Mexico is Chapter II of the same Revelation. Tell
'em this in Washington.

The remaining task will be done too and I think pretty
soon. For that I need well-loaded shells. I'll supply
the gunpowder.

And don't you concern yourself about the English.
They're all right—a little slow, but all right.

Heartily yours,
WALTER H. PAGE.

To Edward M. House

Newtimber Place, Hassocks, Sussex,
Sunday, November 23, 1913.

DEAR HOUSE:

Your letter telling me about Tyrrell and the President
brought me great joy. Tyrrell is in every way a square
fellow, much like his Chief; and, you may depend on it,
they are playing fair—in their slow way. They always
think of India and of Egypt—never of Cuba. Lord!
Lord! the fun I've had, the holy joy I am having (I never
expected to have such exalted and invigorating felicity)
in delivering elementary courses of instruction in democracy to the British Government. Deep down at the
bottom, they don't know what Democracy means.
Their Empire is in the way. Their centuries of land-
stealing are in the way. Their unsleeping watchfulness
of British commerce is in the way. "You say you'll
shoot men into self-government," said Sir Edward.
"Doesn't that strike you as comical?" And I answered,
"It is comical only to the Briton and to others who have
associated shooting with subjugation. We associate
shooting with freedom." Half this blessed Sunday at
this country house I have been ramming the idea down

the throat of the Lord Chancellor.[1] *He* sees it, too, being a Scotchman. I take the members of the Government, as I get the chance or can make it, and go over with them the A B C of the President's principle: no territorial annexation; no trafficking with tyrants; no stealing of American governments by concession or financial thimble-rigging. They'll not recognize another Huerta—they're sick of that. And they'll not endanger our friendship. They didn't see the idea in the beginning. Of course the real trouble has been in Mexico City—Carden. They don't know yet just what he did. But they will, if *I* can find out. I haven't yet been able to make them tell me at Washington. Washington is a deep hole of silence toward ambassadors. By gradual approaches, I'm going to prove that Carden can do—and in a degree has already done—as much harm as Bryce did good—and all about a paltry few hundreds of million dollars' worth of oil. What the devil does the oil or the commerce of Mexico or the investments there amount to in comparison with the close friendship of the two nations? Carden can't be good long: he'll break out again presently. He has no political imagination. That's a rather common disease here, too. Few men have. It's good fun. I'm inviting the Central and South American Ministers to lunch with me, one by one, and I'm incidentally loading them up. I have all the boys in the Embassy full of zeal and they are tackling the Secretaries of the Central and South American legations. We've got a *principle* now to deal by with them. They'll see after a while.

English people are all right, too—except the Doctrinaires. They write much rank ignorance. But the learned men learn things last of all.

---

[1] Viscount Haldane, Lord High Chancellor of Great Britain since 1912.

I thank you heartily for your good news about Tyrrell, about the President (but I'm sorry he's tired: make him quit eating meat and play golf); about the Panama tolls; about the Currency Bill (my love to McAdoo); about my own little affairs.—We are looking with the very greatest pleasure to the coming of the young White House couple. I've got two big dinners for them—Sir Edward, the Lord Chancellor, a duchess or two, some good folk, Ruth Bryan, a couple of ambassadors, etc., etc., etc.   Then we'll take 'em to a literary speaking-feast or two, have 'em invited to a few great houses; then we'll give 'em another dinner, and then we'll get a guide for them to see all the reforming institutions in London, to their hearts' content—lots of fun.

Lots of fun: I got the American Society for its Thanksgiving dinner to invite the Lord Chancellor to respond to a toast to the President. He's been to the United States lately and he is greatly pleased. So far, so good. Then I came down here—where he, too, is staying. After five or six hours' talk about everything else he said, "By the way, your countrymen have invited me," etc., etc. "Now what would be appropriate to talk about?" Then I poured him full of the New Principle as regards Central and South America; for, if he will talk on that, what he says will be reported and read on both continents.   He's a foxy Scot, and he didn't say he would, but he said that he'd consider it. "Consider it" means that he will confer with Sir Edward. I'm beginning to learn their vocabulary. Anyhow the Lord Chancellor is in line.

It's good news you send always. Keep it up—keep it up. The volume of silence that I get is oppressive. You remember the old nigger that wished to pick a quarrel with another old nigger?   Nigger No. 1 swore and stormed at nigger No. 2, and kept on swearing and storming, hoping to provoke him. Nigger No. 2 said not a word, but kept at his work. Nigger No. 1 swore and stormed more. Nigger No. 2 said not a word. Nigger No. 1 frothed still more. Nigger No. 2, still silent. Nigger No. 1 got desperate and said: "Look here, you kinky-headed, flat-nosed, slab-footed nigger, I warns you 'fore God, don't you keep givin' me none o' your damned silence!" I wish you'd tell all my friends that story.

Always heartily yours,

WALTER H. PAGE.

CHAPTER VII

PERSONALITIES OF THE MEXICAN PROBLEM

PAGE'S remarks about the "trouble in Mexico City" and the "remaining task" refer, of course, to Sir Lionel Carden. "As I make Carden out," he wrote about this time, "he's a slow-minded, unimaginative, commercial Briton, with as much nimbleness as an elephant. British commerce is his deity, British advantage his duty and mission; and he goes about his work with blunt dullness and ineptitude. That's his mental calibre as I read him—a dull, commercial man."

Although Sir Lionel Carden had been compelled to harmonize himself with the American policy, Page regarded his continued presence in Mexico City as a standing menace to British-American relations. He therefore set himself to accomplish the minister's removal. The failure of President Taft's attempt to obtain Carden's transfer from Havana, in 1912, showed that Page's new enterprise was a delicate and difficult one; yet he did not hesitate.

The part that the wives of diplomats and statesmen play in international relations is one that few Americans understand. Yet in London, the Ambassador's wife is almost as important a person as the Ambassador himself. An event which now took place in the American Embassy emphasized this point. A certain lady, well known in London, called upon Mrs. Page and gave her a message on Mexican affairs for the Ambassador's benefit. The purport was that the activities of certain British commercial interests in Mexico, if not checked, would produce a serious situation between Great Britain and the United States. The lady in question was herself a sincere worker for Anglo-American amity, and this was the motive that led her to take an unusual step.

"It's all being done for the benefit of one man," she said.

The facts were presented in the form of a memorandum, which Mrs. Page copied and gave the Ambassador. This, in turn, Page sent to President Wilson.

To Edward M. House

London, November 26, 1913.

DEAR HOUSE:

Won't you read the enclosed and get it to the President? It is somewhat extra-official but it is very confidential, and I have a special reason for wishing it to go through your hands. Perhaps it will interest you.

The lady that wrote it is one of the very best-informed women I know, one of those active and most influential women in the high political society of this Kingdom, at whose table statesmen and diplomats meet and important things come to pass. . . .

I am sure she has no motive but the avowed one. She has taken a liking to Mrs. Page and this is merely a friendly and patriotic act.

I had heard most of the things before as gossip—never before as here put together by a responsible hand.

Mrs. Page went to see her and, as evidence of our appreciation and safety, gave the original back to her. We have kept no copy, and I wish this burned, if you please. It would raise a riot here, if any breath of it were to get out, that would put bedlam to shame.

Lord Cowdray has been to see me for four successive days. I have a suspicion (though I don't know) that, instead of his running the Government, the Government has now turned the tables and is running him. His government contract is becoming a bad thing to sleep with. He told me this morning that he (through Lord Murray) had withdrawn the request for any concession in Colombia.[1] I congratulated him. "That, Lord Cowdray, will save you as well as some other people I know a good deal of possible trouble." I have explained to him the whole New Principle *in extenso*, "so that you may see clearly where the line of danger runs." Lord! how he's changed! Several weeks ago when I ran across him accidentally he was humorous, almost cynical. Now he's very serious. I explained to him that the only thing that had kept South America from being parcelled out as Africa has been is the Monroe Doctrine and the United States behind it. He granted that.

"In Monroe's time," said I, "the only way to take a part of South America was to take land. Now finance has new ways of its own!"

"Perhaps," said he.

"Right there," I answered, "where you put your 'perhaps,' I put a danger signal. That, I assure you, you will read about in the histories as 'The Wilson Doctrine'!"

You don't know how easy it all is with our friend and leader in command. I've almost grown bold. You feel steady ground beneath you. They are taking to their tents.

"What's going to happen in Mexico City?"

---

[1]This was another manifestation of British friendliness. When the American excitement was most acute, it became known that British capitalists had secured oil concessions in Colombia. At the demand of the British Government they gave them up.

"A peaceful tragedy, followed by emancipation."

"And the great industries of Mexico?"

"They will not have to depend on adventurers' favours!"

"But in the meantime, what?"

"Patience, looking towards justice!"

Yours heartily and in health (you bet!)

W. H. P.

From Edward M. House

145 East 35th Street,
New York City.
December 12, 1913.

DEAR PAGE:

Your budget under dates, November 15th, 23rd, and 26th came to me last week, just after the President had been here.   I saved the letters until I went to Washington, from which place I have just returned.

The President has been in bed for nearly a week and Doctor Grayson permitted no one to see him but me. Yesterday before I left he was feeling so well that I asked him if he did not want to feel better and then I read him your letters.   Mrs. Wilson was present.

I cannot tell you how pleased he was.   He laughed repeatedly at the different comments you made and he was delighted with what you had to say concerning Lord Cowdray.   We do not love him for we think that between Cowdray and Carden a large part of our troubles in Mexico has been made.   Your description of his attitude at the beginning and his present one pleased us much.

After I had read the confidential letter the President said "now let me see if I have the facts."   He then recited them in consecutive order just as the English lady had written them, almost using the same phrases, showing the well-trained mind that he has.   I then dropped the letter in the grate.

He enjoyed heartily the expression "Washington is a deep hole of silence towards ambassadors," and again "The volume of silence that I get is oppressive," and of course the story apropos of this last remark.

I was with him for more than an hour and he was distinctly better when I left.   I hated to look at him in bed for I could not help realizing what his life means to the Democratic Party, to the Nation and almost to the world.

Of course you know that I only read your letters to him.   Mr. Bryan was my guest on Wednesday and I returned to Washington with him but I made no mention of our correspondence and I never have.   The President seems to like our way of doing things and further than that I do not care.

Upon my soul I do not believe the President could be better pleased than he is with the work you are doing.

Faithfully yours,
E. M. House.

From now on the Ambassador exerted a round-about pressure—the method of "gradual approach" already referred to—upon the Foreign Office for Carden's removal. An extract from a letter to the President gives a hint concerning this method:

I have already worked upon Sir Edward's mind about his Minister to Mexico as far as I could.   Now that the other matter is settled and while Carden is behaving, I go at it.   Two years ago Mr. Knox made a bad blunder in protesting against Carden's "anti-Americanism" in Cuba.   Mr. Knox sent Mr. Reid no definite facts nor even

accusations to base a protest on.   The result was a failure
—a bad failure.   I have again asked Mr. Bryan for all
the definite reports he has heard about Carden.   That
man, in my judgment, has caused nine tenths of the
trouble here.

Naturally Page did not ask the Minister's removal
directly—that would have been an unpardonable blunder.   His meetings during this period with Sir Edward
were taking place almost every day, and Carden, in
one way or another, kept coming to the front in their
conversation.   Sir Edward, like Page, would sacrifice
much in the cause of Anglo-American relations; Page
would occasionally express his regret that the British Minister to Mexico was not a man who shared
their enthusiasm on this subject; in numerous other ways
the impression was conveyed that the two countries
could solve the Mexican entanglement much better if a
more congenial person represented British interests in
the Southern Republic.   This reasoning evidently produced the desired results.   In early January, 1914, a
hint was unofficially conveyed to the American Ambassador that Carden was to be summoned to London for
a "conversation" with Sir Edward Grey, and that his
return to Mexico would depend upon the outcome of that
interview.   There was a likelihood that, in future, Sir
Lionel Carden would represent the British Empire in
Brazil.

This news, sent in discreet cipher to Washington, delighted the Administration.   "It is fine about Carden,"
wrote Colonel House on January 10th.   "I knew you had
done it when I saw it in the papers, but I did not know just
how.   You could not have brought it about in a more
diplomatic and effectual way."

And the following came from the President:

From President Wilson

Pass Christian,
January 6, 1914.

MY DEAR PAGE:

I have your letter of December twenty-first, which I have greatly enjoyed.

Almost at the very time I was reading it, the report came through the Associated Press from London that Carden was to be transferred immediately to Brazil. If this is true, it is indeed a most fortunate thing and I feel sure it is to be ascribed to your tactful and yet very plain representations to Sir Edward Grey. I do not think you realize how hard we worked to get from either Lind or O'Shaughnessy[1] definite items of speech or conduct which we could furnish you as material for what you had to say to the Ministers about Carden. It simply was not obtainable. Everything that we got was at second or third hand. That he was working against us was too plain for denial, and yet he seems to have done it in a very astute way which nobody could take direct hold of. I congratulate you with all my heart on his transference.

I long, as you do, for an opportunity to do constructive work all along the line in our foreign relations, particularly with Great Britain and the Latin-American states, but surely, my dear fellow, you are deceiving yourself in supposing that constructive work is not now actually going on, and going on at your hands quite as much as at ours. The change of attitude and the growing ability to understand what we are thinking about and purposing on the part of the official circle in London is directly attributable

[1] Mr. Nelson O'Shaughnessy, Chargé d'Affaires in Mexico.

to what you have been doing, and I feel more and more grateful every day that you are our spokesman and interpreter there. This is the only possible constructive work in foreign affairs, aside from definite acts of policy.

So far as the policy is concerned, you may be sure I will strive to the utmost to obtain both a repeal of the discrimination in the matter of tolls and a renewal of the arbitration treaties, and I am not without hope that I can accomplish both at this session. Indeed this is the session in which these things must be done if they are to be done at all.

Back of the smile which came to my face when you spoke of the impenetrable silence of the State Department toward its foreign representatives lay thoughts of very serious concern. We must certainly manage to keep our foreign representatives properly informed. The real trouble is to conduct genuinely confidential correspondence except through private letters, but surely the thing can be changed and it will be if I can manage it.

We are deeply indebted to you for your kindness and generous hospitality to our young folks[1] and we have learned with delight through your letters and theirs of their happy days in England.

With deep regard and appreciation,

Cordially and faithfully yours,

WOODROW WILSON.

HON. WALTER H. PAGE,
American Embassy,
London, England.

Yet for the American Ambassador the experience was not one of unmixed satisfaction. These letters have contained references to the demoralized condition of the

[1]Mr. and Mrs. Francis B. Sayre.

State Department under Mr. Bryan and the succeeding ones will contain more; the Carden episode portrayed the stupidity and ignorance of that Department at their worst. By commanding Carden to cease his anti-American tactics and to support the American policy the Foreign Office had performed an act of the utmost courtesy and consideration to this country. By quietly "promoting" the same minister to another sphere, several thousand miles away from Mexico and Washington, it was now preparing to eliminate all possible causes of friction between the two countries. The British, that is, had met the wishes of the United States in the two great matters that were then making serious trouble— Huerta and Carden. Yet no government, Great Britain least of all, wishes to be placed in the position of moving its diplomats about at the request of another Power. The whole deplorable story appears in the following letter.

To Edward M. House

January 8th, 1914.

My dear House:

Two days ago I sent a telegram to the Department saying that I had information from a private, *unofficial* source that the report that Carden would be transferred was true, and from another source that Marling would succeed him. The Government here has given out nothing. I know nothing from official sources. Of course the only decent thing to do at Washington was to sit still till this Government should see fit to make an announcement. But what do they do? Give my telegram to the press! It appears here almost verbatim in this morning's *Mail.*—I have to make an humiliating explanation to the Foreign Office. This is the third time I've had to make such an humiliating explanation to Sir Edward. It's getting a little monotonous. He's getting tired, and so am I. They now deny at the Foreign Office that anything has been decided about Carden, and this meddling by us (as they look at it) will surely cause a delay and may even cause a change of purpose.

That's the practical result of their leaking at Washington. On a previous occasion they leaked the same way. When I telegraphed a remonstrance, they telegraphed back to me that the leak had been *here!* That was the end of it—except that I had to explain to Sir Edward the best I could. And about a lesser matter, I did the same thing a third time, in a conversation. Three times this sort of thing has happened.—On the other hand, the King's Master of Ceremonies called on me on the President's Birthday and requested for His Majesty that I send His Majesty's congratulations. Just ten days passed before a telegraphic answer came! The very hour it came, I was myself making up an answer for the President that I was going to send, to save our face.

Now, I'm trying with all my might to do this job. I spend all my time, all my ingenuity, all my money at it. I have organized my staff as a sort of Cabinet. We meet every day. We go over everything conceivable that we may do or try to do. We do good team work. I am not sure but I doubt whether these secretaries have before been taken into just such a relation to their chief. They are enthusiastic and ambitious and industrious and— *safe.* There's no possibility of any leak. We arrange our dinners with reference to the possibility of getting information and of carrying points. Mrs. Page gives and accepts invitations with the same end in view. We're on the job to the very limit of our abilities.

And I've got the Foreign Office in such a relation that

they are frank and friendly. (I can't keep 'em so, if this sort of thing goes on.)

Now the State Department seems (as it touches us) to be utterly chaotic—silent when it ought to respond, loquacious when it ought to be silent. There are questions that I have put to it at this Government's request to which I can get no answer.

It's hard to keep my staff enthusiastic under these conditions. When I reached the Chancery this morning, they were in my room, with all the morning papers marked, on the table, eagerly discussing what we ought to do about this publication of my dispatch. The enthusiasm and buoyancy were all gone out of them. By their looks they said, "Oh! what's the use of our bestirring ourselves to send news to Washington when they use it to embarrass us?"—While we are thus at work, the only two communications from the Department to-day are two letters from two of the Secretaries about—presenting "Democratic" ladies from Texas and Oklahoma at court! And Bryan is now lecturing in Kansas.

Since I began to write this letter, Lord Cowdray came here to the house and stayed two and a half hours, talking about possible joint intervention in Mexico. Possibly he came from the Foreign Office. I don't know whether to dare send a despatch to the State Department, telling what he told me, for fear they'd leak. And to leak this— Good Lord! Two of the Secretaries were here to dinner, and I asked them if I should send such a despatch. They both answered instantly: "No, sir, don't dare: *write* it to the President." I said: "No, I have no right to bother the President with regular business nor with frequent letters." To that they agreed; but the interesting and somewhat appalling thing is, they're actually afraid to have a confidential despatch go to the State Department.

I see nothing to do but to suggest to the President to put somebody in the Department who will stay there and give intelligent attention to the diplomatic telegrams and letters—some conscientious assistant or clerk. For I hear mutterings, somewhat like these mutterings of mine, from some of the continental embassies.—The whole thing is disorganizing and demoralizing beyond description.

All these and more are *my* troubles. I'll take care of them. But remember what I am going to write on the next sheet. For here may come a trouble for *you:*

Mrs. Page has learned something more about Secretary Bryan's proposed visit here in the spring. He's coming to talk his peace plan which, you know, is a sort of grape-juice arbitration—a distinct step backward from a real arbitration treaty. Well, if he comes with *that*, when you come to talk about reducing armaments, you'll wish you'd never been born. Get your ingenuity together, then, and prevent that visit.[1]

Not the least funny thing in the world is—Senator X turned up to-day. As he danced around the room begging everybody's pardon (nobody knew what for) he complimented everybody in sight, explained the forged letter, dilated on state politics, set the Irish question on the right end, cleared Bacon[2] of all hostility to me, declined tea because he had insomnia and explained just how it works to keep you awake, danced more and declared himself happy and bowed himself out—well pleased. He's as funny a cuss as I've seen in many a day. Lord Cowdray, who was telling Mexican woes to Katharine in the corner, looked up and asked, "Who's the little

---

[1]Colonel House succeeded in preventing it.

[2]Senator Augustus O. Bacon, of Georgia who was reported to nourish ill-feeling toward Page for his authorship of " The Southerner."

dancing gentleman?'' Suppose X had known he was dancing for—Lord Cowdray's amusement, what do y' suppose he'd 've thought? There are some strange combinations in our house on Mrs. Page's days at home. Cowdray has, I am sure, lost (that is, failed to make) a hundred million dollars that he had within easy reach by this Wilson Doctrine, but he's game. He doesn't lie awake. He's a dead-game sport, and he knows he's knocked out in that quarter and he doesn't squeal. His experiences will serve us many a good turn in the future—as a warning. I rather like him. He eats out of my hand in the afternoon and has one of his papers jump on me in the morning. Some time in the twenty-four hours, he must attain about the normal temperature—say about noon. He admires the President greatly—sincerely. Force meets force, you see. With the President behind me I could really enjoy Cowdray centuries after X had danced himself into oblivion.

By the way, Cowdray said to me to-day: "Whatever the United States and Great Britain agree on the world must do." He's right. (1) The President must come here, perhaps in his second term; (2) these two Governments must enter a compact for peace and for gradual disarmament. Then we can go about our business for (say) a hundred years.

Heartily,

W. H. P.

In spite of the continued pressure of the United States and the passive support of its anti-Huerta policy by Great Britain, the Mexican usurper refused to resign. President Wilson now began to espouse the interests of Villa and Carranza. His letters to Page indicate that he took these men at their own valuation, believed that they were sincere patriots working for the cause of democracy" and "constitutionalism" and that their triumph would usher in a day of enlightenment and progress for Mexico. It was the opinion of the Foreign Office that Villa and Carranza were worse men than Huerta and that any recognition of their revolutionary activities would represent no moral gain.

From the President

> The White House, Washington,
> May 18, 1914.

MY DEAR PAGE:

.   .   . As to the attitude of mind on that side of the water toward the Constitutionalists, it is based upon prejudices which cannot be sustained by the facts. I am enclosing a copy of an interview by a Mr. Reid[1] which appeared in one of the afternoon papers recently and which sums up as well as they could be summed up my own conclusions with regard to the issues and the personnel of the pending contest in Mexico. I can verify it from a hundred different sources, most of them sources not in the least touched by predilections for such men as our friends in London have supposed Carranza and Villa to be.

> Cordially and faithfully yours,
> WOODROW WILSON.

HON. WALTER H. PAGE,
   U. S. Embassy,
      London, England.

> The White House, Washington,
> June 1, 1914.

MY DEAR PAGE:

.   .   . The fundamental thing is that they (British critics of Villa) are all radically mistaken. There has

---

[1] Probably an error for John Reed, at that time a newspaper correspondent in Mexico—afterward well known as a champion of the Bolshevist régime in Russia.

been less disorder and less danger to life where the Constitutionalists have gained control than there has been where Huerta is in control. I should think that if they are getting correct advices from Tampico, people in England would be very much enlightened by what has happened there. Before the Constitutionalists took the place there was constant danger to the oil properties and to foreign residents. Now there is no danger and the men who felt obliged to leave the oil wells to their Mexican employees are returning, to find, by the way, that their Mexican employees guarded them most faithfully without wages, and in some instances almost without food. I am told that the Constitutionalists cheered the American flag when they entered Tampico.

I believe that Mexico City will be much quieter and a much safer place to live in after the Constitutionalists get there than it is now. The men who are approaching and are sure to reach it are much less savage and much more capable of government than Huerta.

These, I need not tell you, are not fancies of mine but conclusions I have drawn from facts which are at last becoming very plain and palpable, at least to us on this side of the water. If they are not becoming plain in Great Britain, it is because their papers are not serving them with the truth. Our own papers were prejudiced enough in all conscience against Villa and Carranza and everything that was happening in the north of Mexico, but at last the light is dawning on them in spite of themselves and they are beginning to see things as they really are. I would be as nervous and impatient as your friends in London are if I feared the same things that they fear, but I do not. I am convinced that even Zapata would restrain his followers and leave, at any rate, all

foreigners and all foreign property untouched if he were
the first to enter Mexico City.

Cordially and faithfully yours,

WOODROW WILSON.

HON. WALTER H. PAGE,
    American Embassy,
        London, England.

On this issue, however, the President and his Ambassador to Great Britain permanently disagreed. The
events which took place in April, 1914—the insult to the
American flag at Tampico, the bombardment and capture
of Vera Cruz by American forces—made stronger Page's
conviction, already set forth in this correspondence, that
there was only one solution of the Mexican problem.

To Edward M. House

April 27, 1914.

DEAR HOUSE:

. . . And, as for war with Mexico—I confess I've
had a continually growing fear of it for six months. I've
no confidence in the Mexican leaders—none of 'em. We
shall have to Cuba-ize the country, which means thrashing 'em first—I fear, I fear, I fear; and I feel sorry for us
all, the President in particular. It's inexpressibly hard
fortune for him. I can't tell you with what eager fear
we look for despatches every day and twice a day hurry
to get the newspapers. All England believes we've got
to fight it out.

Well, the English are with us, you see. Admiral
Cradock, I understand, does not approve our policy, but
he stands firmly with us whatever we do. The word to
stand firmly with us has, I am very sure, been passed
along the whole line—naval, newspaper, financial, dip-

lomatic.   Carden won't give us any more trouble during the rest of his stay in Mexico.   The yellow press's abuse of the President and me has actually helped us here.

Heartily yours,

W. H. P.

CHAPTER VIII

HONOUR AND DISHONOUR IN PANAMA

IN THE early part of January, 1914, Colonel House wrote Page, asking whether he would consider favourably an offer to enter President Wilson's Cabinet, as Secretary of Agriculture. Mr. David F. Houston, who was then most acceptably filling that position, was also an authority on banking and finance; the plan was to make him governor of the new Federal Reserve Board, then in process of formation, and to transfer Page to the vacant place in the Cabinet. The proposal was not carried through, but Page's reply took the form of a review of his ambassadorship up to date, of his vexations, his embarrassments, his successes, and especially of the very important task which still lay before him. There were certain reasons, it will appear, why he would have liked to leave London; and there was one impelling reason why he preferred to stay. From the day of his arrival in England, Page had been humiliated, and his work had been constantly impeded, by the almost studied neglect with which Washington treated its diplomatic service. The fact that the American Government provided no official residence for its Ambassador, and no adequate financial allowance for maintaining the office, had made his position almost an intolerable one. All Page's predecessors for twenty-five years had been rich men who could advance the cost of the Embassy from their own private purses; to meet these expenses, however, Page had been obliged to encroach on the savings of a life-

time, and such liberality on his part necessarily had its
limitations.

To Edward M. House

London, England,
February 13, 1914.

MY DEAR HOUSE:

. . . Of course I am open to the criticism of having
taken the place at all. But I was both uninformed and
misinformed about the cost as well as about the frightful
handicap of having no Embassy. It's a kind of scandal
in London and it has its serious effect. Everybody talks
about it all the time: "Will you explain to me why it is
that your great Government has no Embassy: it's very
odd!" "What a frugal Government you have!" "It's a
damned mean outfit, your American Government." Mrs.
Page collapses many an evening when she gets to her room.
"If they'd only quit talking about it!" The other Ambassadors, now that we're coming to know them fairly well,
commiserate us. It's a constant humiliation. Of course
this aspect of it doesn't worry me much—I've got hard-
ened to it. But it is a good deal of a real handicap, and
it adds that much dead weight that a man must over-
come; and it greatly lessens the respect in which our
Government and its Ambassador are held. If I had
known this fully in advance, I should not have had the
courage to come here. Now, of course, I've got used
to it, have discounted it, and can "bull" it through—
could "bull" it through if I could afford to pay the bill.
But I shouldn't advise any friend of mine to come here
and face this humiliation without realizing precisely what
it means—wholly apart, of course, from the cost of
it. . . .

My dear House, on the present basis much of the diplomatic business is sheer humbug. It will always be so till we have our own Embassies and an established position in consequence. Without a home or a house or a fixed background, every man has to establish his own position for himself; and unless he be unusual, this throws him clean out of the way of giving emphasis to the right things. . . .

As for our position, I think I don't fool myself. The job at the Foreign Office is easy because there is no real trouble between us, and because Sir Edward Grey is pretty nearly an ideal man to get on with. I think he likes me, too, because, of course, I'm straightforward and frank with him, and he likes the things we stand for. Outside this official part of the job, of course, we're commonplace—a successful commonplace, I hope. But that's all. We don't know how to try to be anything but what we naturally are. I dare say we are laughed at here and there about this and that. Sometimes I hear criticisms, now and then more or less serious ones. Much of it comes of our greenness; some of it from the very nature of the situation. Those who expect to find us brilliant are, of course, disappointed. Nor are we *smart*, and the smart set (both American and English) find us uninteresting. But we drive ahead and keep a philosophical temper and simply do the best we can, and, you may be sure, a good deal of it. It *is* laborious. For instance, I've made two trips lately to speak before important bodies, one at Leeds, the other at Newcastle, at both of which, in different ways, I have tried to explain the President's principle in dealing with Central American turbulent states—and, incidentally, the American ideals of government. The audiences see it, approve it, applaud it. The newspaper editorial writers never quite go the length—it involves a denial of the divine right of the British Empire; at least they fear so. The fewest possible Englishmen really understand our governmental aims and ideals. I have delivered unnumbered and innumerable little speeches, directly or indirectly, about them; and they seem to like them. But it would take an army of oratorical ambassadors a lifetime to get the idea into the heads of them all. In some ways they are incredibly far back in mediævalism—incredibly.

If I have to leave in the fall or in December, it will be said and thought that I've failed, unless there be some reason that can be made public. I should be perfectly willing to tell the reason—the failure of the Government to make it financially possible. I've nothing to conceal —only definite amounts. I'd never say what it has cost —only that it costs more than I or anybody but a rich man can afford. If then, or in the meantime, the President should wish me to serve elsewhere, *that* would, of course, be a sufficient reason for my going.

Now another matter, with which I shall not bother the President—he has enough to bear on that score. It was announced in one of the London papers the other day that Mr. Bryan would deliver a lecture here, and probably in each of the principal European capitals, on Peace. Now, God restrain me from saying, much more from doing, anything rash. But if I've got to go home at all, I'd rather go before he comes. It'll take years for the American Ambassadors to recover what they'll lose if he carry out this plan. They now laugh at him here. Only the President's great personality saves the situation in foreign relations. Of course the public here doesn't know how utterly unorganized the State Department is— how we can't get answers to important questions, and how they publish most secret despatches or allow them to leak out. But "bad breaks" like this occur. **Mr. Z,** of the 100-years'-Peace Committee,[1] came here a week ago, with a letter from Bryan to the Prime Minister! Z told me that this 100-year business gave a chance to bind the nations together that ought not to be missed. Hence Bryan had asked him to take up the relations of the countries with the Prime Minister! Bryan sent a telegram to Z to be read at a big 100-year meeting here. As for the personal indignity to me—I overlook that. I don't think he means it. But if he doesn't mean it, what does he mean? That's what the Prime Minister asks himself. Fortunately Mr. Asquith and I get along mighty well. He met Bryan once, and he told me with a smile that he regarded him as "a peculiar product of your country." But the Secretary is always doing things like this. He dashes off letters of introduction to people asking me to present them to Mr. Asquith, Mr. Lloyd George, etc.

In the United States we know Mr. Bryan. We know his good points, his good services, his good intentions. We not only tolerate him; we like him. But when he comes here as "the American Prime Minister"[2]—goodbye, John! All that we've tried to do to gain respect for our Government (as they respect our great nation) will disappear in one day. Of course they'll feel obliged to give him big official dinners, etc. And——

Now you'd just as well abandon your trip if he comes; and (I confess) I'd rather be gone. No member of another government ever came here and lectured. T. R. did it as a private citizen, and even then he split the heavens asunder.[3] Most Englishmen will regard it as a

---

[1] The Committee to celebrate the centennial of the signing of the Treaty of Ghent, which ended the War of 1812. The plan to make this an elaborate commemoration of a 100 years' peace between the English-speaking peoples was upset by the outbreak of the World War.

[2] This was the designation Mr. Bryan's admirers sometimes gave him.

[3] The reference is to President Roosevelt's speech at the Guildhall in June, 1910.

piece of effrontery.   Of course, I'm not in the least concerned about mere matters of taste.   It's only the bigger
effects that I have in mind in *queering* our Government in
their eyes.   He must be kept at home on the Mexican
problem, or some other.

Yours faithfully,

WALTER H. PAGE.

P. S.   But, by George, it's a fine game!   This Government and ours are standing together all right, especially
since the President has taken hold of our foreign relations
himself.   With such a man at the helm at home, we can
do whatever we wish to do with the English, as I've often
told you.   (But it raises doubts every time the shoe-
string necktie, broad-brimmed black hat, oratorical, old-
time, River Platte kind of note is heard.)   We've come
a long way in a year—a very joyful long way, full of
progress and real understanding; there's no doubt about
that.   A year ago they knew very well the failure that
had saddled them with the tolls trouble and the failure
of arbitration, and an unknown President had just come
in.   Presently an unknown Ambassador arrived.   Mexico
got worse; would we not recognize Huerta?   They send
Carden.   We had nothing to say about the tolls—simply
asked for time.   They were very friendly; but our slang
phrase fits the situation—"nothin' doin'."   They declined
San Francisco.[1]   Then presently they began to see some
plan in Mexico; they began to see our attitude on the
tolls; they began to understand our attitude toward concessions and governments run for profit; they began dimly
to see that Carden was a misfit; the Tariff Bill passed;
the Currency Bill; the President loomed up; even the

---

[1]This refers to the declination of the British Government to be represented at
the San Francisco world exhibition, held in 1915.

Ambassador, they said, really believed what he preached; he wasn't merely making pretty, friendly speeches.—Now, when we get this tolls job done, we've got 'em where we can do any proper and reasonable thing we want. It's been a great three quarters of a year—immense, in fact. No man has been in the White House who is so regarded since Lincoln; in fact, they didn't regard Lincoln while he lived.

Meantime, I've got to be more or less at home. The Prime Minister dines with me, the Foreign Secretary, the Archbishop, the Colonial Secretary—all the rest of 'em; the King talks very freely; Mr. Asquith tells me some of his troubles; Sir Edward is become a good personal friend; Lord Bryce warms up; the Lord Chancellor is chummy; and so it goes.

So you may be sure we are all in high feather after all; and the President's (I fear exaggerated) appreciation of what I've done is very gratifying indeed. I've got only one emotion about it all—gratitude; and gratitude begets eagerness to go on. Of course I can do future jobs better than I have done any past ones.

There are two shadows in the background—not disturbing, but shadows none the less:

1. The constant reminder that the American Ambassador's homeless position (to this Government and to this whole people) shows that the American Government and the American people know nothing about foreign relations and care nothing—regard them as not worth buying a house for. This leaves a doubt about any continuity of any American policy. It even suggests a sort of fear that we don't really care.

The other is (2) the dispiriting experience of writing and telegraphing about important things and never hearing a word concerning many of them, and the consequent fear of some dead bad break in the State Department. The clubs are full of stories of the silly and incredible things that are *said* to happen there.

After all, these are old troubles. They are not new— neither of them. And we are the happiest group you ever saw.

W. H. P.

Page's letters of this period contain many references to his inability to maintain touch with the State Department. His letters remained unacknowledged, his telegrams un- answered; and he was himself left completely in the dark as to the plans and opinions at Washington.

To Edward M. House

February 28, 1914.

DEAR HOUSE:

. . . *Couldn't the business with Great Britain be put into Moore's¹ hands?* It is surely important enough at times to warrant separate attention—or (I might say) attention. You know, after eight or nine months of this sort of thing, the feeling grows on us all here that perhaps many of our telegrams and letters may not be read by anybody at all. You begin to feel that they may not be deciphered or even opened. Then comes the feeling (for a moment), why send any more? Why do anything but answer such questions as come now and then? Cor- responding with Nobody—can you imagine how that feels?—What the devil *do* you suppose does become of the letters and telegrams that I send, from which and about which I never hear a word? As a mere matter of curi- osity I should like to know who receives them and what he does with them!

¹John Bassett Moore, at that time the very able counsellor of the State Depart- ment.

I've a great mind some day to send a despatch saying that an earthquake has swallowed up the Thames, that a suffragette has kissed the King, and that the statue of Cromwell has made an assault on the House of Lords—just to see if anybody deciphers it.

After the Civil War an old fellow in Virginia was tired of the world. He'd have no more to do with it. He cut a slit in a box in his house and nailed up the box. Whenever a letter came for him, he'd read the postmark and say "Baltimore—Baltimore—there isn't anybody in Baltimore that I care to hear from." Then he'd drop the letter unopened through the slit into the box. "Philadelphia? I have no friend in Philadelphia"—into the box, unopened. When he died, the big box was nearly full of unopened letters. When I get to Washington again, I'm going to look for a big box that must now be nearly full of my unopened letters and telegrams.

W. H. P.

The real reason why the Ambassador wished to remain in London was to assist in undoing a great wrong which the United States had done itself and the world. Page was attempting to perform his part in introducing new standards into diplomacy. His discussions of Mexico had taken the form of that "idealism" which he was apparently having some difficulty in persuading British statesmen and the British public to accept. He was doing his best to help bring about that day when, in Gladstone's famous words, "the idea of public right would be the governing idea" of international relations. But while the American Ambassador was preaching this new conception, the position of his own country on one important matter was a constant impediment to his efforts. Page was continually confronted by the fact that the

United States, high-minded as its foreign policy might pretend to be, was far from "idealistic" in the observance of the treaty that it had made with Great Britain concerning the Panama Canal.   There was a certain em·barrassment involved in preaching unselfishness in Mexico and Central America at a time when the United States was practising selfishness and dishonesty in Panama. For, in the opinion of the Ambassador and that of most other dispassionate students of the Panama treaty, the American policy on Panama tolls amounted to nothing less.

To one unskilled in legal technicalities, the Panama controversy involved no great difficulty.   Since 1850 the United States and Great Britain had had a written understanding upon the construction of the Panama Canal. The Clayton-Bulwer Treaty, which was adopted that year, provided that the two countries should share equally in the construction and control of the proposed waterway across the Isthmus.   This idea of joint control had always rankled in the United States, and in 1901 the American Government persuaded Great Britain to abrogate the Clayton-Bulwer Treaty and agree to another—the Hay-Pauncefote—which transferred the rights of ownership and construction exclusively to this country.   In consenting to this important change, Great Britain had made only one stipulation.   "The Canal," so read Article III of the Convention of 1901, "shall be free and open to the vessels of commerce and war of all nations observing these rules, on terms of entire equality, so that there shall be no discrimination against any such nation, or its citizens or subjects, in respect of the conditions or charges of traffic, or otherwise."   It would seem as though the English language could utter no thought more clearly than this.   The agreement said, not inferentially, but in so many words, that the "charges" levied on the ships of "all nations" that used the Canal should be the same. The history of British-American negotiations on the subject of the Canal had always emphasized this same point. All American witnesses to drawing the Treaty have testified that this was the American understanding. The correspondence of John Hay, who was Secretary of State at the time, makes it clear that this was the agreement. Mr. Elihu Root, who, as Secretary of War, sat next to John Hay in the Cabinet which authorized the treaty, has taken the same stand. The man who conducted the preliminary negotiations with Lord Salisbury, Mr. Henry White, has emphasized the same point. Mr. Joseph H. Choate, who, as American Ambassador to Great Britain in 1901, had charge of the negotiations, has testified that the British and American Governments "meant what they said and said what they meant."

In the face of this solemn understanding, the American Congress, in 1912, passed the Panama Canal Act, which provided that "no tolls shall be levied upon vessels engaged in the coastwise trade of the United States." A technical argument, based upon the theory that "all nations" did not include the United States, and that, inasmuch as this country had obtained sovereign rights upon the Isthmus, the situation had changed, persuaded President Taft to sign this bill. Perhaps this line of reasoning satisfied the legal consciences of President Taft and Mr. Knox, his Secretary of State, but it really cut little figure in the acrimonious discussion that ensued. Of course, there was only one question involved; that was as to whether the exemption violated the Treaty. This is precisely the one point that nearly all the controversialists avoided. The statement that the United States had built the Canal with its own money and its own genius, that it had achieved a great success where other nations had achieved a great failure, and that it had the right of passing its own ships through its own highway without assessing tolls—this was apparently argument enough. When Great Britain protested the exemption as a violation of the Treaty, there were not lacking plenty of elements in American politics and journalism to denounce her as committing an act of high-handed impertinence, as having intruded herself in matters which were not properly her concern, and as having attempted to rob the American public of the fruits of its own enterprise. That animosity to Great Britain, which is always present in certain parts of the hyphenated population, burst into full flame.

Clear as were the legal aspects of the dispute, the position of the Wilson Administration was a difficult one. The Irish-American elements, which have specialized in making trouble between the United States and Great Britain, represented a strength to the Democratic Party in most large cities. The great mass of Democratic Senators and Congressmen had voted for the exemption bill. The Democratic platform of 1912 had endorsed this same legislation. This declaration was the handiwork of Senator O'Gorman, of New York State, who had long been a leader of the anti-British crusade in American politics. More awkward still, President Wilson, in the course of his Presidential campaign, had himself spoken approvingly of free tolls for American ships. The probability is that, when the President made this unfortunate reference to this clause in the Democratic programme, he had given the matter little personal investigation; it must be held to his credit that, when the facts were clearly presented to him, his mind quickly grasped the real point at issue—that it was not a matter of commercial advantage or disadvantage, but one simply of national honour, of whether the United States proposed to keep its word or to break it.

Page's contempt for the hair-drawn technicalities of lawyers was profound, and the tortuous effort to make the Hay-Pauncefote Treaty mean something quite different from what it said, inevitably moved him to righteous wrath. Before sailing for England he spent several days in the State Department studying the several questions that were then at issue between his country and Great Britain. A memorandum contains his impressions of the free tolls contention:

"A little later I went to Washington again to acquaint myself with the business between the United States and Great Britain. About that time the Senate confirmed my appointment, and I spent a number of days reading the recent correspondence between the two governments. The two documents that stand out in my memory are the wretched lawyer's note of Knox about the Panama tolls (I never read a less sincere, less convincing, more purely artificial argument) and Bryce's brief reply, which did have the ring of sincerity in it. The diplomatic correspondence in general seemed to me very dull stuff, and, after wading through it all day, on several nights as I went to bed the thought came to me whether this sort of activity were really worth a man's while."

Anything which affected British shipping adversely touched Great Britain in a sensitive spot; and Page had not been long in London before he perceived the acute nature of the Panama situation. In July, 1913, Col. Edward M. House reached the British capital. A letter of Page's to Sir Edward Grey gives such a succinct description of this new and influential force in American public life that it is worth quoting:

To Sir Edward Grey

Coburg Hotel, London.
[No date.]

DEAR SIR EDWARD:

There is an American gentleman in London, the like of whom I do not know. Mr. Edward M. House is his name. He is "the silent partner" of President Wilson—that is to say, he is the most trusted political adviser and the nearest friend of the President. He is a private citizen, a man without personal political ambition, a modest, quiet, even shy fellow. He helps to make Cabinets, to shape policies, to select judges and ambassadors and suchlike merely for the pleasure of seeing that these tasks are well done.

He is suffering from over-indulgence in advising, and he has come here to rest. I cannot get him far outside his hotel, for he cares to see few people. But he is very eager to meet you.

I wonder if you would do me the honour to take luncheon at the Coburg Hotel with me, to meet him either on July 1, or 3, or 5—if you happen to be free? I shall have only you and Mr. House.

Very sincerely yours,
WALTER H. PAGE.

The chief reason why Colonel House wished to meet the British Foreign Secretary was to bring him a message from President Wilson on the subject of the Panama tolls. The three men—Sir Edward, Colonel House, and Mr. Page—met at the suggested luncheon on July 3rd.

Colonel House informed the Foreign Secretary that President Wilson was now convinced that the Panama Act violated the Hay-Pauncefote Treaty and that he intended to use all his influence to secure its repeal. The matter, the American urged, was a difficult one, since it would be necessary to persuade Congress to pass a law acknowledging its mistake. The best way in which Great Britain could aid in the process was by taking no public action. If the British should keep protesting or discussing the subject acrimoniously in the press and Parliament, such a course would merely reënforce the elements that would certainly oppose the President. Any protests would give them the opportunity to set up the cry of "British dictation," and a change in the Washington policy would subject it to the criticism of having yielded to British pressure. The inevitable effect would be to defeat the whole proceeding. Colonel House therefore suggested that President Wilson be left to handle the matter in his own way and in his own time, and he assured the British statesman that the result would be satisfactory to both countries. Sir Edward Grey at once saw that Colonel House's statement of the matter was simply common sense, and expressed his willingness to leave the Panama matter in the President's hands.

Thus, from July 3, 1913, there was a complete understanding between the British Government and the Washington Administration on the question of the tolls. But neither the British nor the American public knew that President Wilson had pledged himself to a policy of repeal. All during the summer and fall of 1913 this matter was as generally discussed in England as was Mexico. Everywhere the Ambassador went—country houses, London dinner tables, the colleges and the clubs— he was constantly confronted with what was universally regarded as America's great breach of faith. How deeply he felt in the matter his letters show.

To Edward M. House

August 25, 1913.

DEAR HOUSE:

. . . The English Government and the English people without regard to party—I hear it and feel it everywhere—are of one mind about this: they think we have acted dishonourably. They really think so—it isn't any mere political or diplomatic pretense. We made a bargain, they say, and we have repudiated it. If it were a mere bluff or game or party contention— that would be one thing. We could "bull" it through or live it down. But they look upon it as we look upon the repudiation of a debt by a state. Whatever the arguments by which the state may excuse itself, we never feel the same toward it—never quite so safe about it. They say, "You are a wonderful nation and a wonderful people. We like you. But your Government is not a government of honour. Your honourable men do not seem to get control." You can't measure the damage that this does us. Whatever the United States may propose till this is fixed and forgotten will be regarded with a certain hesitancy. They will not fully trust the honour of our Government. They say, too, "See, you've preached arbitration and you propose peace agreements, and yet you will not arbitrate this: you know you are wrong, and this attitude proves it." Whatever Mr. Hay might or could have done, he made a bargain. The Senate ratified it. We accepted it. Whether it were a good bargain or a bad one, we ought to keep it. The English feeling was shown just the other week when Senator Root received an honourary degree at Oxford.

The thing that gave him fame here was his speech on this treaty.[1] There is no end of ways in which they show their feeling and conviction.

Now, if in the next regular session the President takes a firm stand against the ship subsidy that this discrimination gives, couldn't Congress be carried to repeal this discrimination? For this economic objection also exists.

No Ambassador can do any very large constructive piece of work so long as this suspicion of the honour of our Government exists. Sir Edward Grey will take it up in October or November. If I could say then that the President will exert all his influence for this repeal— that would go far. If, when he takes it up, I can say nothing, it will be practically useless for me to take up any other large plan. This is the most important thing for us on the diplomatic horizon.

To the President

Dornoch, Scotland,
September 10, 1913.

DEAR MR. PRESIDENT:

I am spending ten or more of the dog days visiting the Englishman and the Scotchman in their proper setting— their country homes—where they show themselves the best of hosts and reveal their real opinions. There are, for example, in the house where I happen to be to-day, the principals of three of the Scotch universities, and a Member of Parliament, and an influential editor.

They have, of course—I mean all the educated folk I meet—the most intelligent interest in American affairs, and they have an unbounded admiration for the American people—their energy, their resourcefulness, their wealth,

[1]Mr. Root's masterly speech on Panama tolls was made in the United States Senate, January 21, 1913.

their economic power and social independence. I think that no people ever really admired and, in a sense, envied another people more. They know we hold the keys of the future.

But they make a sharp distinction between our people and our Government. They are sincere, God-fearing people who speak their convictions. They cite Tammany, the Thaw case, Sulzer, the Congressional lobby, and sincerely regret that a democracy does not seem to be able to justify itself. I am constantly amazed and sometimes dumbfounded at the profound effect that the yellow press (including the American correspondents of the English papers) has had upon the British mind. Here is a most serious journalistic problem, upon which I have already begun to work seriously with some of the editors of the better London papers. But it is more than a journalistic problem. It becomes political. To eradicate this impression will take years of well-planned work. I am going to make this the subject of one of the dozen addresses that I must deliver during the next six months —"The United States as an Example of Honest and Honourable Government."

And everywhere—in circles the most friendly to us, and the best informed—I receive commiseration because of the dishonourable attitude of our Government about the Panama Canal tolls. This, I confess, is hard to meet. We made a bargain—a solemn compact—and we have broken it. Whether it were a good bargain or a bad one, a silly one or a wise one; that's far from the point. Isn't it? I confess that this bothers me. . . .

And this Canal tolls matter stands in the way of everything. It is in their minds all the time—the minds of all parties and all sections of opinion. They have no respect for Mr. Taft, for they remember that he might have vetoed the bill; and they ask, whenever they dare, what you will do about it.   They hold our Government in shame so long as this thing stands.

As for the folly of having made such a treaty—that's now passed.   As for our unwillingness to arbitrate it— that's taken as a confession of guilt.   .   .   .

We can command these people, this Government, this tight island, and its world-wide empire; they honour us, they envy us, they see the time near at hand when we shall command the capital and the commerce of the world if we unfetter our mighty people; they wish to keep very close to us.   But they are suspicious of our Government because, they contend, it has violated its faith.   Is it so or is it not?

Life meantime is brimful of interest; and, despite this reflex result of the English long-blunder with Ireland (how our sins come home to roost), the Great Republic casts its beams across the whole world and I was never so proud to be an American democrat, as I see it light this hemisphere in a thousand ways.

All health and mastery to you!

WALTER H. PAGE.

The story of Sir William Tyrrell's[1] visit to the White House in November, 1913, has already been told.   On this occasion, it will be recalled, not only was an agreement reached on Mexico, but President Wilson also repeated the assurances already given by Colonel House on the repeal of the tolls legislation.   Now that Great Britain had accepted the President's leadership in Mexico, the time was approaching when President Wilson might be expected to take his promised stand on Panama

[1]Ante: page 202.

tolls. Yet it must be repeated that there had been no definite diplomatic bargain. But Page was exerting all his efforts to establish the best relations between the two countries on the basis of fair dealing and mutual respect. Great Britain had shown her good faith in the Mexican matter; now the turn of the United States had come.

To the President

London, 6 Grosvenor Square.
January 6, 1914.

DEAR MR. PRESIDENT:

We've travelled a long way since this Mexican trouble began—a long way with His Majesty's Government. When your policy was first flung at 'em, they showed at best a friendly incredulity: what! set up a moral standard for government in Mexico? Everybody's mind was fixed merely on the restoring of order—the safety of investments. They thought of course our army would go down in a few weeks. I recall that Sir Edward Grey asked me one day if you would not consult the European governments about the successor to Huerta, speaking of it as a problem that would come up next week. And there was also much unofficial talk about joint intervention.

Well, they've followed a long way. They apologized for Carden (that's what the Prime Minister's speech was); they ordered him to be more prudent. Then the real meaning of concessions began to get into their heads. They took up the dangers that lurked in the Government's contract with Cowdray for oil; and they pulled Cowdray out of Colombia and Nicaragua—granting the application of the Monroe Doctrine to concessions that might imperil a country's autonomy. Then Sir Edward asked me if you would not consult him about such concessions—a long way had been travelled since his other question! Lord Haldane made the Thanksgiving speech that I suggested to him. And now they have transferred Carden. They've done all we asked and more; and, more wonderful yet, they've come to understand what we are driving at.

As this poor world goes, all this seems to me rather handsomely done. At any rate, it's square and it's friendly.

Now in diplomacy, as in other contests, there must be give and take; it's our turn.

If you see your way clear, it would help the Liberal Government (which needs help) and would be much appreciated if, before February 10th, when Parliament meets, you could say a public word friendly to our keeping the Hay-Pauncefote Treaty—on the tolls. You only, of course, can judge whether you would be justified in doing so. I presume only to assure you of the most excellent effect it would have here. If you will pardon me for taking a personal view of it, too, I will say that such an expression would cap the climax of the enormously heightened esteem and great respect in which recent events and achievements have caused you to be held here. It would put the English of all parties in the happiest possible mood toward you for whatever subsequent dealings may await us. It was as friendly a man as Kipling who said to me the night I spent with him: "You know your great Government, which does many great things greatly, does *not* lie awake o' nights to keep its promises."

It's our turn next, whenever you see your way clear.

Most heartily yours,

WALTER H. PAGE.

From Edward M. House

145 East 35th Street,
New York City.
January 24, 1914.

DEAR PAGE:

I was with the President for twenty-four hours and we went over everything thoroughly.

He decided to call the Senate Committee on Foreign Relations to the White House on Monday and tell them of his intentions regarding Panama tolls. We discussed whether it would be better to see some of them individually, or to take them collectively. It was agreed that the latter course was better. It was decided, however, to have Senator Jones poll the Senate in order to find just how it stood before getting the Committee together.

The reason for this quick action was in response to your letter urging that something be done before the 10th of February. . . .

Faithfully yours,
E. M. HOUSE.

On March 5th the President made good his promise by going before Congress and asking the two Houses to repeal that clause in the Panama legislation which granted preferential treatment to American coastwise shipping. The President's address was very brief and did not discuss the matter in the slightest detail. Mr. Wilson made the question one simply of national honour. The exemption, he said, clearly violated the Hay-Pauncefote Treaty and there was nothing left to do but to set the matter right. The part of the President's address that aroused the greatest interest was the conclusion:

"I ask this of you in support of the foreign policy of

the Administration.   I shall not know how to deal with other matters of even greater delicacy and nearer consequence, if you do not grant it to me in ungrudging measure."

The impression that this speech made upon the statesman who then presided over the British Foreign office is evident from the following letter that he wrote to the Ambassador in Washington.

Sir Edward Grey to Sir C. Spring Rice

Foreign Office,
March 13, 1914.

SIR:

In the course of a conversation with the American Ambassador to-day, I took the opportunity of saying how much I had been struck by President Wilson's Message to Congress about the Panama Canal tolls. When I read it, it struck me that, whether it succeeded or failed in accomplishing the President's object, it was something to the good of public life, for it helped to lift public life to a higher plane and to strengthen its morale.

I am, &c.,
E. GREY.

Two days after his appearance before Congress the President wrote to his Ambassador:

From the President

The White House, Washington,
March 7, 1914.

MY DEAR PAGE:

I have your letters of the twenty-second and twenty-fourth of February and I thank you for them most warmly. Happily, things are clearing up a little in the matters which have embarrassed our relations with Great Britain, and I hope that the temper of public opinion is in fact changing there, as it seems to us from this distance to be changing.

Your letters are a lamp to my feet. I feel as I read that their analysis is searching and true.

Things over here go on a tolerably even keel. The prospect at this moment for the repeal of the tolls exemption is very good indeed. I am beginning to feel a considerable degree of confidence that the repeal will go through, and the Press of the country is certainly standing by me in great shape.

My thoughts turn to you very often with gratitude and affectionate regard. If there is ever at any time anything specific you want to learn, pray do not hesitate to ask it of me directly, if you think best.

Carden was here the other day and I spent an hour with him, but I got not even a glimpse of his mind. I showed him all of mine that he cared to see.

With warmest regards from us all,

Faithfully yours,
WOODROW WILSON.

The debate which now took place in Congress proved to be one of the stormiest in the history of that body. The proceeding did not prove to be the easy victory that the Administration had evidently expected. The struggle was protracted for three months; and it signalized Mr. Wilson's first serious conflict with the Senate—that same Senate which was destined to play such a vexatious and destructive rôle in his career. At this time, however, Mr. Wilson had reached the zenith of his control over the law-making bodies. It was early in his Presidential term, and in these early days Senators are likely to be careful about quarrelling with the White House—especially the Senators who are members of the President's political party. In this struggle, moreover, Mr. Wilson had the intelligence and the character of the Senate largely on his side, though, strangely enough, his strongest supporters were Republicans and his bitterest opponents were Democrats. Senator Root, Senator Burton, Senator Lodge, Senator Kenyon, Senator McCumber, all Republicans, day after day and week after week upheld the national honour; while Senators O'Gorman, Chamberlain, Vardaman, and Reed, all members of the President's party, just as persistently led the fight for the baser cause. The debate inspired an outburst of Anglophobia which was most distressing to the best friends of the United States and Great Britain. The American press, as a whole, honoured itself by championing the President, but certain newspapers made the debate an occasion for unrestrained abuse of Great Britain, and of any one who believed that the United States should treat that nation honestly. The Hearst organs, in cartoon and editorial page, shrieked against the ancient enemy. All the well-known episodes and characters in American history—Lexington, Bunker Hill, John Paul Jones, Washington, and Franklin—were paraded as arguments against the repeal of an illegal discrimination. Petitions from the Ancient Order of Hibernians and other Irish societies were showered upon Congress—in almost unending procession they clogged the pages of the *Congressional Record;* public meetings were held in New York and elsewhere denouncing an administration that disgraced the country by "truckling" to Great Britain. The President was accused of seeking an Anglo-American Alliance and of sacrificing American shipping to the glory of British trade, while the history of our diplomatic rela tions was surveyed in detail for the purpose of proving that Great Britain had broken every treaty she had ever made.   In the midst of this deafening hubbub the quiet voice of Senator McCumber—"we are too big in national power to be too little in national integrity"—and that of Senator Root, demolishing one after another the pettifogging arguments of the exemptionists, demonstrated that, after all, the spirit and the eloquence that had given the Senate its great fame were still influential forces in that body.

In all this excitement, Page himself came in for his share of hard knocks.   Irish meetings "resolved" against the Ambassador as a statesman who "looks on English claims as superior to American rights," and demanded that President Wilson recall him.   It has been the fate of practically every American ambassador to Great Britain to be accused of Anglomania.   Lowell, John Hay, and Joseph H. Choate fell under the ban of those elements in American life who seem to think that the main duty of an American diplomat in Great Britain is to insult the country of which he has become the guest. In 1895 the House of Representatives solemnly passed a resolution censuring Ambassador Thomas F. Bayard for a few sentiments friendly to Great Britain which he had uttered at a public banquet.   That Page was no undiscriminating idolater of Great Britain these letters have abundantly revealed.   That he had the profoundest respect for the British character and British institutions has been made just as clear.   With Page this was no sudden enthusiasm; the conviction that British conceptions of liberty and government and British ideals of life represented the fine flower of human progress was one that he felt deeply.   The fact that these fundamentals had had the opportunity of even freer develop-

ment in America he regarded as most fortunate both for
the United States and for the world. He had never concealed his belief that the destinies of mankind depended
more upon the friendly coöperation of the United States
and Great Britain than upon any other single influence.
He had preached this in public addresses, and in his
writings for twenty-five years preceding his mission to
Great Britain. But the mere fact that he should hold
such convictions and presume to express them as American
Ambassador apparently outraged those same elements
in this country who railed against Great Britain in this
Panama Tolls debate.

On August 16, 1913, the City of Southampton, England, dedicated a monument in honour of the *Mayflower*
Pilgrims—Southampton having been their original point
of departure for Massachusetts. Quite appropriately
the city invited the American Ambassador to deliver an
address on this occasion; and quite appropriately the
Ambassador acknowledged the debt that Americans of
to-day owed to the England that had sent these adventurers to lay the foundations of new communities on
foreign soil. Yet certain historic truths embodied in
this very beautiful and eloquent address aroused considerable anger in certain parts of the United States.
"Blood," said the Ambassador, "carries with it that
particular trick of thought which makes us all English
in the last resort. . . . And Puritan and Pilgrim
and Cavalier, different yet, are yet one in that they are
English still. And thus, despite the fusion of races and
of the great contributions of other nations to her 100 millions of people and to her incalculable wealth, the United
States is yet English-led and English-ruled." This was
merely a way of phrasing a great historic truth—that
overwhelmingly the largest element in the American

population is British in origin[1]; that such vital things as its speech and its literature are English; and that our political institutions, our liberty, our law, our conceptions of morality and of life are similarly derived from the British Isles.   Page applied the word "English" to Americans in the same sense in which that word is used by John Richard Green, when he traces the history of the English race from a German forest to the Mississippi Valley and the wilds of Australia.   But the anti-British elements on this side of the water, taking "English-led and English-ruled" out of its context, misinterpreted the phrase as meaning that the American Ambassador had approvingly called attention to the fact that the United States was at present under the political control of Great Britain!   Senator Chamberlain of Oregon presented a petition from the *Staatsverband Deutschsprechender Vereine von Oregon*, demanding the Ambassador's removal, while the Irish-American press and politicians became extremely vocal.

Animated as was this outburst, it was mild compared with the excitement caused by a speech that Page made while the Panama debate was raging in Congress. At a dinner of the Associated Chambers of Commerce, in early March, the Ambassador made a few impromptu remarks.   The occasion was one of good fellowship and good humour, and Page, under the inspiration of the occasion, indulged in a few half-serious, half-jocular references to the Panama Canal and British-American good-feeling, which, when inaccurately reported, caused a great disturbance in the England-baiting press.   "I

---

[1] This is the fact that is too frequently lost sight of in current discussions of the melting pot.   In the *Atlantic Monthly* for August, 1920, Mr. William S. Rossiter, for many years chief clerk of the United States Census and a statistician of high standing, shows that, of the 95,000,000 white people of the United States, 55,000-000 trace their origin to England, Scotland, and Wales.

would not say that we constructed the Panama Canal even for you," he said, "for I am speaking with great frankness and not with diplomatic indirection. We built it for reasons of our own. But I will say that it adds to the pleasure of that great work that you will profit by it. You will profit most by it, for you have the greatest carrying trade." A few paragraphs on the Monroe Doctrine, which practically repeated President Wilson's Mobile speech on that subject, but in which Mr. Page used the expression, "we prefer that European Powers shall acquire no more territory on this continent," alarmed those precisians in language, who pretended to believe that the Ambassador had used the word "prefer" in its literal sense, and interpreted the sentence to mean that, while the United States would "prefer" that Europe should not overrun North and South America, it would really raise no serious objection if Europe did so.

Senator Chamberlain of Oregon, who by this time had apparently become the Senatorial leader of the anti-Page propaganda, introduced a resolution demanding that the Ambassador furnish the Senate a complete copy of this highly pro-British outgiving. The copy was furnished forthwith—and with that the tempest subsided.

To the President

American Embassy, London,
March 18, 1914.

DEAR MR. PRESIDENT:

About this infernal racket in the Senate over my poor speech, I have telegraphed you all there is to say. Of course, it was a harmless courtesy—no bowing low to the British or any such thing—as it was spoken and heard. Of course, too, nothing would have been said about it but for the controversy over the Canal tolls. That was my mistake—in being betrayed by the friendly dinner and the high compliments paid to us into mentioning a subject under controversy.

I am greatly distressed lest possibly it may embarrass you. I do hope not.

I think I have now learned *that* lesson pretty thoroughly. These Anglophobiacs—Irish and Panama—hound me wherever I go. I think I told you of one of their correspondents, who one night got up and yawned at a public dinner as soon as I had spoken and said to his neighbours: "Well, I'll go, the Ambassador didn't say anything that I can get him into trouble about."

I shall, hereafter, write out my speeches and have them gone over carefully by my little Cabinet of Secretaries. Yet something (perhaps not much) will be lost. For these people are infinitely kind and friendly and courteous.

They cannot be driven by anybody to do anything, but they can be led by us to do anything—by the use of spontaneous courtesy. It is by spontaneous courtesy that I have achieved whatever I have achieved, and it is for this that those like me who do like me. Of course, what some of the American newspapers have said is true —that I am too free and too untrained to be a great Ambassador. But the conventional type of Ambassador would not be worth his salt to represent the United States here now, when they are eager to work with us for the peace of the world, if they are convinced of our honour and right-mindedness and the genuineness of our friendship.

I talked this over with Sir Edward Grey the other day, and after telling me that I need fear no trouble at this end of the line, he told me how severely he is now criticized by a "certain element" for "bowing too low to the

Americans." We then each bowed low to the other. The yellow press and Chamberlain would give a year's growth for a photograph of us in that posture!

I am infinitely obliged to you for your kind understanding and your toleration of my errors.

Yours always heartily,
WALTER H. PAGE.

To the President.

P. S.   The serious part of the speech—made to convince the financial people, who are restive about Mexico, that we do not mean to forbid legitimate investments in Central America—has had a good effect here. I have received the thanks of many important men.

W. H. P.

From the President

The White House, Washington,
March 25, 1914.

MY DEAR PAGE:

Thank you for your little note of March thirteenth.[1] You may be sure that none of us who knew you or read the speech felt anything but admiration for it. It is very astonishing to me how some Democrats in the Senate themselves bring these artificial difficulties on the Administration, and it distresses me not a little. Mr. Bryan read your speech yesterday to the Cabinet, who greatly enjoyed it. It was at once sent to the Senate and I hope will there be given out for publication in full.

I want you to feel constantly how I value the intelligent and effective work you are doing in London. I do not know what I should do without you.

The fight is on now about the tolls, but I feel perfectly confident of winning in the matter, though there

─────────
[1] The Ambassador's letter is dated March 18th.

is not a little opposition in Congress—more in the House, it strangely turns out, where a majority of the Democrats originally voted against the exemption, than in the Senate, where a majority of the Democrats voted for it. The vicissitudes of politics are certainly incalculable.

With the warmest regard, in necessary haste,

Cordially and faithfully yours,
WOODROW WILSON.

HON. WALTER H. PAGE,
  American Embassy,
    London, England.

To the President

American Embassy, London,
March 2, 1914.

DEAR MR. PRESIDENT:

I have read in the newspapers here that, after you had read my poor, unfortunate speech, you remarked to callers that you regarded it as proper. I cannot withhold this word of affectionate thanks.

I do not agree with you, heartily as I thank you. The speech itself, in the surroundings and the atmosphere, was harmless and was perfectly understood. But I ought not to have been betrayed into forgetting that the subject was about to come up for fierce discussion in Congress. . . .

Of course, I know that the whole infernal thing is cooked up to beat you, if possible. But that is the greater reason why you must win. I am willing to be sacrificed, if that will help—for forgetting the impending row or for any reason you will.

I suppose we've got to go through such a struggle to pull our Government and our people up to an understanding of our own place in the world—a place so high and big and so powerful that all the future belongs to us. From an economic point of view, we *are* the world; and from a political point of view also. How any man who sees this can have any feeling but pity for the Old World, passes understanding. Our rôle is to treat it most courteously and to make it respect our character—nothing more. Time will do the rest.

I congratulate you most heartily on the character of most of your opposition—the wild Irish (they must be sat upon some time, why not now?), the Clark[1] crowd (characteristically making a stand on a position of dishonour), the Hearst press, and demagogues generally. I have confidence in the people.

This stand is necessary to set us right before the world, to enable us to build up an influential foreign policy, to make us respected and feared, and to make the Democratic Party the party of honour, and to give it the best reason to live and to win.

May I make a suggestion?

The curiously tenacious hold that Anglophobia has on a certain class of our people—might it not be worth your while to make, at some convenient time and in some natural way, a direct attack on it—in a letter to someone, which could be published, or in some address, or possibly in a statement to a Senate committee, which could be given to the press? Say how big and strong and sure-of-the-future we are; so big that we envy nobody, and that those who have Anglophobia or any Europe-phobia are the only persons who "truckle" to any foreign folk or power; that in this tolls-fight all the Continental governments are a unit; that we respect them all, fear none, have no favours, except proper favours among friendly

---

[1] Mr. Champ Clark, Speaker of the House of Representatives, was one of the most blatant opponents of Panama repeal.

nations, to ask of anybody; and that the idea of a "trade" with England for holding off in Mexico is (if you will excuse my French) a common gutter lie.

This may or may not be wise; but you will forgive me for venturing to suggest it. It is *we* who are the proud and erect and patriotic Americans, fearing nobody; but the other fellows are fooling some of the people in making them think that *they* are.

Yours most gratefully,
WALTER H. PAGE.

To the President.

From the President

The White House, Washington,
April 2, 1914.

MY DEAR PAGE:

Please do not distress yourself about that speech. I think with you that it was a mistake to touch upon that matter while it was right hot, because any touch would be sure to burn the finger; but as for the speech itself, I would be willing to subscribe to every bit of it myself, and there can be no rational objection to it. We shall try to cool the excited persons on this side of the water and I think nothing further will come of it. In the meantime, pray realize how thoroughly and entirely you are enjoying my confidence and admiration.

Your letter about Cowdray and Murray was very illuminating and will be very serviceable to me. I have come to see that the real knowledge of the relations between countries in matters of public policy is to be gained at country houses and dinner tables, and not in diplomatic correspondence; in brief, that when we know the men and the currents of opinion, we know more than foreign ministers can tell us; and your letters give me, in a thoroughly dignified way, just the sidelights that are necessary to illuminate the picture. I am heartily obliged to you.

All unite with me in the warmest regards as always.

In haste,

Faithfully yours,

WOODROW WILSON.

HON. WALTER H. PAGE,
   American Embassy,
      London, England.

A note of a conversation with Sir Edward Grey touches the same point: "April 1, 1914. Sir Edward Grey recalled to me to-day that he had waited for the President to take up the Canal tolls controversy at his convenience. 'When he took it up at his own time to suit his own plans, he took it up in the most admirable way possible.' This whole story is too good to be lost. If the repeal of the tolls clause passes the Senate, I propose to make a speech in the House of Commons on 'The Proper Way for Great Governments to Deal with One Another,' and use this experience.

"Sir Edward also spoke of being somewhat 'depressed' by the fierce opposition to the President on the tolls question—the extent of Anglophobia in the United States.

"Here is a place for a campaign of education—Chautauqua and whatnot.

"The amount of Anglophobia *is* great. But I doubt if it be as great as it seems; for it is organized and is very vociferous. If you collected together or thoroughly organized all the people in the United States who have birthmarks on their faces, you'd be 'depressed' by the number of them."

Nothing could have more eloquently proved the truth of this last remark than the history of this Panama bill itself.   After all the politicians in the House and Senate had filled pages of the *Congressional Record* with denunciations of Great Britain—most of it intended for the entertainment of Irish-Americans and German-Americans in the constituencies—the two Houses proceeded to the really serious business of voting.   The House quickly passed the bill by 216 to 71, and the Senate by 50 to 35.   Apparently the amount of Anglophobia was not portentous, when it came to putting this emotion to the test of counting heads.   The bill went at once to the President, was signed—and the dishonour was atoned for.

Mr. and Mrs. Page were attending a ball in Buckingham Palace when the great news reached London.   The gathering represented all that was most distinguished in the official and diplomatic life of the British capital.   The word was rapidly passed from guest to guest, and the American Ambassador and his wife soon found themselves the centre of a company which could hardly restrain itself in expressing its admiration for the United States.   Never in the history of the country had American prestige stood so high as on that night.   The King and the Prime Minister were especially affected by this display of fair-dealing in Washington.   The slight commercial advantage which Great Britain had obtained was not the thought that was uppermost in everybody's mind.   The thing that really moved these assembled statesmen and diplomats was the fact that something new had appeared in the history of legislative chambers.   A great nation had committed an outrageous wrong—that was something that had happened many times before in all countries.   But the unprecedented thing was that this same nation had exposed its fault boldly to the world—had lifted up its hands and cried, "We have sinned!" and then had publicly undone its error. Proud as Page had always been of his country, that moment was perhaps the most triumphant in his life. The action of Congress emphasized all that he had been saying of the ideals of the United States, and gave point to his arguments that justice and honour and right, and not temporary selfish interest, should control the foreign policy of any nation which really claimed to be enlightened. The general feeling of Great Britain was perhaps best expressed by the remark made to Mrs. Page, on this occasion, by Lady D——:

"The United States has set a high standard for all nations to live up to. I don't believe that there is any other nation that would have done it."

One significant feature of this great episode was the act of Congress in accepting the President's statement that the repeal of the Panama discrimination was a necessary preliminary to the success of American foreign policy. Mr. Wilson's declaration, that, unless this legislation should be repealed, he would not "know how to deal with other matters of even greater delicacy and nearer consequence" had puzzled Congress and the country. The debates show the keenest curiosity as to what the President had in mind. The newspapers turned the matter over and over, without obtaining any clew to the mystery. Some thought that the President had planned to intervene in Mexico, and that the tolls legislation was the consideration demanded by Great Britain for a free hand in this matter. But this correspondence has already demolished that theory. Others thought that Japan was in some way involved—but that explanation also failed to satisfy.

Congress accepted the President's statement trustfully and blindly, and passed the asked-for legislation. Up to the present moment this passage in the Presidential message has been unexplained. Page's papers, however, disclose what seems to be a satisfactory solution to the mystery. They show that the President and Colonel House and Page were at this time engaged in a negotiation of the utmost importance. At the very time that the tolls bill was under discussion Colonel House was making arrangements for a visit to Great Britain, France, and Germany, the purpose of which was to bring these nations to some kind of an understanding that would prevent a European war. This evidently was the great business that could not be disclosed at the time and for which the repeal of the tolls legislation was the necessary preliminary.

CHAPTER IX

AMERICA TRIES TO PREVENT THE EUROPEAN WAR

PAGE'S mind, from the day of his arrival in England, had been filled with that portent which was the most outstanding fact in European life. Could nothing be done to prevent the dangers threatened by European militarism? Was there no way of forestalling the war which seemed every day to be approaching nearer? The dates of the following letters, August, 1913, show that this was one of the first ideas which Page presented to the new Administration.

To Edward M. House

Aug. 28, 1913.

MY DEAR HOUSE:

. . . Everything is lovely and the goose hangs high. We're having a fine time. Only, only, only—I do wish to do something constructive and lasting. Here are great navies and armies and great withdrawals of men from industry—an enormous waste. Here are kings and courts and gold lace and ceremonies which, without producing anything, require great cost to keep them going. Here are all the privileges and taxes that this state of things implies—every one a hindrance to human progress. We are free from most of these. We have more people and more capable people and many times more territory than both England and Germany; and we have more *potential* wealth than all Europe. They know that.

They'd like to find a way to escape.   The Hague pro-
grammes, for the most part, just lead them around a
circle in the dark back to the place where they started.
Somebody needs to *do* something.   If we could find some
friendly use for these navies and armies and kings and
things—in the service of humanity—they'd follow us.   We
ought to find a way to use them in cleaning up the tropics
under our leadership and under our code of ethics—that
everything must be done for the good of the tropical
peoples and that nobody may annex a foot of land.   They
want a job.   Then they'd quit sitting on their haunches,
growling at one another.

I wonder if we couldn't serve notice that the land-
stealing game is forever ended and that the cleaning up
of backward lands is now in order—for the people that
live there; and then invite Europe's help to make the
tropics as healthful as the Panama Zone?

There's no future in Europe's vision—no long look
ahead.   They give all their thought to the immediate
danger.   Consider this Balkan War; all European energy
was spent merely to keep the Great Powers at peace.
The two wars in the Balkans have simply impoverished
the people—left the world that much worse than it was
before.   Nobody has considered the well-being or the
future of those peoples nor of their land.   The Great
Powers are mere threats to one another, content to
check, one the other!   There can come no help to the
progress of the world from this sort of action—no step
forward.

Work on a world-plan.   Nothing but blue chips, you
know.   Is it not possible that Mexico may give an entering wedge for this kind of thing?

Heartily yours,
WALTER H. PAGE.

In a memorandum, written about the same time, Mr. Page explains his idea in more detail:

Was there ever greater need than there is now of a first-class mind unselfishly working on world problems? The ablest ruling minds are engaged on domestic tasks. There is no world-girdling intelligence at work in government. On the continent of Europe, the Kaiser is probably the foremost man. Yet he cannot think far beyond the provincial views of the Germans. In England, Sir Edward Grey is the largest-visioned statesman. All the Europeans are spending their thought and money in watching and checkmating one another and in maintaining their armed and balanced *status quo*.

A way must be found out of this stagnant watching. Else a way will have to be fought out of it; and a great European war would set the Old World, perhaps the whole world, back a long way; and thereafter, the present armed watching would recur; we should have gained nothing. It seems impossible to talk the Great Powers out of their fear of one another or to "Hague" them out of it. They'll never be persuaded to disarm. The only way left seems to be to find some common and useful work for these great armies to do. Then, perhaps, they'll *work* themselves out of their jealous position. Isn't this sound psychology?

To produce a new situation, the vast energy that now spends itself in maintaining armies and navies must find a new outlet. Something new must be found for them to do, some great unselfish task that they can do together.

Nobody can lead in such a new era but the United States.

May there not come such a chance in Mexico—to clean out bandits, yellow fever, malaria, hookworm—all to make the country healthful, safe for life and investment, and for orderly self-government at last? What we did in Cuba might thus be made the beginning of a new epoch in history—conquest for the sole benefit of the conquered, worked out by a sanitary reformation. The new sanitation will reclaim all tropical lands; but the work must be first done by military power—probably from the outside.

May not the existing military power of Europe conceivably be diverted, gradually, to this use? One step at a time, as political and financial occasions arise? As presently in Mexico?

This present order must change. It holds the Old World still. It keeps all parts of the world apart, in spite of the friendly cohesive forces of trade and travel. It keeps back self-government and the progress of man.

And the tropics cry out for sanitation, which is at first an essentially military task.

A strange idea this may have seemed in August, 1913, a year before the outbreak of the European war; yet the scheme is not dissimilar to the "mandatory" principle, adopted by the Versailles Peace Conference as the only practical method of dealing with backward peoples. In this work, as in everything that would help mankind on its weary way to a more efficient and more democratic civilization, Page regarded the United States, Great Britain, and the British Dominions as inevitable partners. Anything that would bring these two nations into a closer coöperation he looked upon as a step making for human advancement. He believed that any opportunity of sweeping away misconceptions and prejudices and of impressing upon the two peoples their common mission should be eagerly seized by the statesmen of the two countries. And circumstances at this particular moment, Page believed, presented a large opportunity of this kind. It is one of the minor ironies of modern history that the United States and Great Britain should have selected 1914 as a year for a great peace celebration. That year marked the one hundredth anniversary of the signing of the Treaty of Ghent, which ended the War of 1812, and in 1913 comprehensive plans had already been formed for observing this impressive centennial. The plan was to make it more than the mere observance of a hundred years of peaceful intercourse; it was the intention to use the occasion to emphasize the fundamental identity of American and British ideals and to lay the foundation of a permanent understanding and friendship. The erection of a monument to Abraham Lincoln at Westminster—a plan that has since been realized— was one detail of this programme. Another was the restoration of Sulgrave Manor, the English country seat of the Washingtons, and its preservation as a place where the peoples of both countries could share their common traditions. Page now dared to hope that President Wilson might associate himself with this great purpose to the extent of coming to England and accepting this gift in the name of the American nation. Such a Presidential visit, he believed, would exercise a mighty influence in forestalling a threatening European war. The ultimate purpose, that is, was world peace—precisely the same motive that led President Wilson, in 1919, to make a European pilgrimage.

This idea was no passing fancy with Page: it was with him a favourite topic of conversation. Such a presidential visit, he believed, would accomplish more than any other influences in dissipating the clouds that were darkening the European landscape. He would elaborate the idea at length in discussions with his intimates.

"What I want," he would say, "is to have the President of the United States and the King of England stand up side by side and let the world take a good look at them!"

To Edward M. House

August 25, 1913.

. . . I wrote him (President Wilson) my plan—a mere outline. He'll only smile now. But when the tariff and the currency and Mexico are off his hands, and when he can be invited to come and deliver an oration on George Washington next year at the presentation of the old Washington homestead here, he may be " pushed over." You do the pushing. Mrs. Page has invited the young White House couple to visit us on their honeymoon.[1] Encourage that and that may encourage the larger plan later. Nothing else would give such a friendly turn to the whole world as the President's coming here. The old Earth would sit up and rub its eyes and take notice to whom it belongs. This visit might prevent an English-German war and an American-Japanese war, by this mere show of friendliness. It would be one of the greatest occasions of our time. Even at my little speeches, they "whoop it up!" What would they do over the President's!

But at that time Washington was too busy with its domestic programme to consider such a proposal seriously. "Your two letters," wrote Colonel House in reply, "have come to me and lifted me out of the rut of things and given me a glimpse of a fair land. What you are thinking of and what you want this Administration to do is

---

[1] Mr. and Mrs. Francis B. Sayre, son-in-law and daughter of President Wilson.

beyond the power of accomplishment for the moment. My desk is covered with matters of no lasting importance, but which come to me as a part of the day's work, and which must be done if I am to help lift the load that is pressing upon the President. It tells me better than anything else what he has to bear, and how utterly futile it is for him to attempt such problems as you present."

From the President

MY DEAR PAGE:

   . . . As for your suggestion that I should myself visit England during my term of office, I must say that I agree with all your arguments for it, and yet the case against the President's leaving the country, particularly now that he is expected to exercise a constant leadership in all parts of the business of the government, is very strong and I am afraid overwhelming. It might be the beginning of a practice of visiting foreign countries which would lead Presidents rather far afield.

It is a most attractive idea, I can assure you, and I turn away from it with the greatest reluctance.

We hear golden opinions of the impression you are making in England, and I have only to say that it is just what I had expected.

Cordially and faithfully yours,
WOODROW WILSON.

HON. WALTER H. PAGE,
   American Embassy,
    London, England.

In December, however, evidently Colonel House's mind had turned to the general subject that had so engaged that of the Ambassador.

From Edward M. House

145 East 35th Street,
New York City.
December 13th, 1913.

DEAR PAGE:

In my budget of yesterday I did not tell you of the suggestion which I made to Sir William Tyrrell when he was here, and which I also made to the President.

It occurred to me that between us all we might bring about the naval holiday which Winston Churchill has proposed. My plan is that I should go to Germany in the spring and see the Kaiser, and try to win him over to the thought that is uppermost in our mind and that of the British Government.

Sir William thought there was a good sporting chance of success. He offered to let me have all the correspondence that had passed between the British and German governments upon this question so that I might be thoroughly informed as to the position of them both. He thought I should go directly to Germany without stopping in England, and that Gerard should prepare the Kaiser for my coming, telling him of my relations with the President. He thought this would be sufficient without any further credentials.

In other words, he would do with the Kaiser what you did with Sir Edward Grey last summer.

I spoke to the President about the matter and he seemed pleased with the suggestion; in fact, I might say, he was enthusiastic. He said, just as Sir William did, that it would be too late for this year's budget; but he made a suggestion that he get the Appropriations Committee to incorporate a clause, permitting him to eliminate certain parts of the battleship budget in the event that other nations declared for a naval holiday. So this will be done and will further the plan.

Now I want to get you into the game. If you think it advisable, take the matter up with Sir William Tyrrell and then with Sir Edward Grey, or directly with Sir Edward, if you prefer, and give me the benefit of your advice and conclusions.

Please tell Sir William that I lunched at the Embassy with the Spring Rices yesterday, and had a satisfactory talk with both Lady Spring Rice and Sir Cecil.

Faithfully yours,

E. M. House.

It is apparent from Page's letters that the suggestion now contained in Colonel House's communication would receive a friendly hearing. The idea that Colonel House suggested was merely the initial stage of a plan which soon took on more ambitious proportions. At the time of Sir William Tyrrell's American visit, the Winston Churchill proposal for a naval holiday was being actively discussed by the British and the American press. In one form or another it had been figuring in the news for nearly two years. Viscount Haldane, in the course of his famous visit to Berlin in February, 1912, had attempted to reach some understanding with the German Government on the limitation of the German and the British fleets. The Agadir crisis of the year before had left Europe with a bad state of nerves, and there was a general belief that only some agreement on shipbuilding could prevent a European war. Lord Haldane and von Tirpitz spent many hours discussing the relative sizes of the two navies, but the discussions led to no definite under-

standing. In March, 1913, Mr. Churchill, then First
Lord of the Admiralty, took up the same subject in a
different form. In this speech he first used the words
"naval holiday," and proposed that Germany and Great
Britain should cease building first-class battleships for one
year, thus giving the two nations a breathing space, during
which time they might discuss their future plans in the hope
of reaching a permanent agreement. The matter lagged
again until October 18, 1913, when, in a speech at Manchester, Mr. Churchill placed his proposal in this form: "Now,
we say to our great neighbour, Germany, 'If you will put off
beginning your two ships for twelve months from the ordinary date when you would have begun them, we will put off
beginning our four ships, in absolute good faith, for exactly the same period.'" About the same time Premier
Asquith made it clear that the Ministry was back of the
suggested programme. In Germany, however, the "naval holiday" soon became an object of derision. The
official answer was that Germany had a definite naval
law and that the Government could not entertain any
suggestion of departing from it. Great Britain then
answered that, for every keel Germany laid down, the
Admiralty would lay down two. The outcome, therefore, of this attempt at friendship was that the two nations
had been placed farther apart than ever.

The dates of this discussion, it will be observed, almost
corresponded with the period covered by the Tyrrell
visit to America. This fact, and Page's letters of this
period, had apparently implanted in Colonel House's mind
an ambition for definite action. He now proposed that
President Wilson should take up the broken threads of
the rapprochement and attempt to bring them together
again. From this, as will be made plain, the plan developed into something more comprehensive. Page's

ideas on the treatment of backward nations had strongly impressed both the President and Colonel House. The discussion on Mexico which had just taken place between the American and the British Governments seemed to have developed ideas that could have a much wider application. The fundamental difficulties in Mexico were not peculiar to that country nor indeed to Latin-America. Perhaps the most prolific cause of war among the more enlightened countries was that produced by the jealousies and antagonisms which were developed by their contacts with unprogressive peoples—in the Balkans, the Ottoman Empire, Asia, and the Far East. The method of dealing with such peoples, which the United States had found so successful in Cuba and the Philippines, had proved that there was just one honourable way of dealing with the less fortunate and more primitive races in all parts of the world. Was it not possible to bring the greatest nations, especially the United States, Great Britain, and Germany, to some agreement on this question, as well as on the question of disarmament? This once accomplished, the way could be prepared for joint action on the numerous other problems which were then threatening the peace of the world. The League of Nations was then not even a phrase, but the plan that was forming in Colonel House's mind was at least some scheme for permanent international coöperation. For several years Germany had been the nation which had proved the greatest obstacle to such international friendliness and arbitration. The Kaiser had destroyed both Hague Conferences as influential forces in the remaking of the world; and in the autumn of 1913 he had taken on a more belligerent attitude than ever. If this attempt to establish a better condition of things was to succeed, Germany's coöperation would be indispensable. This is the reason why Colonel House proposed first of all to visit Berlin.

From Edward M. House

145 East 35th Street,
New York City.
January 4th, 1914.

DEAR PAGE:

. . . Benj. Ide Wheeler[1] took lunch with me the other day.   He is just back from Germany and he is on the most intimate terms with the Kaiser.   He tells me he often takes dinner with the family alone, and spends the evening with them.

I know, now, the different Cabinet officials who have the Kaiser's confidence and I know his attitude toward England, naval armaments, war, and world politics in general.

Wheeler spoke to me very frankly and the information he gave me will be invaluable in the event that my plans carry.   The general idea is to bring about a sympathetic understanding between England, Germany, and America, not only upon the question of disarmament, but upon other matters of equal importance to themselves, and to the world at large.

It seems to me that Japan should come into this pact, but Wheeler tells me that the Kaiser feels very strongly upon the question of Asiatics.   He thinks the contest of the future will be between the Eastern and Western civilizations.   . . .

Your friend always,
E. M. HOUSE.

By January 4, 1914, the House-Wilson plan had thus grown into an Anglo-American-German "pact," to deal

[1] Ex-President of the University of California, Roosevelt Professor at the University of Berlin, 1909–10.

not only with "disarmament, but other matters of equal importance to themselves and to the world at large." Page's response to this idea was consistent and characteristic. He had no faith in Germany and believed that the existence of Kaiserism was incompatible with the extension of the democratic ideal. Even at this early time—eight months before the outbreak of the World War—he had no enthusiasm for anything in the nature of an alliance, or a "pact," that included Germany as an equal partner. He did, however, have great faith in the coöperation of the English-speaking peoples as a force that would make for permanent peace and international justice. In his reply to Colonel House, therefore, Page fell back at once upon his favourite plan for an understanding between the United States, Great Britain, and the British colonies. That he would completely sympathize with the Washington aspiration for disarmament was to be expected.

To Edward M. House

January 2, 1914.

My dear House:

You have set my imagination going. I've been thinking of this thing for months, and now you've given me a fresh start. It can be worked out somehow—doubtless, not in the form that anybody may at first see; but experiment and frank discussion will find a way.

As I think of it, turning it this way and that, there always comes to me just as I am falling to sleep this reflection: the English-speaking peoples now rule the world in all essential facts. They alone and Switzerland have permanent free government. In France there's freedom—but for how long? In Germany and Austria —hardly. In the Scandinavian States—yes, but they are small and exposed as are Belgium and Holland. In the big secure South American States—yes, it's coming. In Japan—? Only the British lands and the United States have secure liberty. They also have the most treasure, the best fighters, the most land, the most ships—the future in fact.

Now, because George Washington warned us against alliances, we've gone on as if an alliance were a kind of smallpox. Suppose there were—let us say for argument's sake—the tightest sort of an alliance, offensive and defensive, between all Britain, colonies and all, and the United States—what would happen? Anything we'd say would go, whether we should say, "Come in out of the wet," or, "Disarm." That might be the beginning of a real world-alliance and union to accomplish certain large results—disarmament, for instance, or arbitration —dozens of good things.

Of course, we'd have to draw and quarter the O'Gormans.[1] But that ought to be done anyhow in the general interest of good sense in the world. We could force any nation into this "trust" that we wanted in it.

Isn't it time we tackled such a job frankly, fighting out the Irish problem once for all, and having done with it?

I'm not proposing a programme. I'm only thinking out loud. I see little hope of doing anything so long as we choose to be ruled by an obsolete remark made by George Washington.

W. H. P.

January 11, 1914.

. . . But this armament flurry is worth serious thought. Lloyd George gave out an interview, seeming to imply the necessity of reducing the navy programme.

---

[1] James A. O'Gorman was the anti-British Senator from New York State at this time working hard against the repeal of the Panama tolls discrimination.

The French allies of the British went up in the air!   They
raised a great howl.   Churchill went to see them, to
soothe them.   They would not be soothed.   Now the
Prime Minister is going to Paris—ostensibly to see his
daughter off to the Riviera.   Nobody believes that reason.
They say he's going to smooth out the French.   Meantime the Germans are gleeful.

And the British Navy League is receiving money and
encouraging letters from British subjects, praying greater
activity to keep the navy up.   You touch the navy and
you touch the quick—that's the lesson.   It's an enormous excitement that this small incident has caused.

W. H. P.

To Edward M. House

London, February 24, 1914.

MY DEAR HOUSE:

You'll be interested in these pamphlets by Sir Max
Waechter, who has opened an office here and is spending
much money to "federate" Europe, and to bring a lessening of armaments.   I enclose also an article about him
from the *Daily Telegraph*, which tells how he has inter-
viewed most of the Old World monarchs.   Get also,
immediately, the new two-volume life of Lord Lyons,
Minister to the United States during the Civil War, and
subsequently Ambassador to France.   You will find an
interesting account of the campaign of about 1870 to reduce armaments, when old Bismarck dumped the whole
basket of apples by marching against France.   You
know I sometimes fear some sort of repetition of that
experience.   Some government (probably Germany) will
see bankruptcy staring it in the face and the easiest way
out will seem a great war.   Bankruptcy before a war
would be ignominious; after a war, it could be charged to

"Glory." It'll take a long time to bankrupt England. It's unspeakably rich; they pay enormous taxes, but they pay them out of their incomes, not out of their principal, except their inheritance tax. That looks to me as if it came out of the principal. . . .

I hope you had a good time in Texas and escaped some cold weather. This deceptive sort of winter here is grippe-laden. I've had the thing, but I'm now getting over it. . . .

This Benton[1]-Mexican business is causing great excitement here.

Always heartily yours,
W. H. P.

P. S. There's nothing like the President. By George! the passage of the arbitration treaty (renewal) almost right off the bat, and apparently the tolls discrimination coming presently to its repeal! Sir Edward Grey remarked to me yesterday: "Things are clearing up!" I came near saying to him: "Have you any miracles in mind that you'd like to see worked?" Wilson stock is at a high premium on this side of the water in spite of the momentary impatience caused by Benton's death.

W. H. P.

From Edward M. House

145 East 35th Street,
New York City.
April 19th, 1914.

DEAR PAGE:

I have had a long talk with Mr. Laughlin.[2] At first he thought I would not have more than one chance in a

---

[1] In February, 1915, William S. Benton, an English subject who had spent the larger part of his life in Mexico, was murdered in the presence of Francisco Villa.

[2] Mr. Irwin Laughlin, first secretary of the American Embassy in London; at this time spending a few weeks in the United States.

million to do anything with the Kaiser, but after talking with him further, he concluded that I would have a fairly good sporting chance.   I have about concluded to take it.

If I can do anything, I can do it in a few days.   I was with the President most of last week.   .   .   .

He spoke of your letters to him and to me as being classics, and said they were the best letters, as far as he knew, that any one had ever written.   Of course you know how heartily I concur in this.   He said that sometime they should be published.

The President is now crystallizing his mind in regard to the Federal Reserve Board, and if you are not to remain in London, then he would probably put Houston on the Board and ask you to take the Secretaryship of Agriculture.

You have no idea the feeling that is being aroused by the tolls question.   The Hearst papers are screaming at all of us every day.   They have at last honoured me with their abuse.   .   .   .

With love and best wishes, I am,

Faithfully yours,

E. M. House.

From Edward M. House

145 East 35th Street,
New York City.
April 20th, 1914.

Dear Page:

.   .   .   It is our purpose to sail on the *Imperator*, May 16th, and go directly to Germany.   I expect to be there a week or more, but Mrs. House will reach London by the 1st or 2nd of June.   .   .   .

Our friend[1] in Washington thinks it is worth while for

---

[1] Obviously President Wilson.

me to go to Germany, and that determines the matter. The press is shrieking to-day over the Mexican situation, but I hope they will be disappointed. It is not the intention to do anything further for the moment than to blockade the ports, and unless some overt act is made from the North, our troops will not cross the border.

Your friend always,
E. M. House.

To Edward M. House

London, April 27, 1914.

MY DEAR HOUSE:

Of course you decided wisely to carry out your original Berlin plan, and you ought never to have had a moment's hesitation, if you did have any hesitation. I do not expect you to produce any visible or immediate results. I hope I am mistaken in this. But you know that the German Government has a well-laid progressive plan for shipbuilding for a certain number of years. I believe that the work has, in fact, already been arranged for. But that has nothing to do with the case. You are going to see what effect you can produce on the mind of a man. Perhaps you will never know just what effect you will produce. Yet the fact that you are who you are, that you make this journey for this especial purpose, that you are everlastingly right—these are enough.

Moreover, you can't ever tell results, nor can you afford to make your plans in this sort of high work with the slightest reference to probable results. That's the bigness and the glory of it. Any ordinary man can, on any ordinary day, go and do a task, the favourable results of which may be foreseen. *That's* easy. The big thing is to go confidently to work on a task, the results of which nobody can possibly foresee—a task so vague and improbable of definite results that small men hesitate. It is in this spirit that very many of the biggest things in history have been done. Wasn't the purchase of Louisiana such a thing? Who'd ever have supposed that that could have been brought about? I applaud your errand and I am eagerly impatient to hear the results. When will *you* get here? I assume that Mrs. House will not go with you to Berlin. No matter so you both turn up here for a good long stay.

I've taken me a little bit of a house about twenty miles out of town whither we are going in July as soon as we can get away from London. I hope to stay down there till far into October, coming up to London about thrice a week. That's the dull season of the year. It's a charming little country place—big enough for you to visit us. . . .

From Edward M. House

An Bord des Dampfers Imperator
den May 21, 1914.

Hamburg-Amerika Linie

DEAR PAGE:

Here we are again. The Wallaces[1] land at Cherbourg, Friday morning, and we of course go on to Berlin. I wish I might have the benefit of your advice just now, for the chances for success in this great adventure are slender enough at best. The President has done his part in the letter I have with me, and it is clearly up to me to do mine. . . .

Faithfully yours,
E. M. HOUSE.

---

[1] Mr. Hugh C. Wallace, afterward Ambassador to France, and Mrs. Wallace. Mr. and Mrs. Wallace accompanied Mr. and Mrs. House on this journey.

It will be observed that Colonel House had taken the advice of Sir William Tyrrell, and had sailed directly to Germany on a German ship—the *Imperator*. Ambassador Gerard had made preparations for his reception in Berlin, and the American soon had long talks with Admiral von Tirpitz, Falkenhayn, Von Jagow, Solf, and others. Von Bethmann-Hollweg's wife died almost on the day of his arrival in Berlin, so it was impossible for him to see the Chancellor—the man who would have probably been the most receptive to these peace ideas. All the leaders of the government, except Von Tirpitz, gave Colonel House's proposals a respectful if somewhat cynical hearing. Von Tirpitz was openly and demonstratively hostile. The leader of the German Navy simply bristled with antagonism at any suggestion for peace or disarmament or world coöperation. He consumed a large part of the time which Colonel House spent with him denouncing England and all its works. Hatred of the "Island Kingdom" was apparently the consuming passion of his existence. On the whole, Von Tirpitz thus made no attempt to conceal his feeling that the purpose of the House mission was extremely distasteful to him. The other members of the Government, while not so tactlessly hostile, were not particularly encouraging. The usual objections to disarmament were urged—the fear of other Powers, the walled-in state of Germany, the vigilant enemies against which it was necessary constantly to be prepared and watchful. Even more than the unsympathetic politeness of the German Cabinet the general atmosphere of Berlin was depressing to Colonel House. The militaristic oligarchy was absolutely in control. Militarism possessed not only the army, the navy, and the chief officers of state, but the populace as well. One almost trivial circumstance has left a lasting

impression on Colonel House's mind.   Ambassador Gerard
took him out one evening for a little relaxation.   Both
Mr. Gerard and Colonel House were fond of target shooting and the two men sought one of the numerous rifle
galleries of Berlin.   They visited gallery after gallery,
but could not get into one.   Great crowds lined up at
every place, waiting their turns at the target; it seemed
as though every able-bodied man in Berlin was spending
all his time improving his marksmanship.   But this was
merely a small indication of the atmosphere of militarism
which prevailed in the larger aspects of life.   Colonel
House found himself in a strange place to preach international accord for the ending of war!

He had come to Berlin not merely to talk with the
Cabinet heads; his goal was the Kaiser himself.   But he
perceived at once a persistent opposition to his plan.
As he was the President's personal representative, and
carried a letter from the President to the Kaiser, an audience could not be refused—indeed, it had already been
duly arranged; but there was a quiet opposition to his
consorting with the "All Highest" alone.   It was not usual,
Colonel House was informed, for His Imperial Majesty
to discuss such matters except in the presence of a representative of the Foreign Office.   Germany had not yet
recovered from the shock which the Emperor's conversation with certain foreign correspondents had given the
nation.   The effects were still felt of the famous interviews
of October 28, 1908, which, when published in the London *Telegraph*, had caused the bitterest resentment in
Great Britain.   The Kaiser had given his solemn word
that he would indulge in no more indiscretions of this
sort, and a private interview with Colonel House was regarded by his advisers as a possible infraction of that
promise.   But the American would not be denied.   He

knew that an interview with a third person present would
be simply time thrown away since his message was intended for the Kaiser's own ears; and ultimately his per-
sistence succeeded. The next Monday would be June
1st—a great day in Germany. It was the occasion of the
Schrippenfest, a day which for many years had been set
aside for the glorification of the German Army. On that
festival, the Kaiser entertained with great pomp representative army officers and representative privates, as
well as the diplomatic corps and other distinguished
foreigners. Colonel House was invited to attend the
Kaiser's luncheon on that occasion, and was informed that,
after this function was over, he would have an opportunity of having a private conversation with His Majesty.

The affair took place in the palace at Potsdam. The
militarism which Colonel House had felt so oppressively
in Berlin society was especially manifest on this occasion.
There were two luncheon parties—that of the Kaiser
and his officers and guests in the state dining room, and
that of the selected private soldiers outside. The Kaiser
and the Kaiserin spent a few moments with their humbler
subjects, drinking beer with them and passing a few com-
radely remarks; they then proceeded to the large dining
hall and took their places with the gorgeously caparisoned
and bemedalled chieftains of the German Army. The
whole proceeding has an historic interest, in that it was
the last Schrippenfest held. Whether another will ever
be held is problematical, for the occasion was an inevitable
part of the trappings of Hohenzollernism. Despite the
gravity of the occasion, Colonel House's chief memory
of this function is slightly tinged with the ludicrous. He
had spent the better part of a lifetime attempting to
rid himself of his military title, but uselessly. He was
now embarrassed because these solemn German officers

persisted in regarding him as an important part of the American Army, and in discussing technical and strategical problems. The visitor made several attempts to explain that he was merely a "geographical colonel"— that the title was constantly conferred in an informal sense on Americans, especially Southerners, and that the handle to his name had, therefore, no military significance. But the round-faced Teutons stared at his explanation in blank amazement; they couldn't grasp the point at all, and continued to ask his opinion of matters purely military.

When the lunch was finished, the Kaiser took Colonel House aside, and the two men withdrew to the terrace, out of earshot of the rest of the gathering. However, they were not out of sight. For nearly half an hour the Kaiser and the American stood side by side upon the terrace, the German generals, at a respectful distance, watching the proceeding, resentful, puzzled, curious as to what it was all about. The quiet demeanour of the American "Colonel," his plain citizen's clothes, and his almost impassive face, formed a striking contrast to the Kaiser's dazzling uniform and the general scene of military display. Two or three of the generals and admirals present were in the secret, but only two or three; the mass of officers watching this meeting little guessed that the purpose of House's visit was to persuade the Kaiser to abandon everything for which the Schrippenfest stood; to enter an international compact with the United States and Great Britain for reducing armaments, to reach an agreement about trade and the treatment of backward peoples, and to form something of a permanent association for the preservation of peace. The one thing which was apparent to the watchers was that the American was only now and then saying a brief word, but that the Kaiser was, as usual,

Walter H. Page, from a photograph taken a few years before he
became American Ambassador to Great Britain

The British Foreign Office, Downing Street

doing a vast amount of talking. His speech rattled on with the utmost animation, his arms were constantly gesticulating, he would bring one fist down into his palm to register an emphatic point, and enforce certain ideas with a menacing forefinger. At times Colonel House would show slight signs of impatience and interrupt the flow of talk. But the Kaiser was clearly absorbed in the subject under discussion. His entourage several times attempted to break up the interview. The Court Chamberlain twice gingerly approached and informed His Majesty that the Imperial train was waiting to take the party back to Berlin. Each time the Kaiser, with an angry gesture, waved the interrupter away. Despairing of the usual resources, the Kaiserin was sent with the same message. The Kaiser did not treat her so summarily, but he paid no attention to the request, and continued to discuss the European situation with the American.

The subject that had mainly aroused the Imperial warmth was the "Yellow Peril." For years this had been an obsession with the Kaiser, and he launched into the subject as soon as Colonel House broached the purpose of his visit. There could be no question of disarmament, the Kaiser vehemently declared, as long as this danger to civilization existed. "We white nations should join hands," he said, "to oppose Japan and the other yellow nations, or some day they will destroy us."

It was with difficulty that Colonel House could get His Majesty away from this subject. Whatever topic he touched upon, the Kaiser would immediately start declaiming on the dangers that faced Europe from the East. His insistence on this accounted partly for the slight signs of impatience which the American showed. He feared that all the time allotted for the interview would be devoted to discussing the Japanese. About another nation, the Kaiser showed almost as much alarm as he did about Japan, and that was Russia. He spoke contemptuously of France and Great Britain as possible enemies, for he apparently had no fear of them. But the size of Russia and the exposed eastern frontier of Germany seemed to appal him. How could Germany join a peace pact, and reduce its army, so long as 175,000,000 Slavs threatened them from this direction?

Another matter that the Kaiser discussed with derision was Mr. Bryan's arbitration treaty. Practically all the great nations had already ratified this treaty except Germany. The Kaiser now laughed at the treaties and pooh-poohed Bryan. Germany, he declared, would never accept such an arbitration plan. Colonel House had particular cause to remember this part of the conversation three years afterward, when the United States declared war on Germany. The outstanding feature of the Bryan treaty was the clause which pledged the high contracting parties not to go to war without taking a breathing spell of one year in which to think the matter over. Had Germany adopted this treaty, the United States, in April, 1917, after Germany had presented a *casus belli* by resuming unrestricted submarine warfare, could not have gone to war. We should have been obliged to wait a year, or until April, 1918, before engaging in hostilities. That is, an honourable observance of this Bryan treaty by the United States would have meant that Germany would have starved Great Britain into surrender, and crushed Europe with her army. Had the Kaiser, on this June afternoon, not notified Colonel House that Germany would not accept this treaty, but, instead, had notified him that he would accept it, William II might now be sitting on the throne of a victorious Germany, with Europe for a footstool.

Despite the Kaiser's hostile attitude toward these details, his general reception of the President's proposals was not outwardly unfriendly. Perhaps he was sincere, perhaps not; yet the fact is that he manifested more cordiality to this somewhat vague "get-together" proposal than had any of his official advisers. He encouraged Colonel House to visit London, talk the matter over with British statesmen, and then return to Berlin.

"The last thing," he said, "that Germany wants is war. We are getting to be a great commercial country. In a few years Germany will be a rich country, like England and the United States. We don't want a war to interfere with our progress."

Any peace suggestion that was compatible with German safety, he said, would be entertained. Yet his parting words were not reassuring.

"Every nation in Europe," he said, "has its bayonets pointed at Germany. But——"—and with this he gave a proud and smiling glance at the glistening representatives of his army gathered on this brilliant occasion—"we are ready!"

Colonel House left Berlin, not particularly hopeful; the Kaiser impressed him as a man of unstable nervous organization—as one who was just hovering on the borderland of insanity. Certainly, this was no man to be entrusted with such powers as the American had witnessed that day at Potsdam. Dangerous as the Kaiser was, however, he did not seem to Colonel House to be as great a menace to mankind as were his military advisers. The American came away from Berlin with the conviction that the most powerful force in Germany was the militaristic clique, and second, the Hohenzollern dynasty. He has always insisted that this represented the real precedence in power. So long as the Kaiser was obedient to the will of militarism, so long could he maintain his standing. He was confident, however, that the militaristic oligarchy was determined to have its will, and would dethrone the Kaiser the moment he showed indications of taking a course that would lead to peace. Colonel House was also convinced that this militaristic oligarchy was determined on war. The coolness with which it listened to his proposals, the attempts it made to keep him from seeing the Kaiser alone, its repeated efforts to break up the conversation after it had begun, all pointed to the inevitable tragedy. The fact that the Kaiser expressed a wish to discuss the matter again, after Colonel House had sounded London, was the one hopeful feature of an otherwise discouraging experience, and accounts for the tone of faint optimism in his letters describing the visit.

From Edward M. House

Embassy of the United States of America,
Berlin,
May 28, 1914.

DEAR PAGE:

. . . I have done something here already—not much, but enough to open negotiations with London. I lunch with the Kaiser on Monday. I was advised to avoid Admiral von Tirpitz as being very unsympathetic. However, I went directly at him and had a most interesting talk. He is a forceful fellow. Von Jagow is pleasant but not forceful. I have had a long talk with him. The Chancellor's wife died last week so I have not got in touch with him. I will write you more fully from Paris. My address there will be Hotel Ritz.

Hastily,
E. M. H.

From Edward M. House

Hotel Ritz, 15, Place Vendôme, Paris.
June 3, 1914.

DEAR PAGE:

I had a satisfactory talk with the Kaiser on Monday. I have now seen everyone worthwhile in Germany except the Chancellor. I am ready now for London. Perhaps you had better prepare the way. The Kaiser knows I am to see them, and I have arranged to keep him in touch with results—if there are any. We must work quickly after I arrive, for it may be advisable for me to return to Germany, and I am counting on sailing for home July 15th or 28th. . . . I am eager to see you and tell you what I know.

Yours,

E. M. H.

Colonel House left that night for Paris, but there the situation was a hopeless one. France was not thinking of a foreign war; it was engrossed with its domestic troubles. There had been three French ministries in two weeks; and the trial of Madame Caillaux for the murder of Gaston Calmette, editor of the Paris *Figaro*, was monopolizing all the nation's capacity for emotion. Colonel House saw that it would be a waste of energy to take up his mission at Paris—there was no government stable enough to make a discussion worth while. He therefore immediately left for London.

The political situation in Great Britain was almost as confused as that in Paris. The country was in a state approaching civil war on the question of Home Rule for Ireland; the suffragettes were threatening to dynamite the Houses of Parliament; and the eternal struggle between the Liberal and the Conservative elements was raging with unprecedented virulence. A European war was far from everybody's mind. It was this utter inability to grasp the realities of the European situation which proved the main impediment to Colonel House's work in England. He met all the important people—Mr. Asquith, Mr. Lloyd George, Sir Edward Grey, and others. With them he discussed his "pact" proposal in great detail.

Naturally, ideas of this sort were listened to sympathetically by statesmen of the stamp of Asquith, Grey, and Lloyd George. The difficulty, however, was that none of these men apprehended an immediate war. They saw no necessity of hurrying about the matter. They had the utmost confidence in Prince Lichnowsky, the German Ambassador in London, and Von Bethmann-Hollweg, the German Chancellor. Both these men were regarded by the Foreign Office as guarantees against a German attack; their continuance in their office was looked upon as an assurance that Germany entertained no immediately aggressive plans. Though the British statesmen did not say so definitely, the impression was conveyed that the mission on which Colonel House was engaged was an unnecessary one—a preparation against a danger that did not exist. Colonel House attempted to persuade Sir Edward Grey to visit the Kiel regatta, which was to take place in a few days, see the Kaiser, and discuss the plan with him. But the Government feared that such a visit would be very disturbing to France and Russia. Already Mr. Churchill's proposal for a "naval holiday" had so wrought up the French that a hurried trip to France by Mr. Asquith had been necessary to quiet them; the consternation that would have been caused in Paris by the presence of Sir Edward Grey at Kiel can only be

imagined. The fact that the British statesmen entertained so little apprehension of a German attack may
possibly be a reflection on their judgment; yet Colonel
House's visit has great historical value, for the experience
afterward convinced him that Great Britain had had no
part in bringing on the European war, and that Germany
was solely responsible. It certainly should have put the
Wilson Administration right on this all-important point,
when the great storm broke.

The most vivid recollection which the British statesmen
whom Colonel House met retain of his visit, was his consternation at the spirit that had confronted him everywhere in Germany. The four men most interested—
Sir Edward Grey, Sir William Tyrrell, Mr. Page, and
Colonel House—met at luncheon in the American Embassy a few days after President Wilson's emissary had
returned from Berlin. Colonel House could talk of little
except the preparations for war which were manifest on
every hand.

"I feel as though I had been living near a mighty
electric dynamo," Colonel House told his friends. "The
whole of Germany is charged with electricity. Everybody's nerves are tense. It needs only a spark to set the
whole thing off."

The "spark" came two weeks afterward with the assassination of the Archduke Ferdinand.

"It is all a bad business," Colonel House wrote to
Page when war broke out, "and just think how near we
came to making such a catastrophe impossible! If
England had moved a little faster and had let me go
back to Germany, the thing, perhaps, could have been
done."

To which Page at once replied:

"No, no, no—no power on earth could have prevented it. The German militarism, which is *the* crime of the last fifty years, has been working for this for twenty-five years. It is the logical result of their spirit and enterprise and doctrine. It *had* to come. But, of course, they chose the wrong time and the wrong issue. Militarism has no judgment. Don't let your conscience be worried. You did all that any mortal man could do. But nobody could have done anything effective.

"We've got to see to it that this system doesn't grow up again. That's all."

CHAPTER X

THE GRAND SMASH

IN THE latter part of July the Pages took a small house at Ockham, in Surrey, and here they spent the fateful week that preceded the outbreak of war. The Ambassador's emotions on this event are reflected in a memorandum written on Sunday, August 2nd—a day that was full of negotiations, ultimatums, and other precursors of the approaching struggle.

> Bachelor's Farm, Ockham, Surrey.
> Sunday, August 2, 1914.

The Grand Smash is come. Last night the German Ambassador at St. Petersburg handed the Russian Government a declaration of war. To-day the German Government asked the United States to take its diplomatic and consular business in Russia in hand. Herrick, our Ambassador in Paris, has already taken the German interests there.

It is reported in London to-day that the Germans have invaded Luxemburg and France.

Troops were marching through London at one o'clock this morning. Colonel Squier[1] came out to luncheon. He sees no way for England to keep out of it. There is no way. If she keep out, Germany will take Belgium and Holland, France would be betrayed, and England would be accused of forsaking her friends.

---

[1] At this time American military attaché.

People came to the Embassy all day to-day (Sunday), to learn how they can get to the United States—a rather hard question to answer. I thought several times of going in, but Greene and Squier said there was no need of it. People merely hoped we might tell them what we can't tell them.

Returned travellers from Paris report indescribable confusion—people unable to obtain beds and fighting for seats in railway carriages.

It's been a hard day here. I have a lot (not a big lot either) of routine work on my desk which I meant to do. But it has been impossible to get my mind off this Great Smash. It holds one in spite of one's self. I revolve it and revolve it—of course getting nowhere.

It will revive our shipping. In a jiffy, under stress of a general European war, the United States Senate passed a bill permitting American registry to ships built abroad. Thus a real emergency knocked the old Protectionists out, who had held on for fifty years! Correspondingly the political parties here have agreed to suspend their Home Rule quarrel till this war is ended. Artificial structures fall when a real wind blows.

The United States is the only great Power wholly out of it. The United States, most likely, therefore, will be able to play a helpful and historic part at its end. It will give President Wilson, no doubt, a great opportunity. It will probably help us politically and it will surely help us economically.

The possible consequences stagger the imagination. Germany has staked everything on her ability to win primacy. England and France (to say nothing of Russia) really ought to give her a drubbing. If they do not, this side of the world will henceforth be German. If they do flog Germany, Germany will for a long time be in discredit.

I walked out in the night a while ago. The stars are bright, the night is silent, the country quiet—as quiet as peace itself. Millions of men are in camp and on warships. Will they all have to fight and many of them die—to untangle this network of treaties and alliances and to blow off huge debts with gunpowder so that the world may start again?

A hurried picture of the events of the next seven days is given in the following letter to the President:

To the President

London, Sunday, August 9, 1914.

DEAR MR. PRESIDENT:

God save us! What a week it has been! Last Sunday I was down here at the cottage I have taken for the summer—an hour out of London—uneasy because of the apparent danger and of what Sir Edward Grey had told me. During the day people began to go to the Embassy, but not in great numbers—merely to ask what they should do in case of war. The Secretary whom I had left in charge on Sunday telephoned me every few hours and laughingly told funny experiences with nervous women who came in and asked absurd questious. Of course, we all knew the grave danger that war might come but nobody could by the wildest imagination guess at what awaited us. On Monday I was at the Embassy earlier than I think I had ever been there before and every member of the staff was already on duty. Before breakfast time the place was filled—packed like sardines. This was two days before war was declared. There was no chance to talk to individuals, such was the jam. I got on a chair and explained that I had already telegraphed to Washington—on Saturday—suggesting the sending of money and ships, and asking them to be patient. I made a speech to them several times during the day, and kept the Secretaries doing so at intervals. More than 2,000 Americans crowded into those offices (which are not large) that day. We were kept there till two o'clock in the morning. The Embassy has not been closed since.

Mr. Kent of the Bankers Trust Company in New York volunteered to form an American Citizens' Relief Committee. He and other men of experience and influence organized themselves at the Savoy Hotel. The hotel gave the use of nearly a whole floor. They organized themselves quickly and admirably and got information about steamships and currency, etc. We began to send callers at the Embassy to this Committee for such information. The banks were all closed for four days. These men got money enough—put it up themselves and used their English banking friends for help—to relieve all cases of actual want of cash that came to them. Tuesday the crowd at the Embassy was still great but smaller. The big space at the Savoy Hotel gave them room to talk to one another and to get relief for immediate needs. By that time I had accepted the volunteer services of five or six men to help us explain to the people—and they have all worked manfully day and night. We now have an orderly organization at four places: The Embassy, the Consul-General's Office, the Savoy, and the American Society in London, and everything is going well. Those two first days, there was, of course, great confusion. Crazy men and weeping women were imploring and cursing and demanding—God knows it was bedlam

turned loose. I have been called a man of the greatest
genius for an emergency by some, by others a damned
fool, by others every epithet between these extremes.
Men shook English banknotes in my face and demanded
United States money and swore our Government and its
agents ought all to be shot. Women expected me to
hand them steamship tickets home. When some found
out that they could not get tickets on the transports
(which they assumed would sail the next day) they accused me of favouritism. These absurd experiences will
give you a hint of the panic. But now it has worked out
all right, thanks to the Savoy Committee and other
helpers.

Meantime, of course, our telegrams and mail increased
almost as much as our callers. I have filled the place
with stenographers, I have got the Savoy people to ar swer
certain classes of letters, and we have caught up. My
own time and the time of two of the secretaries has been
almost wholly taken with governmental problems; hundreds of questions have come in from every quarter that
were never asked before. But even with them we have
now practically caught up—it has been a wonderful week!

Then the Austrian Ambassador came to give up his Embassy—to have me take over his business. Every detail was
arranged. The next morning I called on him to assume
charge and to say good-bye, when he told me that he was
not yet going! That was a stroke of genius by Sir Edward
Grey, who informed him that Austria had not given
England cause for war. That *may* work out, or it may
not. Pray Heaven it may! Poor Mensdorff, the Austrian Ambassador, does not know where he is. He is
practically shut up in his guarded Embassy, weeping and
waiting the decree of fate.

Then came the declaration of war, most dramatically.

Tuesday night, five minutes after the ultimatum had expired, the Admiralty telegraphed to the fleet "Go." In a few minutes the answer came back "Off." Soldiers began to march through the city going to the railway stations. An indescribable crowd so blocked the streets about the Admiralty, the War Office, and the Foreign Office, that at one o'clock in the morning I had to drive in my car by other streets to get home.

The next day the German Embassy was turned over to me. I went to see the German Ambassador at three o'clock in the afternoon. He came down in his pajamas, a crazy man. I feared he might literally go mad. He is of the anti-war party and he had done his best and utterly failed. This interview was one of the most pathetic experiences of my life. The poor man had not slept for several nights. Then came the crowds of frightened Germans, afraid that they would be arrested. They besieged the German Embassy and our Embassy. I put one of our naval officers in the German Embassy, put the United States seal on the door to protect it, and we began business there, too. Our naval officer has moved in—sleeps there. He has an assistant, a stenographer, a messenger: and I gave him the German automobile and chauffeur and two English servants that were left there. He has the job well in hand now, under my and Laughlin's supervision. But this has brought still another new lot of diplomatic and governmental problems—a lot of them. Three enormous German banks in London have, of course, been closed. Their managers pray for my aid. Howling women come and say their innocent German husbands have been arrested as spies. English, Germans, Americans—everybody has daughters and wives and invalid grandmothers alone in Germany. In God's name, they ask, what can I do for them? Here come stacks of letters sent under the impression that I can send them to Germany. But the German business is already well in hand and I think that that will take little of my own time and will give little trouble. I shall send a report about it in detail to the Department the very first day I can find time to write it. In spite of the effort of the English Government to remain at peace with Austria, I fear I shall yet have the Austrian Embassy too. But I can attend to it.

Now, however, comes the financial job of wisely using the $300,000 which I shall have to-morrow. I am using Mr. Chandler Anderson as counsel, of course. I have appointed a Committee—Skinner, the Consul-General, Lieut.-Commander McCrary of our Navy, Kent of the Bankers Trust Company, New York, and one other man yet to be chosen—to advise, after investigation, about every proposed expenditure. Anderson has been at work all day to-day drawing up proper forms, etc., to fit the Department's very excellent instructions. I have the feeling that more of that money may be wisely spent in helping to get people off the continent (except in France, where they seem admirably to be managing it, under Herrick) than is immediately needed in England. All this merely to show you the diversity and multiplicity of the job.

I am having a card catalogue, each containing a sort of who's who, of all Americans in Europe of whom we hear. This will be ready by the time the *Tennessee*[1] comes. Fifty or more stranded Americans—men and women—are doing this work free.

I have a member of Congress[2] in the general reception

---

[1]The American Government, on the outbreak of war, sent the U. S. S. *Tennessee* to Europe, with large supplies of gold for the relief of stranded Americans.

[2]The late Augustus P. Gardner, of Massachusetts.

room of the Embassy answering people's questions—three other volunteers as well.

We had a world of confusion for two or three days. But all this work is now well organized and it can be continued without confusion or cross purposes. I meet committees and lay plans and read and write telegrams from the time I wake till I go to bed. But, since it is now all in order, it is easy. Of course I am running up the expenses of the Embassy—there is no help for that; but the bill will be really exceedingly small because of the volunteer work—for awhile. I have not and shall not consider the expense of whatever it seems absolutely necessary to do—of other things I shall always consider the expense most critically. Everybody is working with everybody else in the finest possible spirit. I have made out a sort of military order to the Embassy staff, detailing one man with clerks for each night and forbidding the others to stay there till midnight. None of us slept more than a few hours last week. It was not the work that kept them after the first night or two, but the sheer excitement of this awful cataclysm. All London has been awake for a week. Soldiers are marching day and night; immense throngs block the streets about the government offices. But they are all very orderly. Every day Germans are arrested on suspicion; and several of them have committed suicide. Yesterday one poor American woman yielded to the excitement and cut her throat. I find it hard to get about much. People stop me on the street, follow me to luncheon, grab me as I come out of any committee meeting—to know my opinion of this or that—how can they get home? Will such-and-such a boat fly the American flag? Why did I take the German Embassy? I have to fight my way about and rush to an automobile. I have had to buy me a second one to keep

No. 6 Grosvenor Square, the American Embassy under Mr. Page

Irwin Laughlin, Secretary of the American Embassy at London,
1912–1917, Counsellor 1916–1919

up the racket. Buy?—no—only bargain for it, for I have not any money. But everybody is considerate, and that makes no matter for the moment. This little cottage in an out-of-the-way place, twenty-five miles from London, where I am trying to write and sleep, has been found by people to-day, who come in automobiles to know how they may reach their sick kinspeople in Germany. I have not had a bath for three days: as soon as I got in the tub, the telephone rang an "urgent" call!

Upon my word, if one could forget the awful tragedy, all this experience would be worth a lifetime of common-place. One surprise follows another so rapidly that one loses all sense of time: it seems an age since last Sunday.

I shall never forget Sir Edward Grey's telling me of the ultimatum—while he wept; nor the poor German Ambas-sador who has lost in his high game—almost a demented man; nor the King as he declaimed at me for half-an-hour and threw up his hands and said, "My God, Mr. Page, what else could we do?" Nor the Austrian Ambassador's wringing his hands and weeping and crying out, "My dear Colleague, my dear Colleague."

Along with all this tragedy come two reverend Ameri-can peace delegates who got out of Germany by the skin of their teeth and complain that they lost all the clothes they had except what they had on. "Don't complain," said I, "but thank God you saved your skins." Everybody has forgotten what war means— forgotten that folks get hurt. But they are coming around to it now. A United States Senator telegraphs me: "Send my wife and daughter home on the first ship." Ladies and gentlemen filled the steerage of that ship—not a bunk left; and his wife and daughter are found three days later sitting in a swell hotel waiting for me to bring them stateroom tickets on a silver tray! One of my young fellows in the Embassy rushes into my office saying that a man from Boston, with letters of introduction from Senators and Governors and Secretaries, et al., was demanding tickets of admission to a picture gallery, and a secretary to escort him there.

"What shall I do with him?"

"Put his proposal to a vote of the 200 Americans in the room and see them draw and quarter him."

I have not yet heard what happened. A woman writes me four pages to prove how dearly she loves my sister and invites me to her hotel—five miles away—"please to tell her about the sailing of the steamships." Six American preachers pass a resolution unanimously "urging our Ambassador to telegraph our beloved, peace-loving President to stop this awful war"; and they come with simple solemnity to present their resolution. Lord save us, what a world!

And this awful tragedy moves on to—what? We do not know what is really happening, so strict is the censorship. But it seems inevitable to me that Germany will be beaten, that the horrid period of alliances and armaments will not come again, that England will gain even more of the earth's surface, that Russia may next play the menace; that all Europe (as much as survives) will be bankrupt; that relatively we shall be immensely stronger financially and politically—there must surely come many great changes—very many, yet undreamed of. Be ready; for you will be called on to compose this huge quarrel. I thank Heaven for many things—first, the Atlantic Ocean; second, that you refrained from war in Mexico; third, that we kept our treaty—the canal tolls victory, I mean. Now, when all this half of the world will suffer the unspeakable brutalization of war, we shall preserve our moral strength, our political powers, and our ideals.

God save us!

W. H. P.

Vivid as is the above letter, it lacks several impressive details. Probably the one event that afterward stood out most conspicuously in Page's mind was his interview with Sir Edward Grey, the Foreign Secretary. Sir Edward asked the American Ambassador to call Tuesday afternoon; his purpose was to inform him that Great Britain had sent an ultimatum to Germany. By this time Page and the Foreign Secretary had established not only cordial official relations but a warm friendship. The two men had many things in common; they had the same general outlook on world affairs, the same ideas of justice and fair dealing, the same belief that other motives than greed and aggrandizement should control the attitude of one nation to another. The political tendencies of both men were idealistic; both placed character above everything else as the first requisite of a statesman; both hated war, and looked forward to the time when more rational methods of conducting international relations would prevail. Moreover, their purely personal qualities had drawn Sir Edward and Page closely together. A common love of nature and of out-of-door life had made them akin; both loved trees, birds, flowers, and hedgerows; the same intellectual diversions and similar tastes in reading had strengthened the tie. "I could never mention a book I liked that Mr. Page had not read and liked too," Sir Edward Grey once remarked to the present writer, and the enthusiasm that both men felt for Wordsworth's poetry in itself formed a strong bond of union. The part that the American Ambassador had played in the repeal of the Panama discrimination had also made a great impression upon this British statesman—a man to whom honour means more in international dealings than any other consideration. "Mr. Page is one of the finest illustrations I have ever known," Grey once said, "of the value of character in a public man." In their intercourse for the past year the two men had grown accustomed to disregard all pretense of diplomatic technique; their discussions had been straightforward man-to-man talks; there had been nothing suggestive of pose or finesse, and no attempts at cleverness—merely an effort to get to the bottom of things and to discover a common meeting ground. The Ambassador, moreover, represented a nation for which the Foreign Secretary had always entertained the highest respect and even affection, and he and Page could find no happier common meeting-ground than an effort to bring about the closest coöperation between the two countries. Sir Edward, far-seeing statesman that he was, had already appreciated, even amid the exciting and engrossing experiences through which he was then passing, the critical and almost determining part which the United States was destined to play in the war, and he had now sent for the American Ambassador because he believed that the President was entitled to a complete explanation of the momentous decision which Great Britain had just made.

The meeting took place at three o'clock on Tuesday afternoon, August 4th—a fateful date in modern history. The time represented the interval which elapsed between the transmission of the British ultimatum to Germany and the hour set for the German reply. The place was that same historic room in the Foreign Office where so many interviews had already taken place and where so many were to take place in the next four years. As

Page came in, Sir Edward, a tall and worn and rather pallid figure, was standing against the mantelpiece; he greeted the Ambassador with a grave handshake and the two men sat down. Overwrought the Foreign Secretary may have been, after the racking week which had just passed, but there was nothing flurried or excited in his manner; his whole bearing was calm and dignified, his speech was quiet and restrained, he uttered not one bitter word against Germany, but his measured accents had a sureness, a conviction of the justice of his course, that went home in almost deadly fashion. He sat in a characteristic pose, his elbows resting on the sides of his chair, his hands folded and placed beneath his chin, the whole body leaning forward eagerly and his eyes searching those of his American friend. The British Foreign Secretary was a handsome and an inspiring figure. He was a man of large, but of well knit, robust, and slender frame, wiry and even athletic; he had a large head, surmounted with dark brown hair, slightly touched with gray; a finely cut, somewhat rugged and bronzed face, suggestive of that out-of-door life in which he had always found his greatest pleasure; light blue eyes that shone with straightforwardness and that on this occasion were somewhat pensive with anxiety; thin, ascetic lips that could smile in the most confidential manner or close tightly with grimness and fixed purpose. He was a man who was at the same time shy and determined, elusive and definite, but if there was one note in his bearing that predominated all others, it was a solemn and quiet sincerity. He seemed utterly without guile and magnificently simple.

Sir Edward at once referred to the German invasion of Belgium.

"The neutrality of Belgium," he said, and there was

the touch of finality in his voice, "is assured by treaty. Germany is a signatory power to that treaty. It is upon such solemn compacts as this that civilization rests. If we give them up, or permit them to be violated, what becomes of civilization? Ordered society differs from mere force only by such solemn agreements or compacts. But Germany has violated the neutrality of Belgium. That means bad faith. It means also the end of Belgium's independence. And it will not end with Belgium. Next will come Holland, and, after Holland, Denmark. This very morning the Swedish Minister informed me that Germany had made overtures to Sweden to come in on Germany's side. The whole plan is thus clear. This one great military power means to annex Belgium, Holland, and the Scandinavian states and to subjugate France."

Sir Edward energetically rose; he again stood near the mantelpiece, his figure straightened, his eyes were fairly flashing—it was a picture, Page once told me, that was afterward indelibly fixed in his mind.

"England would be forever contemptible," Sir Edward said, "if it should sit by and see this treaty violated. Its position would be gone if Germany were thus permitted to dominate Europe. I have therefore asked you to come to tell you that this morning we sent an ultimatum to Germany. We have told Germany that, if this assault on Belgium's neutrality is not reversed, England will declare war."

"Do you expect Germany to accept it?" asked the Ambassador.

Sir Edward shook his head.

"No. Of course everybody knows that there will be war."

There was a moment's pause and then the Foreign Secretary spoke again:

"Yet we must remember that there are two Germanys. There is the Germany of men like ourselves—of men like Lichnowsky and Jagow. Then there is the Germany of men of the war party. The war party has got the upper hand."

At this point Sir Edward's eyes filled with tears.

"Thus the efforts of a lifetime go for nothing. I feel like a man who has wasted his life."

"This scene was most affecting," Page said afterward. "Sir Edward not only realized what the whole thing meant, but he showed that he realized the awful responsibility for it."

Sir Edward then asked the Ambassador to explain the situation to President Wilson; he expressed the hope that the United States would take an attitude of neutrality and that Great Britain might look for "the courtesies of neutrality" from this country. Page tried to tell him of the sincere pain that such a war would cause the President and the American people.

"I came away," the Ambassador afterward said, "with a sort of stunned sense of the impending ruin of half the world."[1]

The significant fact in this interview is that the British Foreign Secretary justified the attitude of his country exclusively on the ground of the violation of a treaty. This is something that is not yet completely understood in the United States. The participation of Great Britain in this great continental struggle is usually regarded as having been inevitable, irrespective of the German invasion of Belgium; yet the fact is that, had Germany not invaded Belgium, Great Britain would not have declared war, at least at this critical time. Sir Edward

[1]The materials on which this account is based are a memorandum of the interview made by Sir Edward Grey, now in the archives of the British Foreign Office, a similar memorandum made by Page, and a detailed description given verbally by Page to the writer.

came to Page after a week's experience with a wavering cabinet. Upon the general question of Britain's participation in a European war the Asquith Ministry had been by no means unanimous. Probably Mr. Asquith himself and Mr. Lloyd George would have voted against taking such a step. It is quite unlikely that the cabinet could have carried a majority of the House of Commons on this issue. But the violation of the Belgian treaty changed the situation in a twinkling. The House of Commons at once took its stand in favour of intervention. All members of the cabinet, excepting John Morley and John Burns, who resigned, immediately aligned themselves on the side of war. In the minds of British statesmen the violation of this treaty gave Britain no choice. Germany thus forced Great Britain into the war, just as, two and a half years afterward, the Prussian war lords compelled the United States to take up arms. Sir Edward Grey's interview with the American Ambassador thus had great historic importance, for it makes this point clear. The two men had recently had many discussions on another subject in which the violation of a treaty was the great consideration—that of Panama tolls—and there was a certain appropriateness in this explanation of the British Foreign Secretary that precisely the same point had determined Great Britain's participation in the greatest struggle that has ever devastated Europe.

Inevitably the question of American mediation had come to the surface in this trying time. Several days before Page's interview with Grey, the American Ambassador, acting in response to a cablegram from Washington, had asked if the good offices of the United States could be used in any way. "Sir Edward is very appreciative of our mood and willingness," Page wrote in reference to this visit. "But they don't want peace on the continent—the ruling classes do not. But they will want it presently and then our opportunity will come. Ours is the only great government in the world that is not in some way entangled. Of course I'll keep in daily touch with Sir Edward and with everybody who can and will keep me informed."

This was written about July 27th; at that time Austria had sent her ultimatum to Serbia but there was no certainty that Europe would become involved in war. A demand for American mediation soon became widespread in the United States; the Senate passed a resolution requesting the President to proffer his good offices to that end. On this subject the following communications were exchanged between President Wilson and his chief adviser, then sojourning at his summer home in Massachusetts. Like Mr. Tumulty, the President's Secretary, Colonel House usually addressed the President in terms reminiscent of the days when Mr. Wilson was Governor of New Jersey. Especially interesting also are Colonel House's references to his own trip to Berlin and the joint efforts made by the President and himself in the preceding June to forestall the war which had now broken out.

Edward M. House to the President

Pride's Crossing (Mass.),
August 3, 1914. [Monday.]

THE PRESIDENT,
  The White House, Washington, D. C.
DEAR GOVERNOR:
  Our people are deeply shocked at the enormity of this general European war, and I see here and there regret that you did not use your good offices in behalf of peace.

If this grows into criticism so as to become noticeable I believe everyone would be pleased and proud that you

318 THE LIFE AND LETTERS OF WALTER H. PAGE

had anticipated this world-wide horror and had done all that was humanly possible to avert it.

The more terrible the war becomes, the greater credit it will be that you saw the trend of events long before it was seen by other statesmen of the world.

Your very faithful,

E. M. HOUSE.

P. S.   The question might be asked why negotiations were only with Germany and England and not with France and Russia.   This, of course, was because it was thought that Germany would act for the Triple Alliance and England for the Triple Entente.[1]

The President to Edward M. House

The White House,
Washington, D. C.
August 4th, 1914.   [Tuesday.]

EDWARD M. HOUSE,
Pride's Crossing, Mass.

Letter of third received.   Do you think I could and should act now and if so how?

WOODROW WILSON.

Edward M. House to the President

[Telegram]

Pride's Crossing, Mass.
August 5th, 1914.   [Wednesday.]

THE PRESIDENT,
The White House, Washington, D. C.

Olney[2] and I agree that in response to the Senate reso-

[1]Colonel House, of course, is again referring to his experience in Berlin and London, described in the preceding chapter.

[2]Richard Olney, Secretary of State in the Cabinet of President Cleveland, who was a neighbour of Colonel House at his summer home, and with whom the latter apparently consulted.

lution it would be unwise to tender your good offices at this time. We believe it would lessen your influence when the proper moment arrives. He thinks it advisable that you make a direct or indirect statement to the effect that you have done what was humanly possible to compose the situation before this crisis had been reached. He thinks this would satisfy the Senate and the public in view of your disinclination to act now upon the Senate resolution. The story might be told to the correspondents at Washington and they might use the expression "we have it from high authority."

He agrees to my suggestion that nothing further should be done now than to instruct our different ambassadors to inform the respective governments to whom they are accredited, that you stand ready to tender your good offices whenever such an offer is desired.

Olney agrees with me that the shipping bill[1] is full of lurking dangers.

E. M. HOUSE.

For some reason, however, the suggested statement was not made. The fact that Colonel House had visited London, Paris, and Berlin six weeks before the outbreak of war, in an effort to bring about a plan for disarmament, was not permitted to reach the public ear. Probably the real reason why this fact was concealed was that its publication at that time would have reflected so seriously upon Germany that it would have been regarded as "un-neutral." Colonel House, as already described, had found Germany in a most belligerent frame of mind, its army "ready," to use the Kaiser's own word, for an immediate spring at France; on the other hand he had

[1]This is the bill passed soon after the outbreak of war admitting foreign built ships to American registry. Subsequent events showed that it was "full of lurking dangers."

found Great Britain in a most pacific frame of mind, entirely unsuspicious of Germany, and confident that the European situation was daily improving. It is interesting now to speculate on the public sensation that would have been caused had Colonel House's account of his visit to Berlin been published at that exciting time.

Page's telegrams and letters show that any suggestion at mediation would have been a waste of effort. The President seriously forebore, but the desire to mediate was constantly in his mind for the next few months, and he now interested himself in laying the foundations of future action. Page was instructed to ask for an audience with King George and to present the following document:

From the President of the United States to His Majesty the King

SIR:

As official head of one of the Powers signatory to the Hague Convention, I feel it to be my privilege and my duty under Article 3 of that Convention to say to your Majesty, in a spirit of most earnest friendship, that I should welcome an opportunity to act in the interest of European peace either now or at any time that might be thought more suitable as an occasion, to serve your Majesty and all concerned in a way that would afford me lasting cause for gratitude and happiness.

WOODROW WILSON.

This, of course, was not mediation, but a mere expression of the President's willingness to mediate at any time that such a tender from him, in the opinion of the warring Powers, would serve the cause of peace. Identically the same message was sent to the American Ambassadors at the capitals of all the belligerent Powers for presentation to the heads of state. Page's letter of August 9th, printed above, refers to the earnestness and cordiality with which King George received him and to the freedom with which His Majesty discussed the situation.

In this exciting week Page was thrown into intimate contact with the two most pathetic figures in the diplomatic circle of London—the Austrian and the German Ambassadors. To both of these men the war was more than a great personal sorrow: it was a tragedy. Mensdorff, the Austrian Ambassador, had long enjoyed an intimacy with the British royal family. Indeed he was a distant relative of King George, for he was a member of the family of Saxe-Coburg-Gotha, a fact which was emphasized by his physical resemblance to Prince Albert, the consort of Queen Victoria. Mensdorff was not a robust man, physically or mentally, and he showed his consternation at the impending war in most unrestrained and even unmanly fashion. As his government directed him to turn the Austrian Embassy over to the American Ambassador, it was necessary for Page to call and arrange the details. The interview, as Page's letter indicates, was little less than a paroxysm of grief on the Austrian's part. He denounced Germany and the Kaiser; he paraded up and down the room wringing his hands; he could be pacified only by suggestions from the American that perhaps something might happen to keep Austria out of the war. The whole atmosphere of the Austrian Embassy radiated this same feeling. "Austria has no quarrel with England," remarked one of Mensdorff's assistants to one of the ladies of the American Embassy; and this sentiment was the general one in Austrian diplomatic circles. The disinclination of both Great Britain and

Austria to war was so great that, as Page relates, for several days there was no official declaration.

Even more tragical than the fate of the Austrian Ambassador was that of his colleague, the representative of the German Emperor. It was more tragical because Prince Lichnowsky represented the power that was primarily responsible, and because he had himself been an unwilling tool in bringing on the cataclysm. It was more profound because Lichnowsky was a man of deeper feeling and greater moral purpose than his Austrian colleague, and because for two years he had been devoting his strongest energies to preventing the very calamity which had now become a fact. As the war went on Lichnowsky gradually emerged as one of its finest figures; the pamphlet which he wrote, at a time when Germany's military fortunes were still high, boldly placing the responsibility upon his own country and his own Kaiser, was one of the bravest acts which history records. Through all his brief Ambassadorship Lichnowsky had shown these same friendly traits. The mere fact that he had been selected as Ambassador at this time was little less than a personal calamity. His appointment gives a fair measure of the depths of duplicity to which the Prussian system could descend. For more than fourteen years Lichnowsky had led the quiet life of a Polish country gentleman; he had never enjoyed the favour of the Kaiser; in his own mind and in that of his friends his career had long since been finished; yet from this retirement he had been suddenly called upon to represent the Fatherland at the greatest of European capitals. The motive for this elevation, which was unfathomable then, is evident enough now. Prince Lichnowsky was known to be an Anglophile; everything English—English literature, English country life, English public men—had for him an irresistible charm; and his greatest ambition as a diplomat had been to maintain the most cordial relations between his own country and Great Britain. This was precisely the type of Ambassador that fitted into the Imperial purpose at that crisis. Germany was preparing energetically but quietly for war; it was highly essential that its most formidable potential foe, Great Britain, should be deceived as to the Imperial plans and lulled into a sense of security. The diabolical character of Prince Lichnowsky's selection for this purpose was that, though his mission was one of deception, he was not himself a party to it and did not realize until it was too late that he had been used merely as a tool. Prince Lichnowsky was not called upon to assume a mask; all that was necessary was that he should simply be himself. And he acquitted himself with great success. He soon became a favourite in London society; the Foreign Office found him always ready to coöperate in any plan that tended to improve relations between the two countries. It will be remembered that, when Colonel House returned to London from his interview with the Kaiser in June, 1914, he found British statesmen incredulous about any trouble with Germany. This attitude was the consequence of Lichnowsky's work. The fact is that relations between the two countries had not been so harmonious in twenty years. All causes of possible friction had been adjusted. The treaty regulating the future of the Bagdad Railroad, the only problem that clouded the future, had been initialled by both the British and the German Foreign Offices and was about to be signed at the moment when the ultimatums began to fly through the air. Prince Lichnowsky was thus entitled to look upon his ambassadorship as one of the most successful in modern history, for it had removed all possible cause of war.

And then suddenly came the stunning blow. For several days Lichnowsky's behaviour was that of an irresponsible person. Those who came into contact with him found his mind wandering and incoherent. Page describes the German Ambassador as coming down and receiving him in his pajamas; he was not the only one who had that experience, for members of the British Foreign Office transacted business with this most punctilious of diplomats in a similar condition of personal disarray. And the dishabille extended to his mental operations as well.

But Lichnowsky's and Mensdorff's behaviour merely portrayed the general atmosphere that prevailed in London during that week. This atmosphere was simply hysterical. Among all the intimate participants, however, there was one man who kept his poise and who saw things clearly. That was the American Ambassador. It was certainly a strange trick which fortune had played upon Page. He had come to London with no experience in diplomacy. Though the possibility of such an outbreak as this war had been in every man's consciousness for a generation, it had always been as something certain yet remote; most men thought of it as most men think of death—as a fatality which is inevitable, but which is so distant that it never becomes a reality. Thus Page, when he arrived in London, did not have the faintest idea of the experience that awaited him. Most people would have thought that his quiet and studious and unworldly life had hardly prepared him to become the representative of the most powerful neutral power at the world's capital during the greatest crisis of modern history. To what an extent that impression was justified the happenings of the next four years will disclose; it is enough to point out in this place that in one respect at least the war found the American Ambassador well prepared. From the instant hostilities began his mind seized the significance of it all. "Mr. Page had one fine qualification for his post," a great British statesman once remarked to the present writer. "From the beginning he saw that there was a right and a wrong to the matter. He did not believe that Great Britain and Germany were equally to blame. He believed that Great Britain was right and that Germany was wrong. I regard it as one of the greatest blessings of modern times that the United States had an ambassador in London in August, 1914, who had grasped this overwhelming fact. It seems almost like a dispensation of Providence."

It is important to insist on this point now, for it explains Page's entire course as Ambassador. The confidential telegram which Page sent directly to President Wilson in early September, 1914, furnishes the standpoint from which his career as war Ambassador can be understood:

Confidential to the President

September 11, 3 A. M.
No. 645.

Accounts of atrocities are so inevitably a part of every war that for some time I did not believe the unbelievable reports that were sent from Europe, and there are many that I find incredible even now. But American and other neutral observers who have seen these things in France and especially in Belgium now convince me that the Germans have perpetrated some of the most barbarous deeds in history. Apparently credible persons relate such things without end.

Those who have violated the Belgian treaty, those who have sown torpedoes in the open sea, those who have dropped bombs on Antwerp and Paris indiscriminately with the idea of killing whom they may strike, have taken to heart Bernhardi's doctrine that war is a glorious occupation.   Can any one longer disbelieve the completely barbarous behaviour of the Prussians?

PAGE.

CHAPTER XI

THE months following the outbreak of the war were busy ones for the American Embassy in London. The Embassies of all the great Powers with which Great Britain was contending were handed over to Page, and the citizens of these countries—Germany, Austria, Turkey—who found themselves stranded in England, were practically made his wards. It is a constant astonishment to his biographer that, during all the labour and distractions of this period, Page should have found time to write long letters describing the disturbing scene. There are scores of them, all penned in the beautiful copper-plate handwriting that shows no signs of excitement or weariness, but is in itself an evidence of mental poise and of the sure grip which Page had upon the evolving drama. From the many sent in these autumn and early winter months the following selections are made:

To Edward M. House

September 22nd, 1914.

MY DEAR HOUSE:

When the day of settlement comes, the settlement must make sure that the day of militarism is done and can come no more. If sheer brute force is to rule the world, it will not be worth living in. If German bureaucratic brute force could conquer Europe, presently it would try to conquer the United States; and we should all go back to the era of war as man's chief industry and back to the domination of kings by divine right. It seems to me, therefore, that the Hohenzollern idea must perish—be utterly strangled in the making of peace.

Just how to do this, it is not yet easy to say. If the German defeat be emphatic enough and dramatic enough, the question may answer itself—how's the best way to be rid of the danger of the recurrence of a military bureaucracy? But in any event, this thing must be killed forever—somehow. I think that a firm insistence on this is the main task that mediation will bring. The rest will be corollaries of this.

The danger, of course, as all the world is beginning to fear, is that the Kaiser, after a local victory—especially if he should yet take Paris—will propose peace, saying that he dreads the very sight of blood—propose peace in time, as he will hope, to save his throne, his dynasty, his system. That will be a dangerous day. The horror of war will have a tendency to make many persons in the countries of the Allies accept it. All the peace folk in the world will say "Accept it!" But if he and his throne and his dynasty and his system be saved, in twenty-five years the whole job must be done over again.

We are settling down to a routine of double work and to an oppression of gloom. Dead men, dead men, maimed men, the dull gray dread of what may happen next, the impossibility of changing the subject, the monotony of gloom, the consequent dimness of ideals, the overworking of the emotions and the heavy bondage of thought—the days go swiftly: that's one blessing.

The diplomatic work proper brings fewer difficulties than you would guess. New subjects and new duties come with great rapidity, but they soon fall into formulas —at least into classes. We shall have no sharp crises nor grave difficulties so long as our Government and this Government keep their more than friendly relations.   I see Sir Edward Grey almost every day.   We talk of many things—all phases of one vast wreck; and all the clear-cut points that come up I report by telegraph.   To-day the talk was of American cargoes in British ships and the machinery they have set up here for fair settlement. Then of Americans applying for enlistment in Canadian regiments.   "If sheer brute force conquer Europe," said he, "the United States will be the only country where life will be worth living; and in time you will have to fight against it, too, if it conquer Europe."   He spoke of the letter he had just received from the President, and he asked me many sympathetic questions about you also and about your health.   I ventured to express some solicitude for him.

"How much do you get out now?"

"Only for an automobile drive Sunday afternoon."

This from a man who is never happy away from nature and is at home only in the woods and along the streams. He looks worn.

I hear nothing but satisfaction with our neutrality tight-rope walk.   I think we are keeping it here, by close attention to our work and by silence.

Our volunteer and temporary aids are doing well— especially the army and navy officers.   We now occupy three work-places: (1) the over-crowded embassy; (2) a suite of offices around the corner where the ever-lengthening list of inquiries for persons is handled and where an army officer pays money to persons whose friends have deposited it for them with the Government in Washington—just now at the rate of about $15,000 a day; and (3) two great rooms at the Savoy Hotel, where the admirable relief committee (which meets all trains that bring people from the continent) gives aid to the needy and helps people to get tickets home. They have this week helped about 400 with more or less money—after full investigation.

At the Embassy a secretary remains till bed-time, which generally means till midnight; and I go back there for an hour or two every night.

The financial help we give to German and Austrian subjects (poor devils) is given, of course, at their embassies, where we have men—our men—in charge. Each of these governments accepted my offer to give our Ambassadors (Gerard and Penfield) a sum of money to help Americans if I would set aside an equal sum to help their people here. The German fund that I thus began with was $50,000; the Austrian, $25,000. All this and more will be needed before the war ends.—All this activity is kept up with scrupulous attention to the British rules and regulations. In fact, we are helping this Government much in the management of these "alien enemies," as they call them.

I am amazed at the good health we all keep with this big volume of work and the long hours. Not a man nor a woman has been ill a day. I have known something about work and the spirit of good work in other organizations of various sorts; but I never saw one work in better spirit than this. And remember, most of them are volunteers.

The soldiers here complained for weeks in private about the lethargy of the people—the slowness of men to enlist. But they seemed to me to complain with insufficient reason. For now they come by thousands. They do need more men in the field, and they may conscript them, but I doubt the necessity. But I run across such incidents as these: I met the Dowager Countess of D— yesterday —a woman of 65, as tall as I and as erect herself as a soldier, who might be taken for a woman of 40, prematurely gray. "I had five sons in the Boer War. I have three in this war. I do not know where any one of them is." Mrs. Page's maid is talking of leaving her. "My two brothers have gone to the war and perhaps I ought to help their wives and children." The Countess and the maid are of the same blood, each alike unconquerable. My chauffeur has talked all day about the naval battle in which five German ships were lately sunk.[1] He reminded me of the night two months ago when he drove Mrs. Page and me to dine with Sir John and Lady Jellicoe—Jellicoe now, you know, being in command of the British fleet.

This Kingdom has settled down to war as its one great piece of business now in hand, and it is impossible, as the busy, burdensome days pass, to pick out events or impressions that one can be sure are worth writing. For instance a soldier—a man in the War Office—told me to-day that Lord Kitchener had just told him that the war may last for several years. That, I confess, seems to me very improbable, and (what is of more importance) it is not the notion held by most men whose judgment I respect. But all the military men say it will be long. It would take several years to kill that vast horde of Germans, but it will not take so long to starve them out. Food here is practically as cheap as it was three months ago and the sea routes are all open to England and practically all closed to Germany. The ultimate result, of course, will be Germany's defeat. But the British are now going about the business of war as if they knew they would continue it indefinitely. The grim efficiency of their work even in small details was illustrated to-day by the Government's informing us that a German handy man, whom the German Ambassador left at his Embassy, with the English Govern-

[1]Evidently the battle of Heligoland Bight of August 28, 1914.

ment's consent, is a spy—that he sends verbal messages
to Germany by women who are permitted to go home, and
that they have found letters written by him sewed in some
of these women's undergarments! This man has been at
work there every day under the two very good men whom
I have put in charge there and who have never suspected
him. How on earth they found this out simply passes
my understanding. Fortunately it doesn't bring any embarrassment to us; he was not in our pay and he was left
by the German Ambassador with the British Government's
consent, to take care of the house. Again, when the German Chancellor made a statement two days ago about
the causes of the war, in a few hours Sir Edward Grey
issued a statement showing that the Chancellor had mis-
stated every important historic fact.—The other day a
commercial telegram was sent (or started) by Mr. Bryan
for some bank or trading concern in the United States,
managed by Germans, to some correspondent of theirs in
Germany. It contained the words, "Where is Harry?"
The censor here stopped it. It was brought to me with
the explanation that "Harry" is one of the most notorious
of German spies—whom they would like to catch. The
English were slow in getting into full action, but now they
never miss a trick, little or big.

The Germans have far more than their match in resources and in shrewdness and—in character. As the
bloody drama unfolds itself, the hollow pretence and essential barbarity of Prussian militarism become plainer
and plainer: there is no doubt of that. And so does the
invincibility of this race. A well-known Englishman told
me to-day that his three sons, his son-in-law, and half his
office men are in the military service, "where they belong
in a time like this." The lady who once so sharply criticized this gentleman to Mrs. Page has a son and a brother

in the army in France.   It makes you take a fresh grip on your eyelids to hear either of these talk.   In fact the strain on one's emotions, day in and day out, makes one wonder if the world is real—or is this a vast dream?   From sheer emotional exhaustion I slept almost all day last Sunday, though I had not for several days lost sleep at all.   Many persons tell me of their similar experiences.   The universe seems muffled.   There is a ghostly silence in London (so it seems); and only dim street lights are lighted at night. No experience seems normal.   A vast organization is working day and night down town receiving Belgian refugees.   They become the guests of the English.   They are assigned to people's homes, to boarding houses, to institutions.   They are taking care of them—this government and this people are.   I do not recall when one nation ever did another whole nation just such a hospitable service as this.   You can't see that work going on and remain unmoved.   An old woman who has an income of $15 a week decided that she could live on $7.50.   She buys milk with the other $7.50 and goes to meet every train at one of the big stations with a basket filled with baby bottles, and she gives milk to every hungry-looking baby she sees. Our American committeeman, Hoover, saw her in trouble the other day and asked her what was the matter.   She explained that the police would no longer admit her to the platform because she didn't belong to any relief committee. He took her to headquarters and said: "Do you see this good old lady?   She puts you and me and everybody else to shame—do you understand?"   The old lady now gets to the platform.   Hoover himself gave $5,000 for helping stranded Americans and he goes to the trains to meet them, while the war has stopped his big business and his big income.   This is a sample of the noble American end of the story.

These are the saving class of people to whom life becomes a bore unless they can help somebody. There's just such a fellow in Brussels—you may have heard of him, for his name is Whitlock. Stories of his showing himself a man come out of that closed-up city every week. To a really big man, it doesn't matter whether his post is a little post, or a big post but, if I were President, I'd give Whitlock a big post. There's another fellow somewhere in Germany—a consul—of whom I never heard till the other day. But people have taken to coming in my office —English ladies—who wish to thank "you and your great government" for the courage and courtesy of this consul.[1] Stories about him will follow. Herrick, too, in Paris, somehow causes Americans and English and even Guatemalans who come along to go out of their way to say what he has done for them. Now there is a quality in the old woman with the baby bottles, and in the consul and in Whitlock and Hoover and Herrick and this English nation which adopts the Belgians—a quality that is invincible. When folk like these come down the road, I respectfully do obeisance to them. And—it's this kind of folk that the Germans have run up against. I thank Heaven I'm of their race and blood.

The whole world is bound to be changed as a result of this war. If Germany should win, our Monroe Doctrine would at once be shot in two, and we should have to get "out of the sun." The military party is a party of conquest—absolutely. If England wins, as of course she will, it'll be a bigger and a stronger England, with no strong enemy in the world, with her Empire knit closer than ever—India, Canada, Australia, New Zealand, South Africa, Egypt; under obligations to and in alliance with

---

[1]The reference in all probability is to Mr. Charles L. Hoover, at that time American Consul at Carlsbad.

Russia! England will not need our friendship as much as she now needs it; and there may come governments here that will show they do not. In any event, you see, the world will be changed. It's changed already: witness Bernstorff[1] and Münsterberg[2] playing the part once played by Irish agitators!

All of which means that it is high time we were constructing a foreign service. First of all, Congress ought to make it possible to have half a dozen or more permanent foreign under-secretaries—men who, after service in the Department, could go out as Ministers and Ambassadors; it ought generously to reorganize the whole thing. It ought to have a competent study made of the foreign offices of other governments. Of course it ought to get room to work in. Then it ought at once to give its Ambassadors and Ministers homes and dignified treatment. We've got to play a part in the world whether we wish to or not. Think of these things.

The blindest great force in this world to-day is the Prussian War Party—blind and stupid.—Well, and the most weary man in London just at this hour is

Your humble servant,
W. H. P.

but he'll be all right in the morning.

To Arthur W. Page

[Undated][3]

DEAR ARTHUR:

. . . I recall one night when we were dining at Sir John Jellicoe's, he told me that the Admiralty never slept—that he had a telephone by his bed every night.

[1]German Ambassador in Washington.

[2]Professor of Psychology at Harvard University, whose openly expressed pro-Germanism was making him exceedingly unpopular in the United States.

[3]Evidently written in the latter part of September, 1914.

"Did it ever ring?" I asked.

"No; but it will."

You begin to see pretty clearly how English history has been made and makes itself. This afternoon Lady S—— told your mother of her three sons, one on a warship in the North Sea, another with the army in France, and a third in training to go. "How brave you all are!" said your mother, and her answer was: "They belong to their country; we can't do anything else." One of the daughters-in-law of the late Lord Salisbury came to see me to find out if I could make an inquiry about her son who was reported "missing" after the battle of Mons. She was dry-eyed, calm, self-restrained—very grateful for the effort I promised to make; but a Spartan woman would have envied her self-possession. It turned out that her son was dead.

You hear experiences like these almost every day. These are the kinds of women and the kinds of men that have made the British Empire and the English race. You needn't talk of decadence. All their great qualities are in them here and now. I believe that half the young men who came to Katharine's[1] dances last winter and who used to drop in at the house once in a while are dead in France already. They went as a matter of course. This is the reason they are going to win. Now these things impress you, as they come to you day by day.

There isn't any formal social life now—no dinners, no parties. A few friends dine with a few friends now and then very quietly. The ladies of fashion are hospital nurses and Red Cross workers, or they are collecting socks and blankets for the soldiers. One such woman told your mother to-day that she went to one of the recruiting camps every day and taught the young fellows

---

[1]Miss Katharine A. Page, the Ambassador's daughter.

what colloquial French she could. Every man, woman, and child seems to be doing something. In the ordinary daily life, we see few of them: everybody is at work somewhere.

We live in a world of mystery: nothing can surprise us. The rumour is that a servant in one of the great families sent word to the Germans where the three English cruisers[1] were that German submarines blew up the other day. Not a German in the Kingdom can earn a penny. We're giving thousands of them money at the German Embassy to keep them alive. Our Austrian Embassy runs a soup kitchen where it feeds a lot of Austrians. Your mother went around there the other day and they showed that they thought they owe their daily bread to her. One day she went to one of the big houses where the English receive and distribute the thousands of Belgians who come here, poor creatures, to be taken care of. One old woman asked your mother in French if she were a princess. The lady that was with your mother answered, "Une Grande Dame." That seemed to do as well.

This government doesn't now let anybody carry any food away. But to-day they consented on condition I'd receive the food (for the Belgians) and consign it to Whitlock. This is their way of keeping it out of German hands —have the Stars and Stripes, so to speak, to cover every bag of flour and of salt. That's only one of 1,000 queer activities that I engage in. I have a German princess's[2] jewels in our safe—$100,000 worth of them in my keeping; I have an old English nobleman's check for $40,000 to be sent to men who have been building a house for his daugh-

---

[1] The *Hogue*, the *Cressy*, and the *Aboukir* were torpedoed by a German submarine September 22, 1914. This exploit first showed the world the power of the submarine.

[2] Princess Lichnowsky, wife of the German Ambassador to Great Britain.

ter in Dresden—to be sent as soon as the German Government agrees not to arrest the lady for debt. I have sent Miss Latimer[1] over to France to bring an Austrian baby eight months old whose mother will take it to the United States and bring it up an American citizen! The mother can't go and get it for fear the French might detain her; I've got the English Government's permission for the family to go to the United States. Harold[2] is in Belgium, trying to get a group of English ladies home who went there to nurse wounded English and Belgians and whom the Germans threaten to kidnap and transport to German hospitals—every day a dozen new kinds of jobs.

London is weird and muffled and dark and, in the West End, deserted. Half the lamps are not lighted, and the upper half of the globes of the street lights are painted black—so the Zeppelin raiders may not see them. You've no idea what a strange feeling it gives one. The papers have next to no news. The 23rd day of the great battle is reported very much in the same words as the 3rd day was. Yet nobody talks of much else. The censor erases most of the matter the correspondents write. We're in a sort of dumb as well as dark world. And yet, of course, we know much more here than they know in any other European capital.

To the President

[Undated.]

DEAR MR. PRESIDENT:

When England, France, and Russia agreed the other day not to make peace separately, that cooked the Kaiser's goose. They'll wear him out. Since England thus has Frenchmen and Russians bound, the Allies are strength-

---

[1]Private Secretary to Mrs. Page.

[2]Mr. Harold Fowler, the Ambassador's Secretary.

ened at their only weak place. That done, England is now going in deliberately, methodically, patiently to do the task. Even a fortnight ago, the people of this Kingdom didn't realize all that the war means to them. But the fever is rising now. The wounded are coming back, the dead are mourned, and the agony of hearing only that such-and-such a man is missing—these are having a prodigious effect. The men I meet now say in a matter-of-fact way: "Oh, yes! we'll get 'em, of course; the only question is, how long it will take us and how many of us it will cost. But no matter, we'll get 'em."

Old ladies and gentlemen of the high, titled world now begin by driving to my house almost every morning while I am at breakfast. With many apologies for calling so soon and with the fear that they interrupt me, they ask if I can make an inquiry in Germany for "my son," or "my nephew"—"he's among the missing." They never weep; their voices do not falter; they are brave and proud and self-restrained. It seems a sort of matter-of-course to them. Sometimes when they get home, they write me polite notes thanking me for receiving them. This morning the first man was Sir Dighton Probyn of Queen Alexandra's household—so dignified and courteous that you'd hardly have guessed his errand. And at intervals they come all day. Not a tear have I seen yet. They take it as a part of the price of greatness and of empire. You guess at their grief only by their reticence. They use as few words as possible and then courteously take themselves away. It isn't an accident that these people own a fifth of the world. Utterly unwarlike, they outlast anybody else when war comes. You don't get a sense of fighting here—only of endurance and of high resolve. Fighting is a sort of incident in the struggle to keep their world from German domination. . . .

To Edward M. House

October 11, 1914.

DEAR HOUSE:

There is absolutely nothing to write. It's war, war, war all the time; no change of subject; and, if you changed with your tongue, you couldn't change in your thought; war, war, war—"for God's sake find out if my son is dead or a prisoner"; rumours—they say that two French generals were shot for not supporting French, and then they say only one; and people come who have helped take the wounded French from the field and they won't even talk, it is so horrible; and a lady says that her own son (wounded) told her that when a man raised up in the trench to fire, the stench was so awful that it made him sick for an hour; and the poor Belgians come here by the tens of thousands, and special trains bring the English wounded; and the newspapers tell little or nothing—every day's reports like the preceding days'; and yet nobody talks about anything else.

Now and then the subject of its settlement is mentioned—Belgium and Serbia, of course, to be saved and as far as possible indemnified; Russia to have the Slav-Austrian States and Constantinople; France to have Alsace-Lorraine, of course; and Poland to go to Russia; Schleswig-Holstein and the Kiel Canal no longer to be German; all the South-German States to become Austrian and none of the German States to be under Prussian rule; the Hohenzollerns to be eliminated; the German fleet, or what is left of it, to become Great Britain's; and the German colonies to be used to satisfy such of the Allies as clamour for more than they get.

Meantime this invincible race is doing this revolutionary task marvellously—volunteering; trying to buy arms in the United States (a Pittsburgh manufacturer is now here trying to close a bargain with the War Office!);[1] knitting socks and mufflers; taking in all the poor Belgians; stopping all possible expenditure; darkening London at night; doing every conceivable thing to win as if they had been waging this war always and meant to do nothing else for the rest of their lives—and not the slightest doubt about the result and apparently indifferent how long it lasts or how much it costs.

Every aspect of it gets on your nerves. I can't keep from wondering how the world will seem after it is over—Germany (that is, Prussia and its system) cut out like a cancer; England owning still more of the earth; Belgium—all the men dead; France bankrupt; Russia admitted to the society of nations; the British Empire entering on a new lease of life; no great navy but one; no great army but the Russian; nearly all governments in Europe bankrupt; Germany gone from the sea—in ten years it will be difficult to recall clearly the Europe of the last ten years. And the future of the world more than ever in our hands!

We here don't know what you think or what you know at home; we haven't yet any time to read United States newspapers, which come very, very late; nobody writes us real letters (or the censor gets 'em, perhaps!); and so the war, the war, the war is the one thing that holds our minds.

We have taken a house for the Chancery[2]—almost the size of my house in Grosvenor Square—for the same sum as rent that the landlord proposed hereafter to charge us for the old hole where we've been for twenty-nine years. For the first time Uncle Sam has a decent place

---

[1]Probably a reference to Mr. Charles M. Schwab, President of the Bethlehem Steel Company, who was in London at this time on this errand.

[2]No. 4 Grosvenor Gardens.

in London. We've five times as much room and ten times as much work. Now—just this last week or two—I get off Sundays: that's doing well. And I don't now often go back at night. So, you see, we've much to be thankful for.—Shall we insure against Zeppelins? That's what everybody's asking. I told the Spanish Ambassador yesterday that I am going to ask the German Government for instructions about insuring their Embassy here!

Write and send some news. I saw an American to-day who says he's going home to-morrow. "Cable me," said I, "if you find the continent where it used to be."

Faithfully yours,
WALTER H. PAGE.

P. S. It is strange how little we know what you know on your side and just what you think, what relative value you put on this and what on that. There's a new sort of loneliness sprung up because of the universal absorption in the war.

And I hear all sorts of contradictory rumours about the effect of the German crusade in the United States. Oh well, the world has got to choose whether it will have English or German domination in Europe; that's the single big question at issue. For my part I'll risk the English and then make a fresh start ourselves to outstrip them in the spread of well-being; in the elevation of mankind of all classes; in the broadening of democracy and democratic rule (which is the sheet-anchor of all men's hopes just as bureaucracy and militarism are the destruction of all men's hopes); in the spread of humane feeling and action; in the growth of human kindness; in the tender treatment of women and children and the old; in literature, in art; in the abatement of suffering; in great changes in economic conditions which discourage poverty; and in science which gives us new leases on life and new tools and wider visions.   These are *our* world tasks, with England as our friendly rival and helper.   God bless us.

W. H. P.

To Arthur W. Page

London, November 6, 1914.

DEAR ARTHUR:

Those excellent photographs, those excellent apples, those excellent cigars—thanks.   I'm thinking of sending Kitty[1] over again.   They all spell and smell and taste of home—of the U. S. A.   Even the messenger herself seems Unitedstatesy, and that's a good quality, I assure you.   She's told us less news than you'd think she might for so long a journey and so long a visit; but that's the way with us all.   And, I dare say, if it were all put together it would make a pretty big news-budget.   And luckily for us (I often think we are among the luckiest families in the world) all she says is quite cheerful.   It's a wonderful report she makes of County Line[2]—the country, the place, the house, and its inhabitants.   Maybe, praise God, I'll see it myself some day—it and them.

But—but—I don't know when and can't guess out of this vast fog of war and doom.   The worst of it is nobody knows just what is happening.   I have, for an example, known for a week of the blowing up of a British dreadnaught[3]—thousands of people know it privately—and yet it isn't published!   Such secrecy makes you fear there may be other and even worse secrets.   But I don't really

---

[1]Miss Katharine A. Page had just returned from a visit to the United States.

[2]Mr. Arthur W. Page's country home on Long Island.

[3]Evidently the *Audacious*, sunk by mine off the North of Ireland, October 27, 1914.

believe there are. What I am trying to say is, so far as news (and many other things) go, we are under a military rule.

It's beginning to wear on us badly. It presses down, presses down, presses down in an indescribable way. All the people you see have lost sons or brothers; mourning becomes visible over a wider area all the time; people talk of nothing else; all the books are about the war; ordinary social life is suspended—people are visibly growing older. And there are some aspects of it that are incomprehensible. For instance, a group of American and English military men and correspondents were talking with me yesterday—men who have been on both sides—in Germany and Belgium and in France—and they say that the Germans in France alone have had 750,000 men killed. The Allies have lost 400,000 to 500,000. This in France only. Take the other fighting lines and there must already be a total of 2,000,000 killed. Nothing like that has ever happened before in the history of the world. A flood or a fire or a wreck which has killed 500 has often shocked all mankind. Yet we know of this enormous slaughter and (in a way) are not greatly moved. I don't know of a better measure of the brutalizing effect of war—it's bringing us to take a new and more inhuman standard to measure events by.

As for any political or economic reckoning—that's beyond any man's ability yet. I see strings of incomprehensible figures that some economist or other now and then puts in the papers, summing up the loss in pounds sterling. But that means nothing because we have no proper measure of it. If a man lose $10 or $10,000 we can grasp that. But when nations shoot away so many million pounds sterling every day—that means nothing to me. I do know that there's going to be no money on this side the world for a long time to buy American securities. The whole world is going to be hard up in consequence of the bankruptcy of these nations, the inestimable destruction of property, and the loss of productive men. I fancy that such a change will come in the economic and financial readjustment of the world as nobody can yet guess at.—Are Americans studying these things? It is not only South-American trade; it is all sorts of manufacturers; it is financial influence—if we can quit spending and wasting, and husband our earnings. There's no telling the enormous advantages we shall gain if we are wise.

The extent to which the German people have permitted themselves to be fooled is beyond belief. As a little instance of it, I enclose a copy of a letter that Lord Bryce gave me, written by an English woman who did good social work in her early life—a woman of sense—and who married a German merchant and has spent her married life in Germany. She is a wholly sincere person. This letter she wrote to a friend in England and—she believes every word of it. If she believes it, the great mass of the Germans believe similar things. I have heard of a number of such letters—sincere, as this one is. It gives a better insight into the average German mind than a hundred speeches by the Emperor.

This German and Austrian diplomatic business involves an enormous amount of work. I've now sent one man to Vienna and another to Berlin to straighten out almost hopeless tangles and lies about prisoners and such things and to see if they won't agree to swap more civilians detained in each country. On top of these, yesterday came the Turkish Embassy! Alas, we shall never see old Tewfik[1] again! This business begins briskly to-day

---

[1] Tewfik Pasha, the very popular Turkish Ambassador to Great Britain.

with the detention of every Turkish consul in the British Empire.   Lord!   I dread the missionaries; and I know they're coming now.   This makes four embassies.   We put up a sign, "The American Embassy," on every one of them.   Work?   We're worked to death.   Two nights ago I didn't get time to read a letter or even a telegram that had come that day till 11 o'clock at night. For on top of all these Embassies, I've had to become Commissary-General to feed 6,000,000 starving people in Belgium; and practically all the food must come from the United States.   You can't buy food for export in any country in Europe.   The devastation of Belgium defeats the Germans.—I don't mean in battle but I mean in the after-judgment of mankind.   They cannot recover from that half as soon as they may recover from the economic losses of the war.   The reducing of those people to starvation—that will stick to damn them in history, whatever they win or whatever they lose.

When's it going to end?   Everybody who ought to know says at the earliest next year—next summer.   Many say in two years.   As for me, I don't know.   I don't see how it can end soon.   Neither can lick the other to a frazzle and neither can afford to give up till it is completely licked.   This way of living in trenches and fighting a month at a time in one place is a new thing in warfare. Many a man shoots a cannon all day for a month without seeing a single enemy.   There are many wounded men back here who say they haven't seen a single German. When the trenches become so full of dead men that the living can't stay there longer, they move back to other trenches.   So it goes on.   Each side has several more million men to lose.   What the end will be—I mean when it will come, I don't see how to guess.   The Allies are obliged to win; they have more food and more money, and in the long run, more men.   But the German fighting machine is by far the best organization ever made—not the best men, but the best organization; and the whole German people believe what the woman writes whose letter I send you.   It'll take a long time to beat it.

Affectionately,

W. H. P.

The letter that Page inclosed, and another copy of which was sent to the President, purported to be written by the English wife of a German in Bremen.   It was as follows:

It is very difficult to write, more difficult to believe that what I write will succeed in reaching you.   My husband insists on my urging you—it is not necessary I am sure—to destroy the letter and all possible indications of its origin, should you think it worth translating.   The letter will go by a business friend of my husband's to Holland, and be got off from there.   For our business with Holland is now exceedingly brisk as you may understand.   Her neutrality is most precious to us.[1]

Well, I have of course a divided mind.   I think of those old days in Liverpool and Devonshire—how far off they seem!   And yet I spent all last year in England.   It was in March last when I was with you and we talked of the amazing treatment of your army—I cannot any longer call it *our* army—by ministers crying for the resignation of its officers and eager to make their humiliation an election cry! How far off that seems, too! Let me tell you that it was the conduct of your ministers, Churchill especially, that made people here so confident that your

---

[1]Germany was conducting her trade with the neutral world largely through Dutch and Danish ports.

Government could not fight.   It seemed impossible that
Lloyd George and his following could have the effrontery
to pose as a "war" cabinet; still more impossible that
any sane people could trust them if they did!   Perhaps
you may remember a talk we had also in March about
Matthew Arnold whom I was reading again during my
convalescence at Sidmouth.   You said that "Friendship's Garland" and its Arminius could not be written
now.   I disputed that and told you that it was still true
that your Government talked and "gassed" just as much
as ever, and were wilfully blind to the fact that your
power of action was wholly unequal to your words.   As
in 1870 so now.   Nay, worse, your rulers have always
known it perfectly well, but refused to see it or to admit
it, because they wanted office and knew that to say the
truth would bring the radical vote in the cities upon their
poor heads.   It is the old hypocrisy, in the sense in which
Germans have always accused your nation: alas! and it
is half my nation too.   You pride yourselves on "Keeping
your word" to Belgium.   But you pride yourselves also,
not so overtly just now, on always refusing to prepare
yourselves to keep that word in *deed*.   In the first days
of August you knew, absolutely and beyond all doubt,
that you could do nothing to make good your word.   You
had not the moral courage to say so, and, having said
so, to act accordingly and to warn Belgium that your
promise was "a scrap of paper," and effectively nothing
more.   It *is* nothing more, and has proved to be nothing
more, but you do not see that your indelible disgrace lies
just in this, that you unctuously proclaim that you are
keeping your word when all the time you know, you have
always known, that you refused utterly and completely
to take the needful steps to enable you to translate word
into action.   Have you not torn up your "scrap of

paper" just as effectively as Germany has? As my husband puts it: England gave Belgium a check, a big check, and gave it with much ostentation, but took care that there should be no funds to meet it! Trusting to your check Belgium finds herself bankrupt, sequestrated, blotted out as a nation. But I know England well enough to foresee that English statesmen, with our old friend, the Manchester *Guardian*, which we used to read in years gone by, will always quote with pride how they "guaranteed" the neutrality of Belgium.

As to the future. You cannot win. A nation that has prided itself on making no sacrifice for political power or even independence must pay for its pride. Our house here in Bremen has lately been by way of a centre for naval men, and to a less extent, for officers of the neighbouring commands. They are absolutely confident that they will land ten army corps in England before Christmas. It is terrible to know what they mean to go for. They mean to destroy. Every town which remotely is concerned with war material is to be annihilated. Birmingham, Bradford, Leeds, Newcastle, Sheffield, Northampton are to be wiped out, and the men killed, ruthlessly hunted down. The fact that Lancashire and Yorkshire have held aloof from recruiting is not to save them. The fact that Great Britain is to be a Reichsland will involve the destruction of inhabitants, to enable German citizens to be planted in your country in their place. German soldiers hope that your poor creatures will resist, as patriots should, but they doubt it very much. For resistance will facilitate the process of clearance. Ireland will be left independent, and its harmlessness will be guaranteed by its inevitable civil war.

You may wonder, as I do sometimes, whether this hatred of England is not unworthy, or a form of mental disease. But you must know that it is at bottom not hatred but contempt; fierce, unreasoning scorn for a country that pursues money and ease, from aristocrat to trade-unionist labourer, when it has a great inheritance to defend. I feel bitter, too, for I spent half my life in your country and my dearest friends are all English still; and yet I am deeply ashamed of the hypocrisy and make-believe that has initiated your national policy and brought you down. Now, one thing more. England is, after all, only a stepping stone. From Liverpool, Queenstown, Glasgow, Belfast, we shall reach out across the ocean. I firmly believe that within a year Germany will have seized the new Canal and proclaimed its defiance of the great Monroe Doctrine. We have six million Germans in the United States, and the Irish-Americans behind them. The Americans, believe me, are *as a nation* a cowardly nation, and will never fight organized strength except in defense of their own territories. With the Nova Scotian peninsula and the Bermudas, with the West Indies and the Guianas we shall be able to dominate the Americas. By our possession of the entire Western European seaboard America can find no outlet for its products except by our favour. Her finance is in German hands, her commercial capitals, New York and Chicago, are in reality German cities. It is some years since my father and I were in New York. But my opinion is not very different from that of the forceful men who have planned this war—that with Britain as a base the control of the American continent is under existing conditions the task of a couple of months.

I remember a conversation with Doctor Dohrn, the head of the great biological station at Naples, some four or five years ago. He was complaining of want of adequate subventions from Berlin. "Everything is wanted for the Navy," he said. "And what really does Germany want with such a navy?" I asked. "She is always saying that she certainly does not regard it as a weapon against England." At that Doctor Dohrn raised his eyebrows. "But you, *gnädige Frau*, are a German?" "Of course." "Well, then, you will understand me when I say with all the seriousness I can command that this fleet of ours is intended to deal with smugglers on the shores of the Island of Rügen." I laughed. He became graver still. "The ultimate enemy of our country is America;[1] and I pray that I may see the day of an alliance between a beaten England and a victorious Fatherland against the bully of the Americas." Well, Germany and Austria were never friends until Sadowa had shown the way. Oh! if your country, which in spite of all I love so much, would but "see things clearly and see them whole."

Bremen, September 25, 1914.

To Ralph W. Page[2]

London, Sunday, November 15, 1914.

DEAR RALPH:

You were very good to sit down in Greensboro', or anywhere else, and to write me a fine letter. Do that often. You say there's nothing to do now in the Sandhills. Write us letters: that's a fair job!

God save us, we need 'em. We need anything from the sane part of the world to enable us to keep our balance. One of the commonest things you hear about now is the insanity of a good number of the poor fellows who come back from the trenches as well as of a good many

---

[1] Mr. Irwin Laughlin, first secretary of the American Embassy in London, furnishes this note: "This statement about America was made to me more than once in Germany, between 1910 and 1912, by German officers, military and naval."

[2] Of Pinehurst, North Carolina, the Ambassador's oldest son.

Belgians.   The sights and sounds they've experienced un-
hinge their reason.   If this war keep up long enough—
and it isn't going to end soon—people who have had no
sight of it will go crazy, too—the continuous thought of
it, the inability to get away from it by any device whatever—all this tells on us all.   Letters, then, plenty of
them—let 'em come.

You are in a peaceful land.   The war is a long, long
way off.   You suffer nothing worse than a little idleness
and a little poverty.   They are nothing.   I hope (and
believe) that you get enough to eat.   Be content, then.
Read the poets, improve a piece of land, play with the
baby, learn golf.   That's the happy and philosophic and
fortunate life in these times of world-madness.

As for the continent of Europe—forget it.   We have
paid far too much attention to it.   It has ceased to be
worth it.   And now it's of far less value to us—and will be
for the rest of your life—than it has ever been before.   An
ancient home of man, the home, too, of beautiful things—
buildings, pictures, old places, old traditions, dead civilizations—the place where man rose from barbarism to
civilization—it is now bankrupt, its best young men dead,
its system of politics and of government a failure, its social
structure enslaving and tyrannical—it has little help for
us.   The American spirit, which is the spirit that concerns itself with making life better for the whole mass of
men—that's at home at its best with us.   The whole
future of the race is in the new countries—our country
chiefly.   This grows on one more and more and more.
The things that are best worth while are on our side of the
ocean.   And we've got all the bigger job to do because of
this violent demonstration of the failure of continental
Europe.   It's gone on living on a false basis till its elements got so mixed that it has simply blown itself to

pieces. It is a great convulsion of nature, as an earth-quake or a volcano is. Human life there isn't worth what a yellow dog's life is worth in Moore County. Don't bother yourself with the continent of Europe any more—except to learn the value of a real democracy and the benefits it can confer precisely in proportion to the extent to which men trust to it. Did you ever read my Address delivered before the Royal Institution of Great Britain?[1] I enclose a copy. Now that's my idea of the very milk of the word. To come down to daily, deadly things—this upheaval is simply infernal. Parliament opened the other day and half the old lords that sat in their robes had lost their heirs and a larger part of the members of the House wore khaki. To-morrow they will vote $1,125,000,000 for war purposes. They had already voted $500,000,000. They'll vote more, and more, and more, if necessary. They are raising a new army of 2,000,-000 men. Every man and every dollar they have will go if necessary. That's what I call an invincible people. The Kaiser woke up the wrong passenger. But for fifty years the continent won't be worth living on. My heavens! what bankruptcy will follow death!

Affectionately,
W. H. P.

To Frank C. Page[2]

Sunday, December 20th, 1914.

DEAR OLD MAN:

I envy both you and your mother[3] your chance to make plans for the farm and the house and all the rest of it and

[1]On June 12, 1914. The title of the address was "Some Aspects of the American Democracy."

[2]The Ambassador's youngest son.

[3]Mrs. W. H. Page was at this time spending a few weeks in the United States.

to have one another to talk to. And, most of all, you are where you can now and then change the subject. You can guess somewhat at our plight when Kitty and I confessed to one another last night that we were dead tired and needed to go to bed early and to stay long. She's sleeping yet, the dear kid, and I hope she'll sleep till lunch time. There isn't anything the matter with us but the war; but that's enough, Heaven knows. It's the worst ailment that has ever struck me. Then, if you add to that this dark, wet, foggy, sooty, cold, penetrating climate— you ought to thank your stars that you are not in it. I'm glad your mother's out of it, as much as we miss her; and miss her? Good gracious! there's no telling the hole her absence makes in all our life. But Kitty is a trump, true blue and dead game, and the very best company you can find in a day's journey. And, much as we miss your mother, you mustn't weep for us; we are having some fun and are planning more. I could have no end of fun with her if I had any time. But to work all day and till bedtime doesn't leave much time for sport.

The farm—the farm—the farm—it's yours and Mother's to plan and make and do with as you wish. I shall be happy whatever you do, even if you put the roof in the cellar and the cellar on top of the house.

If you have room enough (16×10 plus a fire and a bath are enough for me), I'll go down there and write a book. If you haven't it, I'll go somewhere else and write a book. I don't propose to be made unhappy by any house or by the lack of any house nor by anything whatsoever.

All the details of life go on here just the same. The war goes as slowly as death because it *is* death, death to millions of men. We've all said all we know about it to one another a thousand times; nobody knows anything else; nobody can guess when it will end; nobody has any doubt about how it will end, unless some totally improbable and unexpected thing happens, such as the falling out of the Allies, which can't happen for none of them can afford it; and we go around the same bloody circle all the time. The papers never have any news; nobody ever talks about anything else; everybody is tired to death; nobody is cheerful; when it isn't sick Belgians, it's aeroplanes; and when it isn't aeroplanes, it's bombarding the coast of England.   When it isn't an American ship held up, it's a fool American-German arrested as a spy; and when it isn't a spy it's a liar who *knows* the Zeppelins are coming to-night.   We don't know anything; we don't believe anybody; we should be surprised at nothing; and at 3 o'clock I'm going to the Abbey to a service in honour of the 100 years of peace!   The world has all got itself so jumbled up that the bays are all promontories, the mountains are all valleys, and earthquakes are necessary for our happiness. We have disasters for breakfast; mined ships for luncheon; burned cities for dinner; trenches in our dreams, and bombarded towns for small talk.

Peaceful seems the sandy landscape where you are, glad the very blackjacks, happy the curs, blessed the sheep, interesting the chin-whiskered clodhopper, innocent the fool darkey, blessed the mule, for it knows no war.   And you have your mother—be happy, boy; you don't know how much you have to be thankful for.

Europe is ceasing to be interesting except as an example of how-not-to-do-it.   It has no lessons for us except as a warning.   When the whole continent has to go fighting— every blessed one of them—once a century, and half of them half the time between and all prepared even when they are not fighting, and when they shoot away all their money as soon as they begin to get rich a little and everybody else's money, too, and make the whole world poor, and when they kill every third or fourth generation of the best men and leave the worst to rear families, and have to start over afresh every time with a worse stock—give me Uncle Sam and his big farm. We don't need to catch any of this European life.   We can do without it all as well as we can do without the judges' wigs and the court costumes.   Besides, I like a land where the potatoes have some flavour, where you can buy a cigar, and get your hair cut and have warm bathrooms.

Build the farm, therefore; and let me hear at every stage of that happy game. May the New Year be the best that has ever come for you!

Affectionately,
W. H. P.

CHAPTER XII

"WAGING NEUTRALITY"

I

THE foregoing letters sufficiently portray Page's attitude toward the war; they also show the extent to which he suffered from the daily tragedy. The great burdens placed upon the Embassy in themselves would have exhausted a physical frame that had never been particularly robust; but more disintegrating than these was the mental distress—the constant spectacle of a civilization apparently bent upon its own destruction. Indeed there were probably few men in Europe upon whom the war had a more depressing effect. In the first few weeks the Ambassador perceptibly grew older; his face became more deeply lined, his hair became grayer, his body thinner, his step lost something of its quickness, his shoulders began to stoop, and his manner became more and more abstracted. Page's kindness, geniality, and consideration had long since endeared him to all the embassy staff, from his chief secretaries to clerks and doormen; and all his associates now watched with affectionate solicitude the extent to which the war was wearing upon him. "In those first weeks," says Mr. Irwin Laughlin, Page's most important assistant and the man upon whom the routine work of the Embassy largely fell, "he acted like a man who was carrying on his shoulders all the sins and burdens of the world. I know no man who seemed to realize so poignantly the misery and sorrow of it all. The sight of an England which he loved bleeding to death in

357

defence of the things in which he most believed was a grief that seemed to be sapping his very life."

Page's associates, however, noted a change for the better after the Battle of the Marne.   Except to his most intimate companions he said little, for he represented a nation that was "neutral"; but the defeat of the Germans added liveliness to his step, gave a keener sparkle to his eye, and even brought back some of his old familiar gaiety of spirit. One day the Ambassador was lunching with Mr. Laughlin and one or two other friends.

"We did pretty well in that Battle of the Marne, didn't we?" he said.

"Isn't that remark **slightly** unneutral, Mr. Ambassador?" asked Mr. Laughlin.

At this a roar of laughter went up from the table that could be heard for a considerable distance.

About this same time Page's personal secretary, Mr. Harold Fowler, came to ask the Ambassador's advice about enlisting in the British Army.   To advise a young man to take a step that might very likely result in his death was a heavy responsibility, and the Ambassador refused to accept it.   It was a matter that the Secretary could settle only with his own conscience.   Mr. Fowler decided his problem by joining the British Army; he had a distinguished career in its artillery and aviation service as he had subsequently in the American Army.   Mr. Fowler at once discovered that his decision had been highly pleasing to his superior.

"I couldn't advise you to do this, Harold," Page said, placing his hand on the young man's shoulder, "but now that you've settled it yourself I'll say this—if I were a young man like you and in your circumstances, I should enlist myself."

Yet greatly as Page abhorred the Prussians and greatly

as his sympathies from the first day of the war were enlisted on the side of the Allies, there was no diplomat in the American service who was more "neutral" in the technical sense. "Neutral!" Page once exclaimed. "There's nothing in the world so neutral as this embassy. Neutrality takes up all our time." When he made this remark he was, as he himself used to say, "the German Ambassador to Great Britain." And he was performing the duties of this post with the most conscientious fidelity. These duties were onerous and disagreeable ones and were made still more so by the unreasonableness of the German Government. Though the American Embassy was caring for the more than 70,000 Germans who were then living in England and was performing numerous other duties, the Imperial Government never realized that Page and the Embassy staff were doing it a service. With characteristic German tactlessness the German Foreign Office attempted to be as dictatorial to Page as though he had been one of its own junior secretaries. The business of the German Embassy in London was conducted with great ability; the office work was kept in the most shipshape condition; yet the methods were American methods and the Germans seemed aggrieved because the routine of the Imperial bureaucracy was not observed. With unparallelled insolence they objected to the American system of accounting—not that it was unsound or did not give an accurate picture of affairs—but simply that it was not German. Page quietly but energetically informed the German Government that the American diplomatic service was not a part of the German organization, that its bookkeeping system was American, not German, that he was doing this work not as an obligation but as a favour, and that, so long as he continued to do it, he would perform the duty in his own way. At this the

Imperial Government subsided. Despite such annoyances Page refused to let his own feelings interfere with the work. The mere fact that he despised the Germans made him over-scrupulous in taking all precautions that they obtained exact justice. But this was all that the German cause in Great Britain did receive. His administration of the German Embassy was faultless in its technique, but it did not err on the side of over-enthusiasm.

His behaviour throughout the three succeeding years was entirely consistent with his conception of "neutrality." That conception, as is apparent from the letters already printed, was not the Wilsonian conception. Probably no American diplomat was more aggrieved at the President's definition of neutrality than his Ambassador to Great Britain. Page had no quarrel with the original neutrality proclamation; that was purely a routine governmental affair, and at the time it was issued it represented the proper American attitude. But the President's famous emendations filled him with astonishment and dismay. "We must be impartial in thought as well as in action," said the President on August 19th,[1] "we must put a curb upon our sentiments as well as upon every transaction that might be construed as a prejudice of one party to the prejudice of another." Page was prepared to observe all the traditional rules of neutrality, to insist on American rights with the British Government, and to do full legal justice to the Germans, but he declined to abrogate his conscience where his personal judgment of the rights and wrongs of the conflict were concerned. "Neutrality," he said in a letter to his brother, Mr. Henry A. Page, of Aberdeen, N. C., "is a

---

[1] In a letter addressed to "My fellow Countrymen" and presented to the Senate by Mr. Chilton.

quality of government—an artificial unit. When a war comes a government must go in it or stay out of it. It must make a declaration to the world of its attitude. That's all that neutrality is. A government can be neutral, but no *man* can be."

"The President and the Government," Page afterward wrote, "in their insistence upon the moral quality of neutrality, missed the larger meaning of the war. It is at bottom nothing but the effort of the Berlin absolute monarch and his group to impose their will on as large a part of the world as they can overrun. The President started out with the idea that it was a war brought on by many obscure causes—economic and the like; and he thus missed its whole meaning. We have ever since been dealing with the chips which fly from the war machine and have missed the larger meaning of the conflict. Thus we have failed to render help to the side of Liberalism and Democracy, which are at stake in the world."

Nor did Page think it his duty, in his private communications to his Government and his friends, to maintain that attitude of moral detachment which Mr. Wilson's pronouncement had evidently enjoined upon him. It was not his business to announce his opinions to the world, for he was not the man who determined the policy of the United States; that was the responsibility of the President and his advisers. But an ambassador did have a certain rôle to perform. It was his duty to collect information and impressions, to discover what important people thought of the United States and of its policies, and to send forward all such data to Washington. According to Page's theory of the Ambassadorial office, he was a kind of listening post on the front of diplomacy, and he would have grievously failed had he not done his best to keep headquarters informed. He did not regard it as "loyalty" merely to forward only that kind of material which Washington apparently preferred to obtain; with a frankness which Mr. Wilson's friends regarded as almost ruthless, Page reported what he believed to be the truth. That this practice was displeasing to the powers of Washington there is abundant evidence. In early December, 1914, Colonel House was compelled to transmit a warning to the American Ambassador at London. "The President wished me to ask you to please be more careful not to express any unneutral feeling, either by word of mouth, or by letter and not even to the State Department. He said that both Mr. Bryan and Mr. Lansing had remarked upon your leaning in that direction and he thought that it would materially lessen your influence. He feels very strongly about this."

Evidently Page did not regard his frank descriptions of England under war as expressing unneutral feeling; at any rate, as the war went on, his letters, even those which he wrote to President Wilson, became more and more outspoken. Page's resignation was always at the President's disposal; the time came, as will appear, when it was offered; so long as he occupied his post, however, nothing could turn him from his determination to make what he regarded as an accurate record of events. This policy of maintaining an outward impartiality, and, at the same time, of bringing pressure to bear on Washington in behalf of the Allies, he called "waging neutrality."

Such was the mood in which Page now prepared to play his part in what was probably the greatest diplomatic drama in history. The materials with which this drama concerned itself were such apparently lifeless subjects as ships and cargoes, learned discourses on such abstract matters as the doctrine of continuous voyage, effective blockade, and conditional contraband; yet the struggle, which lasted for three years, involved the greatest issue of modern times—nothing less than the survival of those conceptions of liberty, government, and society which make the basis of English-speaking civilization. To the newspaper reader of war days, shipping difficulties signified little more than a newspaper headline which he hastily read, or a long and involved lawyer's note which he seldom read at all—or, if he did, practically never understood. Yet these minute and neglected controversies presented to the American Nation the greatest decision in its history. Once before, a century ago, a European struggle had laid before the United States practically the same problem. Great Britain fought Napoleon, just as it had now been compelled to fight the Hohenzollern, by blockade; such warfare, in the early nineteenth century, led to retaliations, just as did the maritime warfare in the recent conflict, and the United States suffered, in 1812, as in 1914, from what were regarded as the depredations of both sides. In Napoleon's days France and Great Britain, according to the international lawyers, attacked American commerce in illegal ways; on strictly technical grounds this infant nation had an adequate cause of war against both belligerents; but the ultimate consequence of a very confused situation was a declaration of war against Great Britain. Though an England which was ruled by a George III or a Prince Regent—an England of rotten boroughs, of an ignorant and oppressed peasantry, and of a social organization in which caste was almost as definitely drawn as in an Oriental despotism—could hardly appeal to the enthusiastic democrat as embodying all the ideals of his system, yet the England of 1800 did represent modern progress when compared with the mediæval autocracy of Napoleon. If we take this broad view, therefore, we must admit that, in 1812, we fought on the side of darkness and injustice against the forces that were making for enlightenment. The war of 1914 had not gone far when the thinking American foresaw that it would present to the American people precisely this same problem. What would the decision be? Would America repeat the experience of 1812, or had the teachings of a century so dissipated hatreds that it would be able to exert its influence in a way more worthy of itself and more helpful to the progress of mankind?

There was one great difference, however, between the position of the United States in 1812 and its position in 1914. A century ago we were a small and feeble nation, of undeveloped industries and resources and of immature character; our entrance into the European conflict, on one side or the other, could have little influence upon its results, and, in fact, it influenced it scarcely at all; the side we fought against emerged triumphant. In 1914, we had the greatest industrial organization and the greatest wealth of any nation and the largest white population of any country except Russia; the energy of our people and our national talent for success had long been the marvel of foreign observers. It mattered little in 1812 on which side the United States took its stand; in 1914 such a decision would inevitably determine the issue. Of all European statesmen there was one man who saw this point with a definiteness which, in itself, gives him a clear title to fame. That was Sir Edward Grey. The time came when a section of the British public was prepared almost to stone the Foreign Secretary in the streets of London, because they believed that his "subservience" to American trade interests was losing the war for Great Britain; his tenure of office was a constant struggle with British naval and military chiefs who asserted that the Foreign Office, in its efforts to maintain harmonious relations with America, was hamstringing the British fleet, was rendering almost impotent its control of the sea, and was thus throwing away the greatest advantage which Great Britain possessed in its life and death struggle. "Some blight has been at work in our Foreign Office for years," said the *Quarterly Review*, "steadily undermining our mastery of the sea."

"The fleet is not allowed to act," cried Lord Charles Beresford in Parliament; the Foreign Office was constantly interfering with its operations. The word "traitor" was not infrequently heard; there were hints that pro-Germanism was rampant and that officials in the Foreign Office were drawing their pay from the Kaiser. It was constantly charged that the navy was bringing in suspicious cargoes only to have the Foreign Office order their release. "I fight Sir Edward about stopping cargoes," Page wrote to Colonel House in December, 1914; "literally fight. He yields and promises this or that. This or that doesn't happen or only half happens. I know why. The military ministers balk him. I inquire through the back door and hear that the Admiralty and the War Office of course value American good-will, but they'll take their chances of a quarrel with the United States rather than let copper get to Germany. The cabinet has violent disagreements. But the military men yield as little as possible. It was rumoured the other day that the Prime Minister threatened to resign; and I know that Kitchener's sister told her friends, with tears in her eyes, that the cabinet shamefully hindered her brother."

These criticisms unquestionably caused Sir Edward great unhappiness, but this did not for a moment move him from his course. His vision was fixed upon a much greater purpose. Parliamentary orators might rage because the British fleet was not permitted to make indiscriminate warfare on commerce, but the patient and far-seeing British Foreign Secretary was the man who was really trying to win the war. He was one of the few Englishmen who, in August, 1914, perceived the tremendous extent of the struggle in which Great Britain had engaged. He saw that the English people were facing the greatest crisis since William of Normandy, in 1066, subjected their island to foreign rule. Was England to become the "Reichsland" of a European monarch, and was the British Empire to pass under the sway of Germany? Proud as Sir Edward Grey was of his country, he was modest in the presence of facts; and one fact of which he early became convinced was that Great Britain could not win unless the United States was ranged upon its side. Here was the country—so Sir Edward reasoned—that contained the largest effective white population in the world; that could train armies larger than those of any other nation; that could make the most munitions, build the largest number of battleships and merchant vessels, and raise food in quantities great enough to feed itself and Europe besides. This power, the Foreign Secretary believed, could determine the issue of the war. If Great Britain secured American sympathy and support, she would win; if Great Britain lost this sympathy and support, she would lose. A foreign policy that would estrange the United States and perhaps even throw its support to Germany would not only lose the war to Great Britain, but it would be perhaps the blackest crime in history, for it would mean the collapse of that British-American coöperation, and the destruction of those British-American ideals and institutions which are the greatest facts in the modern world. This conviction was the basis of Sir Edward's policy from the day that Great Britain declared war. Whatever enemies he might make in England, the Foreign Secretary was determined to shape his course so that the support of the United States would be assured to his country. A single illustration shows the skill and wisdom with which he pursued this great purpose.

Perhaps nothing in the early days of the war enraged the British military chiefs more than the fact that cotton was permitted to go from the United States to Germany. That Germany was using this cotton in the manufacture of torpedoes to sink British ships and of projectiles to kill British soldiers in trenches was well known; nor did many people deny that Great Britain had the right to put cotton on the contraband list. Yet Grey, in the pursuit of his larger end, refused to take this step. He knew that the prosperity of the Southern States depended exclusively upon the cotton crop. He also knew that the South had raised the 1914 crop with no knowledge that a war was impending and that to deny the Southern planters their usual access to the German markets would all but ruin them. He believed that such a ruling would immediately alienate the sympathy of a large section of the United States and make our Southern Senators and Congressmen enemies of Great Britain. Sir Edward was also completely informed of the extent to which the German-Americans and the Irish-Americans were active and he was familiar with the aims of American pacifists. He believed that declaring cotton contraband at this time would bring together in Congress the Southern Senators and Congressmen, the representatives of the Irish and the German causes and the pacifists, and that this combination would exercise an influence that would be disastrous to Great Britain. Two dangers constantly haunted Sir Edward's mind at this time. One was that the enemies of Great Britain would assemble enough votes in Congress to place an embargo upon the shipment of munitions from this country. Such an embargo might well be fatal to Great Britain, for at this time she was importing munitions, especially shells, in enormous quantities from the United States. The other was that such pressure might force the Government to convoy American cargoes with American warships. Great Britain then could stop the cargoes only by attacking our cruisers, and to attack a cruiser is an act of war. Had Congress taken either one of these steps the Allies would have lost the war in the spring of 1915. At a cabinet meeting held to consider this question, Sir Edward Grey set forth this view and strongly advised that cotton should not be made contraband at that time.[1] The Cabinet supported him and events justified the decision. Afterward, in Washington, several of the most influential Senators informed Sir Edward that this action had averted a great crisis.

This was the motive, which, as will appear as the story of our relations with Great Britain progresses, inspired the Foreign Secretary in all his dealings with the United States. His purpose was to use the sea power of Great Britain to keep war materials and foodstuffs out of Germany, but never to go to the length of making an unbridgeable gulf between the United States and Great Britain. The American Ambassador to Great Britain completely sympathized with this programme. It was Page's business to protect the rights of the United States, just as it was Grey's to protect the rights of Great Britain.

---

[1]This was in October, 1914. In August, 1915, when conditions had changed, cotton was declared contraband.

Both were vigilant in protecting such rights, and animated differences between the two men on this point were not infrequent. Great Britain did many absurd and high-handed things in intercepting American cargoes, and Page was always active in "protesting" when the basis for the protest actually existed. But on the great overhanging issue the two men were at one. Like Grey, Page believed that there were more important things involved than an occasional cargo of copper or of oil cake. The American Ambassador thought that the United States should protect its shipping interests, but that it should realize that maritime law was not an exact science, that its principles had been modified by every great conflict in which the blockade had been an effective agency, and that the United States itself, in the Civil War, had not hesitated to make such changes as the changed methods of modern transportation had required. In other words he believed that we could safeguard our rights in a way that would not prevent Great Britain from keeping war materials and foodstuffs out of Germany. And like Sir Edward Grey, Page was obliged to contend with forces at home which maintained a contrary view. In this early period Mr. Bryan was nominally Secretary of State, but the man who directed the national policy in shipping matters was Robert Lansing, then counsellor of the Department. It is somewhat difficult to appraise Mr. Lansing justly, for in his conduct of his office there was not the slightest taint of malice. His methods were tactless, the phrasing of his notes lacked deftness and courtesy, his literary style was crude and irritating; but Mr. Lansing was not anti-British, he was not pro-German; he was nothing more nor less than a lawyer. The protection of American rights at sea was to him simply a "case" in which he had been retained as counsel for the plaintiff. As a good lawyer it was his business to score as many points as possible for his client and the more weak joints he found in the enemy's armour the better did he do his job. It was his duty to scan the law books, to look up the precedents, to examine facts, and to prepare briefs that would be unassailable from a technical standpoint. To Mr. Lansing this European conflict was the opportunity of a lifetime. He had spent thirty years studying the intricate problems that now became his daily companions. His mind revelled in such minute details as ultimate destination, the continuous voyage as applied to conditional contraband, the searching of cargoes upon the high seas, belligerent trading through neutral ports, war zones, orders in council, and all the other jargon of maritime rights in time of war. These topics engrossed him as completely as the extension of democracy and the significance of British-American coöperation engrossed all the thoughts of Page and Grey.

That Page took this larger view is evident from the communications which he now began sending to the President. One that he wrote on October 15, 1914, is especially to the point. The date is extremely important; so early had Page formulated the standards that should guide the United States and so early had he begun his work of attempting to make President Wilson understand the real nature of the conflict. The position which Page now assumed was one from which he never departed.

To the President

In this great argument about shipping I cannot help being alarmed because we are getting into deep water uselessly. The Foreign Office has yielded unquestioningly to all our requests and has shown the sincerest wish to meet all our suggestions, so long as it is not called upon to admit war materials into Germany. It will not give way to us in that. We would not yield it if we were in their place. Neither would the Germans. England will risk a serious quarrel or even hostilities with us rather than yield. You may look upon this as the final word.

Since the last lists of contraband and conditional contraband were published, such materials as rubber and copper and petroleum have developed entirely new uses in war. The British simply will not let Germany import them. Nothing that can be used for war purposes in Germany now will be used for anything else. Representatives of Spain, Holland, and all the Scandinavian states agree that they can do nothing but acquiesce and file protests and claims, and they admit that Great Britain has the right to revise the list of contraband. This is not a war in the sense in which we have hitherto used that word. It is a world-clash of systems of government, a struggle to the extermination of English civilization or of Prussian military autocracy. Precedents have gone to the scrap heap. We have a new measure for military and diplomatic action. Let us suppose that we press for a few rights to which the shippers have a theoretical claim. The American people gain nothing and the result is friction with this country; and that is what a very small minority of the agitators in the United States would like. Great Britain can any day close the Channel to all shipping or can drive Holland to the enemy and blockade her ports.

Let us take a little farther view into the future. If Germany win, will it make any difference what position Great Britain took on the Declaration of London? The Monroe Doctrine will be shot through. We shall have to have a great army and a great navy. But suppose that

England win. We shall then have an ugly academic dispute with her because of this controversy. Moreover, we shall not hold a good position for helping to compose the quarrel or for any other service.

The present controversy seems here, where we are close to the struggle, academic. It seems to us a petty matter when it is compared with the grave danger we incur of shutting ourselves off from a position to be of some service to civilization and to the peace of mankind.

In Washington you seem to be indulging in a more or less theoretical discussion. As we see the issue here, it is a matter of life and death for English-speaking civilization. It is not a happy time to raise controversies that can be avoided or postponed. We gain nothing, we lose every chance for useful coöperation for peace. In jeopardy also are our friendly relations with Great Britain in the sorest need and the greatest crisis in her history. I know that this is the correct view. I recommend most earnestly that we shall substantially accept the new Order in Council or acquiesce in it and reserve whatever rights we may have. I recommend prompt information be sent to the British Government of such action. I should like to inform Grey that this is our decision.

So far as our neutrality obligations are concerned, I do not believe that they require us to demand that Great Britain should adopt for our benefit the Declaration of London. Great Britain has never ratified it, nor have any other nations except the United States. In its application to the situation presented by this war it is altogether to the advantage of Germany.

I have delayed to write you this way too long. I have feared that I might possibly seem to be influenced by sympathy with England and by the atmosphere here. But I write of course solely with reference to our own country's interest and its position after the reorganization of Europe.

Anderson[1] and Laughlin[2] agree with me emphatically.

WALTER H. PAGE.

II

The immediate cause of this protest was, as its context shows, the fact that the State Department was insisting that Great Britain should adopt the Declaration of London as a code of law for regulating its warfare on German shipping. Hostilities had hardly started when Mr. Bryan made this proposal; his telegram on this subject is dated August 7, 1914. "You will further state," said Mr. Bryan, "that this Government believes that the acceptance of these laws by the belligerents would prevent grave misunderstandings which may arise as to the relations between belligerents and neutrals. It therefore hopes that this inquiry may receive favourable consideration." At the same time Germany and the other belligerents were asked to adopt this Declaration.

The communication was thus more than a suggestion; it was a recommendation that was strongly urged. According to Page this telegram was the first great mistake the American Government made in its relations with Great Britain. In September, 1916, the Ambassador submitted to President Wilson a memorandum which he called "Rough notes toward an explanation of the British feeling toward the United States." "Of recent years," he said, "and particularly during the first year of the present Administration, the British feeling toward the United States was most friendly and cordial. About

---

[1]Mr. Chandler P. Anderson, of New York, at this time advising the American Embassy on questions of international law.

[2]Mr. Irwin Laughlin, first secretary of the Embassy.

the time of the repeal of the tolls clause in the Panama Act, the admiration and friendliness of the whole British public (governmental and private) reached the highest point in our history.   In considering the change that has taken place since, it is well to bear this cordiality in mind as a starting point.   When the war came on there was at first nothing to change this attitude.   The hysterical hope of many persons that our Government might protest against the German invasion of Belgium caused some feeling of disappointment, but thinking men did not share it; and, if this had been the sole cause of criticism of us, the criticism would have died out.   The unusually high regard in which the President—and hence our Government—was then held was to a degree new.   The British had for many years held the people of the United States in high esteem: they had not, as a rule, so favourably regarded the Government at Washington, especially in its conduct of foreign relations.   They had long regarded our Government as ignorant of European affairs and amateurish in its cockiness.   When I first got to London I found evidence of this feeling, even in the most friendly atmosphere that surrounded us.   Mr. Bryan was looked on as a joke.   They forgot him—rather, they never took serious notice of him.   But, when the Panama tolls incident was closed, they regarded the President as his own Foreign Secretary; and thus our Government as well as our Nation came into this high measure of esteem.

"The war began.   We, of course, took a neutral attitude, wholly to their satisfaction.   But we at once interfered—or tried to interfere—by insisting on the Declaration of London, which no Great Power but the United States (I think) had ratified and which the British House of Lords had distinctly rejected.   That Declaration would probably have given a victory to Germany if the

Allies had adopted it. In spite of our neutrality we insisted vigorously on its adoption and aroused a distrust in our judgment. Thus we started in wrong, so far as the British Government is concerned."

The rules of maritime warfare which the American State Department so disastrously insisted upon were the direct outcome of the Hague Conference of 1907. That assembly of the nations recognized, what had long been a palpable fact, that the utmost confusion existed in the operations of warring powers upon the high seas. About the fundamental principle that a belligerent had the right, if it had the power, to keep certain materials of commerce from reaching its enemy, there was no dispute. But as to the particular articles which it could legally exclude there were as many different ideas as there were nations. That the blockade, a term which means the complete exclusion of cargoes and ships from an enemy's ports, was a legitimate means of warfare, was also an accepted fact, but as to the precise means in which the blockade could be enforced there was the widest difference of opinion. The Hague Conference provided that an attempt should be made to codify these laws into a fixed system, and the representatives of the nations met in London in 1908, under the presidency of the Earl of Desart, for this purpose. The outcome of their two months' deliberations was that document of seven chapters and seventy articles which has ever since been known as the Declaration of London. Here at last was the thing for which the world had been waiting so long—a complete system of maritime law for the regulation of belligerents and the protection of neutrals, which would be definitely binding upon all nations because all nations were expected to ratify it.

But the work of all these learned gentlemen was thrown away. The United States was the only party to the negotiations that put the stamp of approval upon its labours. All other nations declined to commit themselves. In Great Britain the Declaration had an especially interesting course. In that country it became a football of party politics. The Liberal Government was at first inclined to look upon it favourably; the Liberal House of Commons actually ratified it. It soon became apparent, however, that this vote did not represent the opinion of the British public. In fact, few measures have ever aroused such hostility as this Declaration, once its details became known. For more than a year the hubbub against it filled the daily press, the magazines, the two Houses of Parliament and the hustings; Rudyard Kipling even wrote a poem denouncing it. The adoption of the Declaration, these critics asserted, would destroy the usefulness of the British fleet. In many quarters it was described as a German plot—as merely a part of the preparations which Germany was making for world conquest. The fact is that the Declaration could not successfully stand the analysis to which it was now mercilessly submitted; the House of Lords rejected it, and this action met with more approbation than had for years been accorded the legislative pronouncements of that chamber. The Liberal House of Commons was not in the least dissatisfied with this conclusion, for it realized that it had made a mistake and it was only too happy to be permitted to forget it.

When the war broke out there was therefore no single aspect of maritime law which was quite so odious as the Declaration of London. Great Britain realized that she could never win unless her fleet were permitted to keep contraband out of Germany and, if necessary, completely to blockade that country. The two greatest conflicts of the nineteenth century were the European struggle with Napoleon and the American Civil War. In both the blockade had been the decisive element, and that this great agency would similarly determine events in this even greater struggle was apparent. What enraged the British public against any suggestion of the Declaration was that it practically deprived Great Britain of this indispensable means of weakening the enemy. In this Declaration were drawn up lists of contraband, non-contraband, and conditional contraband, and all of these, in English eyes, worked to the advantage of Germany and against the advantage of Great Britain. How absurd this classification was is evident from the fact that airplanes were not listed as absolute contraband of war. Germany's difficulty in getting copper was one of the causes of her collapse; yet the Declaration put copper for ever on the non-contraband list; had this new code been adopted, Germany could have imported enormous quantities from this country, instead of being compelled to reinforce her scanty supply by robbing housewives of their kitchen utensils, buildings of their hardware, and church steeples of their bells. Germany's constant scramble for rubber formed a diverting episode in the struggle; there are indeed few things so indispensable in modern warfare; yet the Declaration included rubber among the innocent articles and thus opened up to Germany the world's supply. But the most serious matter was that the Declaration would have prevented Great Britain from keeping foodstuffs out of the Fatherland.

When Mr. Bryan, therefore, blandly asked Great Britain to accept the Declaration as its code of maritime warfare, he was asking that country to accept a document which Great Britain, in peace time, had repudiated and which would, in all probability, have caused that country to lose the war. The substance of this request was bad enough, but the language in which it was phrased made

matters much worse.   It appears that only the intervention of Colonel House prevented the whole thing from
becoming a tragedy.

From Edward M. House

115 East 53rd Street,
New York City.
October 3, 1914.

HIS EXCELLENCY,
The American Ambassador, London, England.
DEAR PAGE:

. . . I have just returned from Washington where
I was with the President for nearly four days.   He is
looking well and is well.   Sometimes his spirits droop, but
then, again, he is his normal self.

I had the good fortune to be there at a time when the
discussion of the Declaration of London had reached a
critical stage.   Bryan was away and Lansing, who had
not mentioned the matter to Sir Cecil,[1] prepared a long
communication to you which he sent to the President
for approval.   The President and I went over it and I
strongly urged not sending it until I could have a conference with Sir Cecil.   I had this conference the next day
without the knowledge of any one excepting the President,
and had another the day following.   Sir Cecil told me that
if the dispatch had gone to you as written and you had
shown it to Sir Edward Grey, it would almost have been
a declaration of war; and that if, by any chance, the newspapers had got hold of it as they so often get things from
our State Department, the greatest panic would have prevailed.   He said it would have been the Venezuela incident magnified by present conditions.

At the President's suggestion, Lansing then prepared a

---

[1]Sir Cecil Spring Rice, British Ambassador at Washington.

cablegram to you. This, too, was objectionable and the President and I together softened it down into the one you received.

Faithfully yours,
E. M. HOUSE.

In justice to Mr. Lansing, a passage in a later letter of Colonel House must be quoted: "It seems that Lansing did not write the particular dispatch to you that was objected to. Someone else prepared it and Lansing rather too hastily submitted it to the President, with the result you know."

This suppressed communication is probably for ever lost, but its tenor may perhaps be gathered from instructions which were actually sent to the Ambassador about this time. After eighteen typewritten pages of not too urbanely expressed discussion of the Declaration of London and the general subject of contraband, Page was instructed to call the British Government's attention to the consequences which followed shipping troubles in previous times. It is hard to construe this in any other way than as a threat to Great Britain of a repetition of 1812:

Confidential. You will not fail to impress upon His Excellency[1] the gravity of the issues which the enforcement of the Order in Council seems to presage, and say to him in substance as follows:

It is a matter of grave concern to this Government that the particular conditions of this unfortunate war should be considered by His Britannic Majesty's Government to be such as to justify them in advancing doctrines and advocating practices which in the past aroused strong opposition on the part of the Government of the United

[1] Sir Edward Grey.

States, and bitter feeling among the American people. This Government feels bound to express the fear, though it does so reluctantly, that the publicity, which must be given to the rules which His Majesty's Government announce that they intend to enforce, will awaken memories of controversies, which it is the earnest desire of the United States to forget or to pass over in silence. . . .

Germany, of course, promptly accepted the Declaration, for the suggestion fitted in perfectly with her programme; but Great Britain was not so acquiescent. Four times was Page instructed to ask the British Government to accede unconditionally, and four times did the Foreign Office refuse. Page was in despair. In the following letter he notified Colonel House that if he were instructed again to move in this matter he would resign his ambassadorship.

To Edward M. House

American Embassy, London,
October 22, 1914.

DEAR HOUSE:

This is about the United States and England. Let's get that settled before we try our hands at making peace in Europe.

One of our greatest assets is the friendship of Great Britain, and our friendship is a still bigger asset for her, and she knows it and values it. Now, if either country should be damfool enough to throw this away because old Stone[1] roars in the Senate about something that hasn't happened, then this crazy world would be completely mad

---

[1] Senator William J. Stone, perhaps the leading spokesman of the pro-German cause in the United States Senate. Senator Stone represented Missouri, a state with a large German-American element.

all round, and there would be no good-will left on earth at all.

The case is plain enough to me. England is going to keep war-materials out of Germany as far as she can. We'd do it in her place. Germany would do it. Any nation would do it. That's all she has declared her intention of doing. And, if she be let alone, she'll do it in a way to give *us* the very least annoyance possible; for she'll go any length to keep our friendship and good will. And *she has not confiscated a single one of our cargoes even of unconditional contraband.* She has stopped some of them and bought them herself, but confiscated not one. All right; what do we do? We set out on a comprehensive plan to regulate the naval warfare of the world and we up and ask 'em all, "Now, boys, all be good, damn you, and agree to the Declaration of London."

"Yah," says Germany, "if England will."

Now Germany isn't engaged in naval warfare to count, and she never even paid the slightest attention to the Declaration all these years. But she saw that it would hinder England and help her now, by forbidding England to stop certain very important war materials from reaching Germany. "Yah," said Germany. But England said that her Parliament had rejected the Declaration in times of peace and that she could now hardly be expected to adopt it in the face of this Parliamentary rejection. But, to please us, she agreed to adopt it with only two changes.

Then Lansing to the bat:

"No, no," says Lansing, "you've got to adopt it all."

Four times he's made me ask for its adoption, the last time coupled with a proposition that if England would adopt it, she might issue a subsequent proclamation saying that, since the Declaration is contradictory, she will construe it her own way, and the United States will raise no objection!

Then he sends eighteen pages of fine-spun legal arguments (not all sound by any means) against the sections of the English proclamations that have been put forth, giving them a strained and unfriendly interpretation.

In a word, England has acted in a friendly way to us and will so act, if we allow her. But Lansing, instead of trusting to her good faith and reserving all our rights under international law and usage, imagines that he can force her to agree to a code that the Germans now agree to because, in Germany's present predicament, it will be especially advantageous to Germany. Instead of trusting her, he assumes that she means to do wrong and proceeds to try to bind her in advance. He hauls her up and tries her in court—that's his tone.

Now the relations that I have established with Sir Edward Grey have been built up on frankness, fairness and friendship. I can't have relations of any other sort nor can England and the United States have relations of any other sort. This is the place we've got to now. Lansing seems to assume that the way to an amicable agreement is through an angry controversy.

Lansing's method is the trouble. He treats Great Britain, to start with, as if she were a criminal and an opponent. That's the best way I know to cause trouble to American shipping and to bring back the good old days of mutual hatred and distrust for a generation or two. If that isn't playing into the hands of the Germans, what would be? And where's the "neutrality" of this kind of action?

See here: If we let England go on, we can throw the whole responsibility on her and reserve all our rights under international law and usage and claim damages (and get 'em) for every act of injury, if acts of injury occur; and we can keep her friendship and good-will. Every other neutral nation is doing that. Or we can insist on regulating all naval warfare and have a quarrel and refer it to a Bryan-Peace-Treaty Commission and claim at most the selfsame damages with a less chance to get 'em. We can get damages without a quarrel; or we can have a quarrel and probably get damages. Now, why, in God's name, should we provoke a quarrel?

The curse of the world is little men who for an imagined small temporary advantage throw away the long growth of good-will nurtured by wise and patient men and who cannot see the lasting and far greater future evil they do. Of all the years since 1776 this great war-year is the worst to break the 100 years of our peace, or even to ruffle it. I pray you, good friend, get us out of these incompetent lawyer-hands.

Now about the peace of Europe. Nothing can yet be done, perhaps nothing now can ever be done by us. The Foreign Office doubts our wisdom and prudence since Lansing came into action. The whole atmosphere is changing. One more such move and they will conclude that Dernburg and Bernstorff have seduced us—without our knowing it, to be sure; but their confidence in our judgment will be gone. God knows I have tried to keep this confidence intact and our good friendship secure. But I have begun to get despondent over the outlook since the President telegraphed me that Lansing's proposal would settle the matter. I still believe he did not understand it—he couldn't have done so. Else he could not have approved it. But that tied my hands. If Lansing again brings up the Declaration of London—after four flat and reasonable rejections—I shall resign. I will not be the instrument of a perfectly gratuitous and ineffective insult to this patient and fair and friendly government and people who in my time have done us many kindnesses and never an injury but Carden,[1] and who sincerely try now to meet our wishes. It would be too asinine an act ever to merit forgiveness or ever to be forgotten. I should blame myself the rest of my life. It would grieve Sir Edward more than anything except this war. It would knock the management of foreign affairs by this Administration into the region of sheer idiocy. I'm afraid any peace talk from us, as it is, would merely be whistling down the wind. If we break with England—not on any case or act of violence to our shipping—but on a useless discussion, in advance, of general principles of conduct during the war—just for a discussion—we've needlessly thrown away our great chance to be of some service to this world gone mad. If Lansing isn't stopped, that's what he will do. Why doesn't the President see Spring Rice? Why don't you take him to see him?

Good night, my good friend. I still have hope that the President himself will take this in hand.

Yours always,

W. H. P.

The letters and the cablegrams which Page was sending to Colonel House and the State Department at this time evidently ended the matter. By the middle of October the two nations were fairly deadlocked. Sir Edward Grey's reply to the American proposal had been an acceptance of the Declaration of London with certain modifications. For the list of contraband in the Declaration he had submitted the list already adopted by Great Britain in its Order in Council, and he had also rejected that article which made it impossible for Great Britain

[1]See Chapter VII.

to apply the doctrine of "continuous voyage" to conditional contraband. The modified acceptance, declared Mr. Lansing, was a practical rejection—as of course it was, and as it was intended to be. So the situation remained for several exciting weeks, the State Department insisting on the Declaration in full, precisely as the legal luminaries had published it five years before, the Foreign Office courteously but inflexibly refusing to accede. Only the cordial personal relations which prevailed between Grey and Page prevented the crisis from producing the most disastrous results. Finally, on October 17th, Page proposed by cable an arrangement which he hoped would settle the matter. This was that the King should issue a proclamation accepting the Declaration with practically the modifications suggested above, and that a new Order in Council should be issued containing a new list of contraband. Sir Edward Grey was not to ask the American Government to accept this proclamation; all that he asked was that Washington should offer no objections to it. It was proposed that the United States at the same time should publish a note withdrawing its suggestion for the adoption of the Declaration, and explaining that it proposed to rest the rights of its citizens upon the existing rules of international law and the treaties of the United States. This solution was accepted. It was a defeat for Mr. Lansing, of course, but he had no alternative. The relief that Page felt is shown in the following memorandum, written soon after the tension had ceased:

"That insistence on the Declaration entire came near to upsetting the whole kettle of fish. It put on me the task of insisting on a general code—at a time when the fiercest war in history was every day becoming fiercer and more desperate—which would have prevented the British from putting on their contraband list several of the most important war materials—accompanied by a proposal that would have angered every neutral nation through which supplies can possibly reach Germany and prevented this Government from making friendly working arrangements with them; and, after Sir Edward Grey had flatly declined for these reasons, I had to continue to insist. I confess it did look as if we were determined to dictate to him how he should conduct the war—and in a way that distinctly favoured the Germans.

"I presented every insistence; for I should, of course, not have been excusable if I had failed in any case vigorously to carry out my instructions. But every time I plainly saw matters getting worse and worse; and I should have failed of my duty also if I had not so informed the President and the Department. I can conceive of no more awkward situation for an Ambassador or for any other man under Heaven. I turned the whole thing over in my mind backward and forward a hundred times every day. For the first time in this stress and strain, I lost my appetite and digestion and did not know the day of the week nor what month it was—seeing the two governments rushing toward a very serious clash, which would have made my mission a failure and done the Administration much hurt, and have sowed the seeds of bitterness for generations to come.

"One day I said to Anderson (whose assistance is in many ways invaluable): 'Of course nobody is infallible— least of all we. Is it possible that we are mistaken? You and Laughlin and I, who are close to it all, are absolutely agreed. But may there not be some important element in the problem that we do not see? Summon and nurse every doubt that you can possibly muster up of the correctness of our view, put yourself on the defensive, recall every mood you may have had of the slightest hesitation, and tell me to-morrow of every possible weak place there may be in our judgment and conclusions.' The next day Anderson handed me seventeen reasons why it was unwise to persist in this demand for the adoption of the Declaration of London. Laughlin gave a similar opinion. I swear I spent the night in searching every nook and corner of my mind and I was of the same opinion the next morning. There was nothing to do then but the most unwelcome double duty: (1) Of continuing to carry out instructions, at every step making a bad situation worse and running the risk of a rupture (which would be the only great crime that now remains uncommitted in the world); and (2) of trying to persuade our own Government that this method was the wrong method to pursue. I know it is not my business to make policies, but I conceive it to be my business to report when they fail or succeed. Now if I were commanded to look throughout the whole universe for the most unwelcome task a man may have, I think I should select this. But, after all, a man has nothing but his own best judgment to guide him; and, if he follow that and fail—that's all he *can* do. I do reverently thank God that we gave up that contention. We *may* have trouble yet, doubtless we shall, but it will not be trouble of our own making, as that was.

"Tyrrell[1] came into the reception room at the Foreign Office the day after our withdrawal, while I was waiting to see Sir Edward Grey, and he said: 'I wish to tell you personally—just privately between you and me—how infinite a relief it is to us all that your Government has withdrawn that demand. We couldn't accept it; our refusal was not stubborn nor pig-headed: it was a physical necessity in order to carry on the war with any hope of success.'

---

[1] Private secretary to Sir Edward Grey.

Then, as I was going out, he volunteered this remark: 'I make this guess—that that programme was not the work of the President but of some international prize court enthusiast (I don't know who) who had failed to secure the adoption of the Declaration when parliaments and governments could discuss it at leisure and who hoped to jam it through under the pressure of war and thus get his prize court international.' I made no answer for several reasons, one of which is, I do not know whose programme it was. All that I know is that I have here, on my desk at my house, a locked dispatch book half full of telegrams and letters insisting on it, which I do not wish (now at least) to put in the Embassy files, and the sight of which brings the shuddering memory of the worst nightmare I have ever suffered.

"Now we can go on, without being a party to any general programme, but in an independent position vigorously stand up for every right and privilege under law and usage and treaties; and we have here a government that we can deal with frankly and not (I hope) in a mood to suspect us of wishing to put it at a disadvantage for the sake of a general code or doctrine. A land and naval and air and submarine battle (the greatest battle in the history of the belligerent race of man) within 75 miles of the coast of England, which hasn't been invaded since 1066 and is now in its greatest danger since that time; and this is no time I fear, to force a great body of doctrine on Great Britain. God knows I'm afraid some American boat will run on a mine somewhere in the Channel or the North Sea. There's war there as there is on land in Germany. Nobody tries to get goods through on land on the continent, and they make no complaints that commerce is stopped. Everybody tries to ply the Channel and the North Sea as usual, both of which have German and English mines and torpedo craft and submarines almost as thick as batteries along the hostile camps on land. The British Government (which now issues marine insurance) will not insure a British boat to carry food to Holland en route to the starving Belgians; and I hear that no government and no insurance company will write insurance for anything going across the North Sea. I wonder if the extent and ferocity and danger of this war are fully realized in the United States?

"There is no chance yet effectively to talk of peace.[1] The British believe that their civilization and their Empire are in grave danger. They are drilling an army of a million men here for next spring; more and more troops come from all the Colonies, where additional enlistments are going on. They feel that to stop before a decisive result is reached would simply be provoking another war, after a period of dread such as they have lived through the last ten years; a large and increasing proportion of the letters you see are on black-bordered paper and this whole island is becoming a vast hospital and prisoners' camp— all which, so far from bringing them to think of peace, urges them to renewed effort; and all the while the bitterness grows.

"The Straus incident[1] produced the impression here that it was a German trick to try to shift the responsibility of continuing the war, to the British shoulders. Mr. Sharp's bare mention of peace in Paris caused the French censor to forbid the transmission of a harmless interview; and our insistence on the Declaration left, for the time being at least, a distinct distrust of our judgment and perhaps even of our good-will. It was suspected—I am

---

[1] The reference is to an attempt by Germany to start peace negotiations in September, 1914, after the Battle of the Marne. This is described in the next chapter.

sure—that the German influence in Washington had unwittingly got influence over the Department.   The atmosphere (toward me) is as different now from what it was a week ago as Arizona sunshine is from a London fog, as much as to say, 'After all, perhaps, you don't *mean* to try to force us to play into the hands of our enemies!' "

III

And so this crisis was passed; it was the first great service that Page had rendered the cause of the Allies and his own country.   Yet shipping difficulties had their more agreeable aspects.   Had it not been for the fact that both Page and Grey had an understanding sense of humour, neutrality would have proved a more difficult path than it actually was.   Even amid the tragic problems with which these two men were dealing there was not lacking an occasional moment's relaxation into the lighter aspect of things.   One of the curious memorials preserved in the British Foreign Office is the cancelled $15,000,000 check with which Great Britain paid the *Alabama* claims.   That the British should frame this memento of their great diplomatic defeat and hang it in the Foreign Office is an evidence of the fact that in statesmanship, as in less exalted matters, the English are excellent sportsmen.   The real justification of the honour paid to this piece of paper, of course, is that the settlement of the *Alabama* claims by arbitration signalized a great forward step in international relations and did much to heal a century's troubles between the United States and Great Britain.   Sir Edward Grey used frequently to call Page's attention to this document.   It represented the amount of money, then considered large, which Great Britain had paid the United States for the depredations on American shipping for which she was responsible during the Civil War.

One day the two men were discussing certain detentions of American cargoes—high-handed acts which, in Page's opinion, were unwarranted. Not infrequently, in the heat of discussion, Page would get up and pace the floor. And on this occasion his body, as well as his mind, was in a state of activity. Suddenly his eye was attracted by the framed Alabama check. He leaned over, peered at it intensely, and then quickly turned to the Foreign Secretary:

"If you don't stop these seizures, Sir Edward, some day you'll have your entire room papered with things like that!"

Not long afterward Sir Edward in his turn scored on Page. The Ambassador called to present one of the many State Department notes. The occasion was an embarrassing one, for the communication was written in the Department's worst literary style. It not infrequently happened that these notes, in the form in which Page received them, could not be presented to the British Government; they were so rasping and undiplomatic that Page feared that he would suffer the humiliation of having them returned, for there are certain things which no self-respecting Foreign Office will accept. On such occasions it was the practice of the London Embassy to smooth down the language before handing the paper to the Foreign Secretary. The present note was one of this kind; but Page, because of his friendly relations with Grey, decided to transmit the communication in its original shape.

Sir Edward glanced over the document, looked up, and remarked, with a twinkle in his eye,—

"This reads as though they thought that they are still talking to George the Third."

The roar of laughter that followed was something quite

unprecedented amid the thick and dignified walls of the Foreign Office.

One of Page's most delicious moments came, however, after the Ministry of Blockade had been formed, with Lord Robert Cecil in charge. Lord Robert was high minded and conciliatory, but his knowledge of American history was evidently not without its lapses. One day, in discussing the ill-feeling aroused in the United States by the seizure of American cargoes, Page remarked banteringly:

"You must not forget the Boston Tea Party, Lord Robert."

The Englishman looked up, rather puzzled.

"But you must remember, Mr. Page, that I have never been in Boston. I have never attended a tea party there."

It has been said that the tact and good sense of Page and Grey, working sympathetically for the same end, avoided many an impending crisis. The trouble caused early in 1915 by the ship *Dacia* and the way in which the difficulty was solved, perhaps illustrate the value of this coöperation at its best. In the early days of the War Congress passed a bill admitting foreign ships to American registry. The wisdom and even the "neutrality" of such an act were much questioned at the time. Colonel House, in one of his early telegrams to the President, declared that this bill "is full of lurking dangers." Colonel House was right. The trouble was that many German merchant ships were interned in American harbours, fearing to put to sea, where the watchful British warships lay waiting for them. Any attempt to place these vessels under the American flag, and to use them for trade between American and German ports, would at once cause a crisis with the Allies, for such a paper change in ownership would be altogether too transparent. Great Britain viewed this legislation with disfavour, but did not think it politic to protest such transfers generally; Spring Rice contented himself with informing the State Department that his government would not object so long as this changed status did not benefit Germany. If such German ships, after being transferred to the American flag, engaged in commerce between American ports and South American ports, or other places remotely removed from the Fatherland, Great Britain would make no difficulty. The *Dacia*, a merchantman of the Hamburg-America line, had been lying at her wharf in Port Arthur, Texas, since the outbreak of the war. In early January, 1915, she was purchased by Mr. E. N. Breitung, of Marquette, Michigan. Mr. Breitung caused great excitement in the newspapers when he announced that he had placed the *Dacia* under American registry, according to the terms of this new law, had put upon her an American crew, and that he proposed to load her with cotton and sail for Germany. The crisis had now arisen which the well-wishers of Great Britain and the United States had so dreaded. Great Britain's position was a difficult one. If it acquiesced, the way would be opened for placing under American registry all the German and Austrian ships that were then lying unoccupied in American ports and using them in trade between the United States and the Central Powers. If Great Britain seized the *Dacia*, then there was the likelihood that this would embroil her with the American Government—and this would serve German purposes quite as well.

Sir Cecil Spring Rice, the British Ambassador at Washington, at once notified Washington that the *Dacia* would be seized if she sailed for a German port. The cotton which she intended to carry was at that time not contraband, but the vessel itself was German and was thus subject to apprehension as enemy property. The seriousness of this position was that technically the *Dacia* was now an American ship, for an American citizen owned her, she carried an American crew, she bore on her flagstaff the American flag, and she had been admitted to American registry under a law recently passed by Congress. How could the United States sit by quietly and permit this seizure to take place? When the *Dacia* sailed on January 23rd the excitement was keen; the voyage had obtained a vast amount of newspaper advertising, and the eyes of the world were fixed upon her. German sympathizers attributed the attitude of the American Government in permitting the vessel to sail as a "dare" to Great Britain, and the fact that Great Britain had announced her intention of taking up this "dare" made the situation still more tense.

When matters had reached this pass Page one day dropped into the Foreign Office.

"Have you ever heard of the British fleet, Sir Edward?" he asked.

Grey admitted that he had, though the question obviously puzzled him.

"Yes," Page went on musingly. "We've all heard of the British fleet. Perhaps we have heard too much about it. Don't you think it's had too much advertising?"

The Foreign Secretary looked at Page with an expression that implied a lack of confidence in his sanity.

"But have you ever heard of the French fleet?" the American went on. "France has a fleet too, I believe."

Sir Edward granted that.

"Don't you think that the French fleet ought to have a little advertising?"

"What on earth are you talking about?"

"Well," said Page, "there's the *Dacia*. Why not let the French fleet seize it and get some advertising?"

A gleam of understanding immediately shot across Grey's face. The old familiar twinkle came into his eye.

"Yes," he said, "why not let the Belgian royal yacht seize it?"

This suggestion from Page was one of the great inspirations of the war. It amounted to little less than genius. By this time Washington was pretty wearied of the *Dacia*, for mature consideration had convinced the Department that Great Britain had the right on its side. Washington would have been only too glad to find a way out of the difficult position into which it had been forced, and this Page well understood. But this government always finds itself in an awkward plight in any controversy with Great Britain, because the hyphenates raise such a noise that it has difficulty in deciding such disputes upon their merits. To ignore the capture of this ship by the British would have brought all this hullabaloo again about the ears of the Administration. But the position of France is entirely different; the memories of Lafayette and Rochambeau still exercise a profound spell on the American mind; France does not suffer from the persecution of hyphenate populations, and Americans will stand even outrages from France without getting excited. Page knew that if the British seized the *Dacia*, the cry would go up in certain quarters for immediate war, but that, if France committed the same crime, the guns of the adversary would be spiked. It was purely a case of sentiment and "psychology." And so the event proved. His suggestion was at once acted on; a French cruiser went out into the Channel, seized the offending ship, took it into port, where a French prize court promptly condemned it. The proceeding did not cause even a ripple of hostility. The *Dacia* was sold to Frenchmen, rechristened the *Yser* and put to work in the Mediterranean trade. The episode was closed in the latter part of 1915 when a German submarine torpedoed the vessel and sent it to the bottom.

Such was the spirit which Page and Sir Edward Grey brought to the solution of the shipping problems of 1914–1917. There is much more to tell of this great task of "waging neutrality," and it will be told in its proper place. But already it is apparent to what extent these two men served the cause of English-speaking civilization. Neither would quibble or uphold an argument which he thought unjust, even though his nation might gain in a material sense, and neither would pitch the discussion in any other key than forbearance and mutual accommodation and courtliness. For both men had the same end in view. They were both thinking, not of the present, but of the coming centuries. The coöperation of the two nations in meeting the dangers of autocracy and Prussian barbarism, in laying the foundations of a future in which peace, democracy, and international justice should be the directing ideas of human society— such was the ultimate purpose at which these two statesmen aimed. And no men have ever been more splendidly justified by events. The Anglo-American situation of 1914 contained dangers before which all believers in real progress now shudder. Had Anglo-American diplomacy been managed with less skill and consideration, the United States and Great Britain would have become involved in a quarrel beside which all their previous differences would have appeared insignificant. Mutual hatreds and hostilities would have risen that would have prevented the entrance of the United States into the war on the side of the Allies. It is not inconceivable that the history of 1812 would have been repeated, and that the men and resources of this country might have been used to support purposes which have always been hateful to the American conscience. That the world was saved from this calamity is owing largely to the fact that Great Britain had in its Foreign Office a man who was always solving temporary irritations with his eyes constantly fixed upon a great goal, and that the United States had as ambassador in London a man who had the most exalted view of the mission of his country, who had dedicated his life to the worldwide spread of the American ideal, and who believed that an indispensable part of this work was the maintenance of a sympathetic and helpful coöperation with the English-speaking peoples.

CHAPTER XIII

GERMANY'S FIRST PEACE DRIVES

THE Declaration of London was not the only problem that distracted Page in these early months of the war. Washington's apparent determination to make peace also added to his daily anxieties. That any attempt to end hostilities should have distressed so peace-loving and humanitarian a statesman as Page may seem surprising; it was, however, for the very reason that he was a man of peace that these Washington endeavours caused him endless worry. In Page's opinion they indicated that President Wilson did not have an accurate understanding of the war. The inspiring force back of them, as the Ambassador well understood, was a panic-stricken Germany. The real purpose was not a peace, but a truce; and the cause which was to be advanced was not democracy but Prussian absolutism. Between the Battle of the Marne and the sinking of the *Lusitania* four attempts were made to end the war; all four were set afoot by Germany. President Wilson was the man to whom the Germans appealed to rescue them from their dilemma. It is no longer a secret that the Germans at this time regarded their situation as a tragic one; the success that they had anticipated for forty years had proved to be a disaster. The attempt to repeat the great episodes of 1864, 1866, and 1870, when Prussia had overwhelmed Denmark, Austria, and France in three brief campaigns, had ignominiously failed. Instead of beholding a conquered Europe at her feet, Germany awoke from her illusion to find herself encompassed by a ring of resolute and powerful foes. The fact that the British Empire, with its immense resources, naval, military, and economic, was now leading the alliance against them, convinced the most intelligent Germans that the Fatherland was face to face with the greatest crisis in its history.

Peace now became the underground Germanic programme. Yet the Germans did not have that inexorable respect for facts which would have persuaded them to accept terms to which the Allies could consent. The military oligarchy were thinking not so much of saving the Fatherland as of saving themselves; a settlement which would have been satisfactory to their enemies would have demanded concessions which the German people, trained for forty years to expect an unparalleled victory, would have regarded as a defeat. The collapse of the militarists and of Hohenzollernism would have ensued. What the German oligarchy desired was a peace which they could picture to their deluded people as a triumph, one that would enable them to extricate themselves at the smallest possible cost from what seemed a desperate position, to escape the penalties of their crimes, to emerge from their failure with a Germany still powerful, both in economic resources and in arms, and to set to work again industriously preparing for a renewal of the struggle at a more favourable time. If negotiations resulted in such a truce, the German purpose would be splendidly served; even if they failed, however, the gain for Germany would still be great. Germany could appear as the belligerent which desired peace and the Entente could perhaps be manœuvred into the position of the side responsible for continuing the war. The consideration which was chiefly at stake in these tortuous proceedings was public opinion in the United States. Americans do not yet understand the extent to which their country was regarded as the determining power. Both the German and the British Foreign Offices clearly understood, in August, 1914, that the United States, by throwing its support, especially its economic support, to one side or the other, could settle the result. Probably Germany grasped this point even more clearly than did Great Britain, for, from the beginning, she constantly nourished the hope that she could embroil the United States and Great Britain—a calamity which would have given victory to the German arms. In every German move there were thus several motives, and one of the chief purposes of the subterranean campaigns which she now started for peace was the desire of putting Britain in the false light of prolonging the war for aggressive purposes, and thus turning to herself that public opinion in this country which was so outspoken on the side of the Allies. Such public opinion, if it could be brought to regard Germany in a tolerant spirit, could easily be fanned into a flame by the disputes over blockades and shipping, and the power of the United States might thus be used for the advancement of the Fatherland. On the other hand, if Germany could obtain a peace which would show a profit for her tremendous effort, then the negotiations would have accomplished their purpose.

Conditions at Washington favoured operations of this kind. Secretary Bryan was an ultra-pacifist; like men of one idea, he saw only the fact of a hideous war, and he was prepared to welcome anything that would end hostilities. The cessation of bloodshed was to him the great purpose to be attained: in the mind of Secretary Bryan it was more important that the war should be stopped than that the Allies should win. To President Wilson the European disaster appeared to be merely a selfish struggle for power, in which both sides were almost equally to blame. He never accepted Page's obvious interpretation that the single cause was Germany's determination to embark upon a war of world conquest. From the beginning, therefore, Page saw that he would have great difficulty in preventing intervention from Washington in the interest of Germany, yet this was another great service to which he now unhesitatingly directed his efforts.

The Ambassador was especially apprehensive of these peace moves in the early days of September, when the victorious German armies were marching on Paris. In London, as in most parts of the world, the capture of the French capital was then regarded as inevitable. September 3, 1914, was one of the darkest days in modern times. The population of Paris was fleeing southward; the Government had moved its headquarters to Bordeaux; and the moment seemed to be at hand when the German Emperor would make his long anticipated entry into the capital of France. It was under these circumstances that the American Ambassador to Great Britain sent the following message directly to the President:

To the President

American Embassy, London,
Sep. 3, 4 A. M.

Everybody in this city confidently believes that the Germans, if they capture Paris, will make a proposal for peace, and that the German Emperor will send you a message declaring that he is unwilling to shed another drop of blood. Any proposal that the Kaiser makes will be simply the proposal of a conqueror. His real purpose will be to preserve the Hohenzollern dynasty and the imperial bureaucracy. The prevailing English judgment is that, if Germany be permitted to stop hostilities, the war will have accomplished nothing. There is a determination here to destroy utterly the German bureaucracy, and Englishmen are prepared to sacrifice themselves to any extent in men and money. The preparations that are being made here are for a long war; as I read the disposition and the character of Englishmen they will not stop until they have accomplished their purpose. There is a general expression of hope in this country that neither the American Government nor the public opinion of our country will look upon any suggestion for peace as a serious one which does not aim, first of all, at the absolute destruction of the German bureaucracy.

From such facts as I can obtain, it seems clear to me that the opinion of Europe—excluding of course, Germany—is rapidly solidifying into a severe condemnation of the German Empire. The profoundest moral judgment of the world is taking the strongest stand against Germany and German methods. Such incidents as the burning of Louvain and other places, the slaughter of civilian populations, the outrages against women and children—outrages of such a nature that they cannot be printed, but which form a matter of common conversation everywhere—have had the result of arousing Great Britain to a mood of the grimmest determination.

PAGE.

This message had hardly reached Washington when the peace effort of which it warned the President began to take practical form. In properly estimating these manœuvres it must be borne in mind that German diplomacy always worked underground and that it approached its negotiations in a way that would make the other side appear as taking the initiative. This was a phase of German diplomatic technique with which every European Foreign Office had long been familiar. Count Bern-storff arrived in the United States from Germany in the latter part of August, evidently with instructions from his government to secure the intercession of the United States. There were two unofficial men in New York who were ideally qualified to serve the part of intermediaries. Mr. James Speyer had been born in New York; he had received his education at Frankfort-on-the-Main, Germany, and had spent his apprenticeship also in the family banking house in that city. As the head of an American banking house with important German affiliations, his interests and sympathies were strong on the side of the Fatherland; indeed, he made no attempt to conceal his strong pro-Germanism.

Mr. Oscar S. Straus had been born in Germany; his father had been a German revolutionist of 'Forty-eight; like Carl Schurz, Abraham Jacobi, and Franz Sigel, he had come to America to escape Prussian militarism and the Prussian autocracy, and his children had been educated in a detestation of the things for which the German Empire stood. Mr. Oscar Straus was only two years old when he was brought to this country, and he had given the best evidences of his Americanism in a distinguished public career. Three times he had served the United States as Ambassador to Turkey; he had filled the post of Secretary of Commerce and Labour in President Roosevelt's cabinet, and had held other important public commissions. Among his other activities, Mr. Straus had played an important part in the peace movement of the preceding quarter of a century and he had been a member of the Permanent Court of Arbitration at The Hague. Mr. Straus was on excellent terms with the German, the British, and the French ambassadors at Washington. As far back as 1888, when he was American

Minister at Constantinople, Bernstorff, then a youth, was an attaché at the German Embassy; the young German was frequently at the American Legation and used to remind Mr. Straus, whenever he met him in later years, how pleasantly he remembered his hospitality. With Sir Cecil Spring Rice, the British Ambassador, and M. Jules Jusserand, the French Ambassador, Mr. Straus had also become friendly in Constantinople and in Washington. This background, and Mr. Straus's well-known pro-British sentiments, would have made him a desirable man to act as a liaison agent between the Germans and the Allies, but there were other reasons why this ex-ambassador would be useful at this time. Mr. Straus had been in Europe at the outbreak of the war; he had come into contact with the British statesmen in those exciting early August days; in particular he had discussed all phases of the conflict with Sir Edward Grey, and before leaving England, he had given certain interviews which the British statesmen declared had greatly helped their cause in the United States. Of course, the German Government knew all about these activities.

On September 4th, Mr. Straus arrived at New York on the *Mauretania*. He had hardly reached this country when he was called upon the telephone by Mr. Speyer, a friend of many years' standing. Count Bernstorff, the German Ambassador, Mr. Speyer said, was a guest at his country home, Waldheim, at Scarboro, on the Hudson; Mr. Speyer was giving a small, informal dinner the next evening, Saturday, September 5th, and he asked Mr. and Mrs. Straus to come. The other important guests were Mr. Frank A. Vanderlip, president of the National City Bank, and Mrs. Vanderlip. Mr. Straus accepted the invitation, mentally resolving that he would not discuss the war himself, but merely listen. It would certainly have been a difficult task for any man to avoid this subject on this particular evening; the date was September 5th, the day when the German Army suddenly stopped in its progress toward Paris, and began retreating, the French and the British forces in pursuit. A few minutes before Count Bernstorff sat down at Mr. Speyer's table, with Mr. Straus opposite, he had learned that the magnificent enterprise which Germany had planned for forty years had failed, and that his country was facing a monstrous disaster. The Battle of the Marne was raging in all its fury while this pacific conversation at Mr. Speyer's house was taking place.

Of course the war became the immediate topic of discussion. Count Bernstorff at once plunged into the usual German point of view—that Germany did not want war in the first place, that the Entente had forced the issue, and the like.

"The Emperor and the German Government stood for peace," he said.

Naturally, a man who had spent a considerable part of his life promoting the peace cause pricked up his ears at this statement.

"Does that sentiment still prevail in Germany?" asked Mr. Straus.

"Yes," replied the German Ambassador.

"Would your government entertain a proposal for mediation now?" asked Mr. Straus.

"Certainly," Bernstorff promptly replied. He hastened to add, however, that he was speaking unofficially. He had had no telegraphic communication from Berlin for five days, and therefore could not definitely give the attitude of his government. But he was quite sure that the Kaiser would be glad to have President Wilson take steps to end the war.

The possibility that he might play a part in bringing hostilities to a close now occurred to Mr. Straus. He had come to the dinner determined to avoid the subject altogether, but Count Bernstorff had precipitated the issue in a way that left the American no option. Certainly Mr. Straus would have been derelict if he had not reported this conversation to the high quarters for which Count Bernstorff had evidently intended it.

"That is a very important statement you have made, Mr. Ambassador," said Mr. Straus, measuring every word. "May I make use of it?"

"Yes."

"May I use it in any way I choose?"

"You may," replied Bernstorff.

Mr. Straus saw in this acquiescent mood a chance to appeal directly to President Wilson.

"Do you object to my laying this matter before our government?"

"No, I do not."

Mr. Straus glanced at his watch; it was 10:15 o'clock.

"I think I shall go to Washington at once—this very night. I can get the midnight train."

Mr. Speyer, who has always maintained that this proceeding was casual and in no way promoted by himself and Bernstorff, put in a word of caution.

"I would sleep on it," he suggested.

But, in a few moments, Mr. Straus was speeding in his automobile through Westchester County in the direction of the Pennsylvania Station. He caught the express, and, the next morning, which was Sunday the sixth, he was laying the whole matter before Secretary Bryan at the latter's house. Naturally, Mr. Bryan was overjoyed at the news; he at once summoned Bernstorff from New York to Washington, and went over the suggestion personally. The German Ambassador repeated the statements which he had made to Mr. Straus—always guardedly qualifying his remarks by saying that the proposal had not come originally from him but from his American friend. Meanwhile Mr. Bryan asked Mr. Straus to discuss the matter with the British and French ambassadors.

The meeting took place at the British Embassy. The two representatives of the Entente, though only too glad to talk the matter over, were more skeptical about the attitude of Bernstorff than Mr. Bryan had been.

"Of course, Mr. Straus," said Sir Cecil Spring Rice, "you know that this dinner was arranged purposely so that the German Ambassador could meet you?"

Mr. Straus demurred at this statement, but the Englishman smiled.

"Do you suppose," Sir Cecil asked, "that any ambassador would make such a statement as Bernstorff made to you without instructions from his government?"

"You and M. Jusserand," replied the American, "have devoted your whole lives to diplomacy with distinguished ability and you can therefore answer that question better than I."

"I can assure you," replied M. Jusserand, "that no ambassador under the German system would dare for a moment to make such a statement without being authorized to do so."

"The Germans," added Sir Cecil, "have a way of making such statements unofficially and then denying that they have ever made them."

Both the British and French ambassadors, however, thought that the proposal should be seriously considered.

"If it holds out one chance in a hundred of lessening

the length of the war, we should entertain it," said Ambassador Jusserand.

"I certainly hope that you will entertain it cordially," said Mr. Straus.

"Not cordially—that is a little too strong."

"Well, sympathetically?"

"Yes, sympathetically," said M. Jusserand, with a smile.

These facts were at once cabled to Page, who took the matter up with Sir Edward Grey. A despatch from the latter to the British Ambassador in Washington gives a splendid summary of the British attitude on such approaches at this time.

Sir Edward Grey to Sir Cecil Spring Rice

Foreign Office,
September 9, 1914.

Sir:

The American Ambassador showed me to-day a communication that he had from Mr. Bryan. It was to the effect that Mr. Straus and Mr. Speyer had been talking with the German Ambassador, who had said that, though he was without instructions, he thought that Germany might be disposed to end the war by mediation. This had been repeated to Mr. Bryan, who had spoken to the German Ambassador, and had heard the same from him. Mr. Bryan had taken the matter up, and was asking direct whether the German Emperor would accept mediation if the other parties who were at war would do the same.

The American Ambassador said to me that this information gave him a little concern. He feared that, coming after the declaration that we had signed last week with France and Russia about carrying on the war in common,[1] the peace parties in the United States might be given the impression that Germany was in favour of peace, and that the responsibility for continuing the war was on others.

I said that the agreement that we had made with France and Russia was an obvious one; when three countries were at war on the same side, one of them could not honourably make special terms for itself and leave the others in the lurch. As to mediation, I was favourable to it in principle, but the real question was: On what terms could the war be ended? If the United States could devise anything that would bring this war to an end and prevent another such war being forced on Europe I should welcome the proposal.

The Ambassador said that before the war began I had made suggestions for avoiding it, and that these suggestions had been refused.

I said that this was so, but since the war began there were two further considerations to be borne in mind: We were fighting to save the west of Europe from being dominated by Prussian militarism; Germany had prepared to the day for this war, and we could not again have a great military power in the middle of Europe preparing war in this way and forcing it upon us; and the second thing was that cruel wrong had been done to Belgium, for which there should be some compensation. I had no indication whatever that Germany was prepared to make any reparation to Belgium, and, while repeating that in principle I was favourable to mediation, I could see nothing to do but to wait for the reply of the German Emperor to the question that Mr. Bryan had put to him

[1]On September 5, 1914, Great Britain, France, and Russia signed the Pact of London, an agreement which bound the three powers of the Entente to make war and peace as a unit. Each power specifically pledged itself not to make a separate peace.

and for the United States to ascertain on what terms Germany would make peace if the Emperor's reply was favourable to mediation.

The Ambassador made it quite clear that he regarded what the German Ambassador had said as a move in the game. He agreed with what I had said respecting terms of peace, and that there seemed no prospect at present of Germany being prepared to accept them.

I am, &c.,
E. GREY.

A letter from Page to Colonel House gives Page's interpretation of this negotiation:

To Edward M. House

London, September 10, 1914.

MY DEAR HOUSE:

A rather serious situation has arisen: The Germans of course thought that they would take Paris. They were then going to propose a conqueror's terms of peace, which they knew would not be accepted. But they would use their so-called offer of peace purely for publicity purposes. They would say, "See, men of the world, we want peace; we offer peace; the continuance of this awful war is not our doing." They are using Hearst for this purpose. I fear they are trying to use so good a man as Oscar Straus. They are fooling the Secretary.

Every nation was willing to accept Sir Edward Grey's proposals but Germany. She was bent on a war of conquest. Now she's likely to get licked—lock, stock and barrel. She is carrying on a propaganda and a publicity campaign all over the world. The Allies can't and won't accept any peace except on the condition that German militarism be uprooted. They are not going to live again under that awful shadow and fear. They say truly that life on such terms is not worth living. Moreover, if Germany should win the military control of Europe, she would soon—that same war-party—attack the United States. The war will not end until this condition can be imposed—that there shall be no more militarism.

But in the meantime, such men as Straus (a good fellow) may be able to let (by helping) the Germans appear to the Peace people as really desiring peace. Of course, what they want is to save their mutton.

And if we begin mediation talk now on that basis, we shall not be wanted when a real chance for mediation comes. If we are so silly as to play into the hands of the German-Hearst publicity bureau, our chance for real usefulness will be thrown away.

Put the President on his guard.

W. H. P.

In the latter part of the month came Germany's reply. One would never suspect, when reading it, that Germany had played any part in instigating the negotiation. The Kaiser repeated the old charges that the Entente had forced the war on the Fatherland, that it was now determined to annihilate the Central Powers and that consequently there was no hope that the warring countries could agree upon acceptable terms for ending the struggle.

So ended Germany's first peace drive, and in the only possible way that it could end. But the Washington administration continued to be most friendly to mediation. A letter of Colonel House's, dated October 4, 1914, possesses great historical importance. It was written after a detailed discussion with President Wilson, and it indicates not only the President's desire to bring the struggle to a close, but it describes in some detail the principles which the President then regarded as essential to a permanent peace. It furnishes the central idea of the presidential policy for the next four years; indeed, it contains the first statement of that famous "Article X" of the Covenant of the League of Nations which was Mr. Wilson's most important contribution to that contentious document. This was the article which pledges the League "to respect and preserve as against external aggression the territorial integrity and existing political independence" of all its members; it was the article which, more than any other, made the League obnoxious to Americans, who interpreted it as an attempt to involve them perpetually in the quarrels of Europe; and it was the one section of the Treaty of Versailles which was most responsible for the rejection of that document by the United States Senate. There are other suggestions in Colonel House's letter which apparently bore fruit in the League Covenant. It is somewhat astonishing that a letter of Colonel House's, written as far back as October 3, 1914, two months after the outbreak of the war, should contain "Article X" as one of the essential terms of peace, as well as other ideas afterward incorporated in that document, accompanied by an injunction that Page should present the suggestion to Sir Edward Grey:

From Edward M. House

115 East 53rd Street,
New York City.
October 3rd, 1914.

DEAR PAGE:

Frank [the Ambassador's son] has just come in and has given me your letter of September 22nd[1] which is of ab-

[1]Published in Chapter XI, page 327.

sorbing interest.   You have never done anything better
than this letter, and some day, when you give the word,
it must be published.   But in the meantime, it will repose
in the safe deposit box along with your others and with
those of our great President.

I have just returned from Washington where I was with
the President for nearly four days.   He is looking well
and is well.   Sometimes his spirits droop, but then again,
he is his normal self.

Before I came from Prides[1] I was fearful lest Straus,
Bernstorff, and others would drive the President into
doing something unwise.   I have always counselled him
to remain quiet for the moment and let matters unfold
themselves further.   In the meantime, I have been conferring with Bernstorff, with Dumba,[2] and, of course,
Spring Rice.   The President now wants me to keep in
touch with the situation, and I do not think there is
any danger of any one on the outside injecting himself
into it unless Mr. Bryan does something on his own
initiative.

Both Bernstorff and Dumba say that their countries
are ready for peace talks, but the difficulty is with England.   Sir Cecil says their statements are made merely to
place England in a false position.

The attitude, I think, for England to maintain is the
one which she so ably put forth to the world.   That is,
peace must come only upon condition of disarmament
and must be permanent.   I have a feeling that Germany
will soon be willing to discuss terms.   I do not agree
that Germany has to be completely crushed and that
terms must be made either in Berlin or London.   It is
manifestly against England's interest and the interest of

---

[1] Colonel House's summer home in Massachusetts.

[2] Ambassador from Austria-Hungary to the United States.

Europe generally for Russia to become the dominating military force in Europe, just as Germany was. The dislike which England has for Germany should not blind her to actual conditions. If Germany is crushed, England cannot solely write the terms of peace, but Russia's wishes must also largely prevail.

With Russia strong in militarism, there is no way by which she could be reached. Her government is so constituted that friendly conversations could not be had with her as they might be had even with such a power as Germany, and the world would look forward to another cataclysm and in the not too distant future.

When peace conversations begin, at best, they will probably continue many months before anything tangible comes from them. England and the Allies could readily stand on the general proposition that only enduring peace will satisfy them and I can see no insuperable obstacle in the way.

The Kaiser did not want war and was not responsible for it further than his lack of foresight which led him to build up a formidable engine of war which later dominated him. Peace cannot be made until the war party in Germany find that their ambitions cannot be realized, and this, I think, they are beginning to know.

When the war is ended and the necessary territorial alignments made, it seems to me, the best guaranty of peace could be brought by every nation in Europe guaranteeing the territorial integrity of every other nation.[1] By confining the manufacture of arms to the governments themselves and by permitting representatives of all nations to inspect, at any time, the works.[2]

---

[1] This, with certain modifications is Article 10 of the Covenant of the League of Nations.

[2] There is a suggestion of these provisions in Article 8 of the League Covenant.

Then, too, all sources of national irritation should be removed so what at first may be a sore spot cannot grow into a malignant disease.[1] It will not be too difficult, I think, to bring about an agreement that will insure permanent peace, provided all the nations of Europe are honest in their desire for it.

I am writing this to you with the President's knowledge and consent and with the thought that it will be conveyed to Sir Edward. There is a growing impatience in this country because of this war and there is constant pressure upon the President to use his influence to bring about normal conditions. He does not wish to do anything to irritate or offend any one of the belligerent nations, but he has an abiding faith in the efficacy of open and frank discussion between those that are now at war.

As far as I can see, no harm can be done by a dispassionate discussion at this stage, even though nothing comes of it. In a way, it is perhaps better that informal and unofficial conversations are begun and later the principals can take it up themselves.

I am sure that Sir Edward is too great a man to let any prejudices deter him from ending, as soon as possible, the infinite suffering that each day of war entails.

Faithfully yours,
E. M. HOUSE.

It is apparent that the failure of this first attempt at mediation discouraged neither Bernstorff nor the Washington administration. Colonel House was constantly meeting the German and the British Ambassadors; he was also, as his correspondence shows, in touch with Zimmermann, the German Under Foreign Secretary. The German desire for peace grew stronger in the autumn

---

[1]Article 11 of the League Covenant reflects the influence of this idea.

and winter of 1914–1915, as the fact became more and more clear that Great Britain was summoning all her resources for the greatest effort in her history, as the stalemate on the Aisne more and more impressed upon the German chieftains the impossibility of obtaining any decision against the French Army, and as the Russians showed signs of great recuperation after the disaster of Tannenberg. By December 4th Washington had evidently made up its mind to move again.

From Edward M. House

115 East 53rd Street,
New York City.
December 4th, 1914.

DEAR PAGE:

The President desires to start peace parleys at the very earliest moment, but he does not wish to offend the sensibilities of either side by making a proposal before the time is opportune. He is counting upon being given a hint, possibly through me, in an unofficial way, as to when a proffer from him will be acceptable.

Pressure is being brought upon him to offer his services again, for this country is suffering, like the rest of the neutral world, from the effects of the war, and our people are becoming restless.

Would you mind conveying this thought delicately to Sir Edward Grey and letting me know what he thinks?

Would the Allies consider parleys upon a basis of indemnity for Belgium and a cessation of militarism? If so, then something may be begun with the Dual Alliance.

I have been told that negotiations between Russia and Japan were carried on several months before they agreed to meet at Portsmouth. The havoc that is being wrought in human lives and treasure is too great to permit racial feeling or revenge to enter into the thoughts of those who govern the nations at war.

I stand ready to go to Germany at any moment in order to sound the temper of that government, and I would then go to England as I did last June.

This nation would not look with favour upon a policy that held nothing but the complete annihilation of the enemy.

Something must be done sometime, by somebody, to initiate a peace movement, and I can think of no way, at the moment, than the one suggested.

I will greatly appreciate your writing me fully and freely in regard to this phase of the situation.

Faithfully yours,

E. M. House.

To this Page immediately replied:

To Edward M. House

December 12th, 1914.

My dear House:

The English rulers have no feeling of vengeance. I have never seen the slightest traces of that. But they are determined to secure future safety. They will not have this experience repeated if they can help it. They realize now that they have been living under a sort of fear—or dread—for ten years: they sometimes felt that it was bound to come some time and then at other times they could hardly believe it. And they will spend all the men and all the money they have rather than suffer that fear again or have that danger. Now, if anybody could fix a basis for the complete restoration of Belgium, so far as restoration is possible, and for the elimination of militarism, I am sure the *English* would talk on that basis.

But there are two difficulties—Russia wouldn't talk till she has Constantinople, and I haven't found anybody who can say exactly what you mean by the "elimination of militarism." Disarmament? England will have her navy to protect her incoming bread and meat. How, then, can she say to Germany, "You can't have an army"?

You say the Americans are becoming "restless." The plain fact is that the English people, and especially the English military and naval people, don't care a fig what the Americans think and feel. They say, "We're fighting their battle, too—the battle of democracy and freedom from bureaucracy—why don't they come and help us in our life-and-death struggle?" I have a drawer full of letters saying this, not one of which I have ever answered. The official people never say that of course—nor the really responsible people, but a vast multitude of the public do. This feeling comes out even in the present military and naval rulers of this Kingdom—comes indirectly to me. A part of the public, then, and the military part of the Cabinet, don't longer care for American opinion and they resent even such a reference to peace as the President made in his Message to Congress.[1] But the civil part of the Cabinet and the responsible and better part of the public do care very much. The President's intimation about peace, however, got no real response here. They think he doesn't understand the meaning of the war. They don't want war; they are not a warlike people. They don't hate the Germans. There is no feeling of vengeance. They constantly say: "Why

---

[1] From the President's second message to Congress, December 8. 1914: "It is our dearest present hope that this character and reputation may presently, in God's providence, bring us an opportunity, such as has seldom been vouchsafed any nation, to counsel and obtain peace in the world and reconciliation and a healing settlement of many a matter that has cooled and interrupted the friendship of nations."

do the Germans hate us? We don't hate them." But, since Germany set out to rule the world and to conquer Great Britain, they say, "We'll all die first." That's "all there is to it." And they will all die unless they can so fix things that this war cannot be repeated. Lady K—, as kindly an old lady as ever lived, said to me the other day: "A great honour has come to us. Our son has been killed in battle, fighting for the safety of England."

Now, the question which nobody seems to be able to answer is this: How can the military party and the military spirit of Germany be prevented from continuing to prepare for the conquest of Great Britain and from going to work to try it again? That implies a change in the form, spirit, and control of the German Empire. If they keep up a great army, they will keep it up with that end more or less in view. If the military party keeps in power, they will try it again in twenty-five or forty years. This is all that the English care about or think about.

They don't see how it is to be done themselves. All they see yet is that they must show the Germans that they can't whip Great Britain. If England wins decisively the English hope that somehow the military party will be overthrown in Germany and that the Germans, under peaceful leadership, will go about their business—industrial, political, educational, etc.—and quit dreaming of and planning for universal empire and quit maintaining a great war-machine, which at some time, for some reason, must attack somebody to justify its existence. This makes it difficult for the English to make overtures to or to receive overtures from this military war-party which now *is* Germany. But, if it be possible so completely to whip the war party that it will somehow be thrown out of power at home—that's the only way they now see out of it. To patch up a peace, leaving the

German war party in power, they think, would be only to invite another war.

If you can get over this point, you can bring the English around in ten minutes. But they are not going to take any chances on it. Read English history and English literature about the Spanish Armada or about Napoleon. They are acting those same scenes over again, having the same emotions, the same purpose: nobody must invade or threaten England. "If they do, we'll spend the last man and the last shilling. We value," they say truly, "the good-will and the friendship of the United States more than we value anything except our own freedom, but we'll risk even that rather than admit copper to Germany, because every pound of copper prolongs the war."

There you are. I've blinked myself blind and talked myself hoarse to men in authority—from Grey down—to see a way out—without keeping this intolerable slaughter up to the end. But they stand just where I tell you.

And the horror of it no man knows. The news is suppressed. Even those who see it and know it do not realize it. Four of the crack regiments of this kingdom —regiments that contained the flower of the land and to which it was a distinction to belong—have been practically annihilated, one or two of them annihilated twice. Yet their ranks are filled up and you never hear a murmur. Presently it'll be true that hardly a title or an estate in England will go to its natural heir—the heir has been killed. Yet, not a murmur; for England is threatened with invasion. They'll all die first. It will presently be true that more men will have been killed in this war than were killed before in all the organized wars since the Christian era began. The English are willing and eager to stop it if things can be so fixed that there will be no military power in Europe that wishes or prepares to attack and invade England.

I've had many one-hour, two-hour, three-hour talks with Sir Edward Grey. He sees nothing further than I have written. He says to me often that if the United States could see its way to cease to protest against stopping war materials from getting into Germany, they could end the war more quickly—all this, of course, informally; and I say to him that the United States will consider any proposal you will make that does not infringe on a strict neutrality. Violate a rigid neutrality we will not do. And, of course, he does not ask that. I give him more trouble than all the other neutral Powers combined; they all say this. And, on the other side, his war-lord associates in the Cabinet make his way hard.

So it goes—God bless us, it's awful. I never get away from it—war, war, war every waking minute, and the worry of it; and I see no near end of it. I've had only one thoroughly satisfactory experience in a coon's age, and this was this: Two American ships were stopped the other day at Falmouth. I telegraphed the captains to come here to see me. I got the facts from them—all the facts. I telephoned Sir Edward that I wished to see him at once. I had him call in one of his ship-detaining committee. I put the facts on the table. I said, "By what right, or theory of right, or on what excuse, are those ships stopped? They are engaged in neutral commerce. They fly the American flag." One of them was released that night—no more questions asked. The other was allowed to go after giving bond to return a lot of kerosene which was loaded at the bottom of the ship.

If I could get facts, I could do many things. The State Department telegraphs me merely what the shipper says —a partial statement. The British Government tells me (after infinite delay) another set of facts.   The British Government says, "We're sorry, but the Prize Court must decide."   Our Government wires a dissertation on International Law—Protest, protest: (I've done nothing else since the world began!)   One hour with a sensible ship captain does more than a month of cross-wrangling with Government Departments.

I am trying my best, God knows, to keep the way as smooth as possible; but neither government helps me. Our Government merely sends the shipper's ex-parte statement.   This Government uses the Navy's excuse.   .   .   .

At present, I can't for the life of me see a way to peace, for the one reason I have told you.   The Germans wish to whip England, to invade England.   They started with their army toward England.   Till that happened England didn't have an army.   But I see no human power that can give the English now what they are determined to have—safety for the future—till some radical change is made in the German system so that they will no longer have a war-party any more than England has a war-party.   England surely has no wish to make conquest of Germany.   If Germany will show that she has no wish to make conquest of England, the war would end to-morrow.

What impresses me through it all is the backwardness of all the Old World in realizing the true aims of government and the true methods.   I can't see why any man who has hope for the progress of mankind should care to live anywhere in Europe.   To me it is all infinitely sad. This dreadful war is a logical outcome of their condition, their thought, their backwardness.   I think I shall never care to see the continent again, which of course is committing suicide and bankruptcy.   When my natural term of service is done here, I shall go home with more

joy than you can imagine. That's the only home for a
man who wishes his horizon to continue to grow wider.
All this for you and me only—nobody else.

Heartily yours,

WALTER H. PAGE.

Probably Page thought that this statement of the case
—and it was certainly a masterly statement—would end
any attempt to get what he regarded as an unsatisfactory
and dangerous peace. But President Wilson could not
be deterred from pressing the issue. His conviction was
firm that this winter of 1914–1915 represented the most
opportune time to bring the warring nations to terms,
and it was a conviction from which he never departed.
After the sinking of the *Lusitania* the Administration
gazed back regretfully at its frustrated attempts of the
preceding winter, and it was inclined to place the responsibility for this failure upon Great Britain and
France. "The President's judgment," wrote Colonel
House on August 4, 1915, three months after the *Lusitania* went down, "was that last autumn was the time to
discuss peace parleys, and we both saw present possibilities. War is a great gamble at best, and there was too
much at stake in this one to take chances. I believe if
one could have started peace parleys in November, we
could have forced the evacuation of both France and
Belgium, and finally forced a peace which would have
eliminated militarism on land and sea. The wishes of
the Allies were heeded with the result that the war has
now fastened itself upon the vitals of Europe and what
the end may be is beyond the knowledge of man."

This shows that the efforts which the Administration
was making were not casual or faint-hearted, but that
they represented a most serious determination to bring

hostilities to an end.   This letter and the correspondence which now took place with Page also indicate the general terms upon which the Wilson Administration believed that the mighty differences could be composed.   The ideas which Colonel House now set forth were probably more the President's than his own; he was merely the intermediary in their transmission.   They emphasized Mr. Wilson's conviction that a decisive victory on either side would be a misfortune for mankind.   As early as August, 1914, this was clearly the conviction that underlay all others in the President's interpretation of events.   His other basic idea was that militarism should come to an end "on land and sea"; this could mean nothing except that Germany was expected to abandon its army and that Great Britain was to abandon its navy.

From Edward M. House

115 East 53rd Street,
New York City.
January 4th, 1915.

DEAR PAGE:

I believe the Dual Alliance is thoroughly ready for peace and I believe they would be willing to agree upon terms England would accept provided Russia and France could be satisfied.

They would, in my opinion, evacuate both Belgium and France and indemnify the former, and they would, I think, be willing to begin negotiations upon a basis looking to permanent peace.

It would surprise me if the Germans did not come out in the open soon and declare that they have always been for peace, that they are for peace now, and that they are willing to enter into a compact which would insure peace for all time; that they have been misrepresented and maligned and that they leave the entire responsibility for the continuation of the war with the Allies.

If they should do this, it would create a profound impression, and if it was not met with sympathy by the Allies, the neutral sentiment, which is now almost wholly against the Germans, would veer toward them.

Will you not convey this thought to Sir Edward and let me know what he says?

The President is willing and anxious for me to go to England and Germany as soon as there is anything tangible to go on, and whenever my presence will be welcome. The Germans have already indicated this feeling but I have not been able to get from Spring Rice any expression from his Government.

As I told you before, the President does not wish to offend the sensibilities of any one by premature action, but he is, of course, enormously interested in initiating at least tentative conversations.

Will you not advise me in regard to this?

Faithfully yours,

E. M. HOUSE.

From Edward M. House

115 East 53rd Street,
New York City.
January 18, 1915.

DEAR PAGE:

The President has sent me a copy of your confidential dispatch No. 1474, January 15th.

The reason you had no information in regard to what General French mentioned was because no one knew of it outside of the President and myself and there was no safe way to inform you.

As a matter of fact, there has been no direct proposal

made by anybody.   I have had repeated informal talks with the different ambassadors and I have had direct communication with Zimmermann, which has led the President and me to believe that peace conversations may be now initiated in an unofficial way.

This is the purpose of my going over on the *Lusitania*, January 30th.   When I reach London I will be guided by circumstances as to whether I shall go next to France or Germany.

The President and I find that we are going around in a circle in dealing with the representatives in Washington, and he thinks it advisable and necessary to reach the principals direct.   When I explain just what is in the President's mind, I believe they will all feel that it was wise for me to come at this time.

I shall not write more fully for the reason I am to see you so soon.

I am sending this through the kindness of Sir Horace Plunkett.   Faithfully yours,

                                                    E. M. House.

P. S.   We shall probably say, for public consumption, that I am coming to look into relief measures, and see what further can be done.   Of course, no one but you and Sir Edward must know the real purpose of my visit.

Why was Colonel House so confident that the Dual Alliance was prepared at this time to discuss terms of peace?   Colonel House, as his letter shows, was in communication with Zimmermann, the German Under Foreign Secretary.   But a more important approach had just been made, though information bearing on this had not been sent to Page.   The Kaiser had asked President Wilson to transmit to Great Britain a suggestion for making peace on the basis of surrendering Belgium and of

paying for its restoration. It seems incredible that the
Ambassador should not have been told of this, but Page
learned of the proposal from Field Marshal French, then
commanding the British armies in the field, and this accounts for Colonel House's explanation that, "the reason
you had no information, in regard to what General French
mentioned was because no one knew of it outside of the
President and myself and there was no safe way to inform
you." Page has left a memorandum which explains the
whole strange proceeding—a paper which is interesting
not only for its contents, but as an illustration of the unofficial way in which diplomacy was conducted in Washington at this time:

Field Marshal Sir John French, secretly at home from
his command of the English forces in France, invited me
to luncheon. There were his especially confidential friend
Moore, the American who lives with him, and Sir John's
private secretary. The military situation is this: a trench
stalemate in France. Neither army has made appreciable
progress in three months. Neither can advance without
a great loss of men. Neither is whipped. Neither can
conquer. It would require a million more men than the
Allies can command and a very long time to drive the
Germans back across Belgium. Presently, if the Russians
succeed in driving the Germans back to German soil,
there will be another trench stalemate there. Thus the
war wears a practically endless outlook so far as military
operations are concerned. Germany has plenty of men
and plenty of food for a long struggle yet; and, if she use
all the copper now in domestic use in the Empire, she will
probably have also plenty of ammunition for a long struggle. She is not nearly at the end of her rope either in a
military or an economic sense.

What then? The Allies are still stronger—so long as they hold together as one man. But is it reasonable to assume that they can? And, even if they can, is it worth while to win a complete victory at such a cost as the lives of practically all the able-bodied men in Europe? But can the Allies hold together as one man for two or three or four years? Well, what are we going to do? And here came the news of the lunch. General French informed me that the President had sent to England, at the request of the Kaiser, a proposal looking toward peace, Germany offering to give up Belgium and to pay for its restoration.

"This," said Sir John, "is their fourth proposal."

"And," he went on, "if they will restore Belgium and give Alsace-Lorraine to France and Constantinople will go to Russia, I can't see how we can refuse it."

He scouted the popular idea of "crushing out militarism" once for all. It would be desirable, even if it were not necessary, to leave Germany as a first-class power. We couldn't disarm her people forever. We've got to leave her and the rest to do what they think they must do; and we must arm ourselves the best we can against them.

Now—did General French send for me and tell me this just for fun and just because he likes me? He was very eager to know my opinion whether this peace offer were genuine or whether it was a trick of the Germans to— publish it later and thereby to throw the blame for continuing the war on England?

It occurs to me as possible that he was directed to tell me what he told, trusting to me, in spite of his protestations of personal confidence, etc., to get it to the President. Assuming that the President sent the Kaiser's message to the King, this may be a suggested informal answer— that if the offer be extended to give France and Russia what they want, it will be considered, etc. This may or may not be true. Alas! the fact that I know nothing about the offer has no meaning; for the State Department never informs me of anything it takes up with the British Ambassador in Washington. Well, I'll see.

These were therefore the reasons why Colonel House had decided to go to Europe and enter into peace negotiations with the warring powers. Colonel House was wise in taking all possible precautions to conceal the purpose of this visit. His letter intimates that the German Government was eager to have him cross the ocean on this particular mission; it discloses, on the other hand, that the British Government regarded the proposed negotiations with no enthusiasm. Sir Edward Grey and Mr. Asquith would have been glad to end hostilities on terms that would permanently establish peace and abolish the vices which were responsible for the war, and they were ready to welcome courteously the President's representative and discuss the situation with him in a fair-minded spirit. But they did not believe that such an enterprise could serve a useful purpose. Possibly the military authorities, as General French's remarks to Page may indicate, did not believe that either side could win a decisive victory, but this was not the belief of the British public itself. The atmosphere in England at that time was one of confidence in the success of British arms and of suspicion and distrust of the British Government. A strong expectation prevailed in the popular mind, that the three great Powers of the Entente would at an early date destroy the menace which had enshrouded Europe for forty years, and there was no intention of giving Germany a breathing spell during which she could regenerate her forces to resume the onslaught.

In the winter of 1915 Great Britain was preparing for the naval attack on the Dardanelles, and its success was regarded as inevitable. Page had an opportunity to observe the state of optimism which prevailed in high British circles. In March of 1915 he was visiting the Prime Minister at Walmer Castle; one afternoon Mr. Asquith took him aside, informed him of the Dardanelles preparations and declared that the Allies would have possession of Constantinople in two weeks. The Prime Minister's attitude was not one of hope; it was one of confidence. The capture of Constantinople, of course, would have brought an early success to the allied army on all fronts.[1] This was the mood that was spurring on the British public to its utmost exertions, and, with such a determination prevailing everywhere, a step in the direction of peace was the last thing that the British desired; such a step could have been interpreted only as an attempt to deprive the Allies of their victory and as an effort to assist Germany in escaping the consequences of her crimes. Combined with this stout popular resolve, however, there was a lack of confidence in the Asquith ministry. An impression was broadcast that it was pacifist, even "defeatist," in its thinking, and that it harboured a weak humanitarianism which was disposed to look gently even upon the behaviour of the Prussians. The masses suspected that the ministry would welcome a peace with Germany which would mean little more than a cessation of hostilities and which would leave the great problems of the war unsolved. That this opinion was unjust, that, on the contrary, the British Foreign Office was steadily resisting all attempts to end the

---

[1]The opening of the Dardanelles would have given Russian agricultural products access to the markets of the world and thus have preserved the Russian economic structure. It would also have enabled the Entente to munition the Russian Army. With a completely equipped Russian Army in the East and the Entente Army in the West, Germany could not long have survived the pressure.

war on an unsatisfactory basis, Page's correspondence, already quoted, abundantly proves, but this unreasoning belief did prevail and it was an important element in the situation. This is the reason why the British Cabinet regarded Colonel House's visit at that time with positive alarm. It feared that, should the purpose become known, the British public and press would conclude that the Government had invited a peace discussion. Had any such idea seized the popular mind in February and March, 1915, a scandal would have developed which would probably have caused the downfall of the Asquith Ministry. "Don't fool yourself about peace," Page writes to his son Arthur, about this time. "If any one should talk about peace, or doves, or ploughshares here, they'd shoot him."

Colonel House reached London early in February and was soon in close consultation with the Prime Minister and Sir Edward Grey. He made a great personal success; the British statesmen gained a high regard for his disinterestedness and his general desire to serve the cause of decency among nations; but he made little progress in his peace plans, simply because the facts were so discouraging and so impregnable. Sir Edward repeated to him what he had already said to Page many times: that Great Britain was prepared to discuss a peace that would really safeguard the future of Europe, but was not prepared to discuss one that would merely reinstate the régime that had existed before 1914. The fact that the Germans were not ready to accept such a peace made discussion useless. Disappointed at this failure, Colonel House left for Berlin. His letters to Page show that the British judgment of Germany was not unjust and that the warnings which Page had sent to Washington were based on facts:

From Edward M. House

Embassy of the United States of America,
Berlin, Germany,
March 20, 1915.

DEAR PAGE:

I arrived yesterday morning and I saw Zimmermann[1] almost immediately. He was very cordial and talked to me frankly and sensibly.

I tried to bring about a better feeling toward England, and told him how closely their interests touched at certain points. I also told him of the broad way in which Sir Edward was looking at the difficult problems that confronted Europe, and I expressed the hope that this view would be reciprocated elsewhere, so that, when the final settlement came, it could be made in a way that would be to the advantage of mankind.

The Chancellor is out of town for a few days and I shall see him when he returns. I shall also see Ballin, Von Gwinner, and many others. I had lunch yesterday with Baron von Wimpsch who is a very close friend of the Emperor.

Zimmermann said that it was impossible for them to make any peace overtures, and he gave me to understand that, for the moment, even what England would perhaps consent to now, could not be accepted by Germany, to say nothing of what France had in mind.

I shall hope to establish good relations here and then go somewhere and await further developments. I even doubt whether more can be done until some decisive military result is obtained by one or other of the belligerents.

---

[1]German Under Foreign Secretary.

I will write further if there is any change in the situation. I shall probably be here until at least the 27th.

Faithfully yours,

E. M. HOUSE.

From Edward M. House

Embassy of the United States of America,

Berlin, Germany.

March 26, 1915.

DEAR PAGE:

While I have accomplished here much that is of value, yet I leave sadly disappointed that no direct move can be made toward peace.

The Civil Government are ready, and upon terms that would at least make an opening. There is also a large number in military and naval circles that I believe would be glad to begin parleys, but the trouble is mainly with the people. It is a very dangerous thing to permit a people to be misled and their minds inflamed either by the press, by speeches, or otherwise.

In my opinion, no government could live here at this time if peace was proposed upon terms that would have any chance of acceptance. Those in civil authority that I have met are as reasonable and fairminded as their counterparts in England or America, but, for the moment, they are impotent.

I hear on every side the old story that all Germany wants is a permanent guaranty of peace, so that she may proceed upon her industrial career undisturbed.

I have talked of the second convention,[1] and it has been cordially received, and there is a sentiment here, as well as

---

[1] It was the Wilson Administration's plan that there should be two peace gatherings, one of the belligerents to settle the war, and the other of belligerents and neutrals, to settle questions of general importance growing out of the war. This latter is what Colonel House means by "the second convention."

elsewhere, to make settlement upon lines broad enough to prevent a recurrence of present conditions.

There is much to tell you verbally, which I prefer not to write.

Faithfully yours,

E. M. HOUSE.

Colonel House's next letter is most important, for it records the birth of that new idea which afterward became a ruling thought with President Wilson and the cause of almost endless difficulties in his dealings with Great Britain. The "new phase of the situation" to which he refers is "the Freedom of the Seas" and this brief note to Page, dated March 27, 1915, contains the first reference to this idea on record. Indeed, it is evident from the letter itself that Colonel House made this notation the very day the plan occurred to him.

From Edward M. House

Embassy of the United States of America,
Berlin, Germany.
March 27, 1915.

DEAR PAGE:

I have had a most satisfactory talk with the Chancellor. After conferring with Stovall,[1] Page,[2] and Willard,[3] I shall return to Paris and then to London to discuss with Sir Edward a phase of the situation which promises results.

I did not think of it until to-day and have mentioned it to both the Chancellor and Zimmermann, who have received it cordially, and who join me in the belief that it may be the first thread to bridge the chasm.

---

[1]Mr. Pleasant A. Stovall, American Minister to Switzerland.

[2]Mr. Thomas Nelson Page, American Ambassador to Italy.

[3]Mr. Joseph E. Willard, American Ambassador to Spain.

I am writing hastily, for the pouch is waiting to be closed.

Faithfully yours,

E. M. HOUSE.

The "freedom of the seas" was merely a proposal to make all merchant shipping, enemy and neutral, free from attack in time of war. It would automatically have ended all blockades and all interference with commerce. Germany would have been at liberty to send all her merchant ships to sea for undisturbed trade with all parts of the world in war time as in peace, and, in future, navies would be used simply for fighting. Offensively, their purpose would be to bombard enemy fortifications, to meet enemy ships in battle, and to convoy ships which were transporting troops for the invasion of enemy soil; defensively, their usefulness would consist in protecting the homeland from such attacks and such invasions. Perhaps an argument can be made for this new rule of warfare, but it is at once apparent that it is the most startling proposal brought forth in modern times in the direction of disarmament. It meant that Great Britain should abandon that agency of warfare with which she had destroyed Napoleon, and with which she expected to destroy Germany in the prevailing struggle—the blockade. From a defensive standpoint, Colonel House's proposed reform would have been a great advantage to Britain, for an honourable observance of the rule would have insured the British people its food supply in wartime. With Great Britain, however, the blockade has been historically an offensive measure: it is the way in which England has always made war. Just what reception this idea would have had with official London, in April, 1915, had Colonel House been able to present it as his own proposal, is not clear, but the Germans, with characteristic stupidity, prevented the American from having a fair chance. The Berlin Foreign Office at once cabled to Count Bernstorff and Bernhard Dernburg —the latter a bovine publicity agent who was then promoting the German cause in the American press—with instructions to start a "propaganda" in behalf of the "freedom of the seas." By the time Colonel House reached London, therefore, these four words had been adorned with the Germanic label. British statesmen regarded the suggestion as coming from Germany and not from America, and the reception was worse than cold.

And another horror now roughly interrupted President Wilson's attempts at mediation. Page's letters have disclosed that he possessed almost a clairvoyant faculty of foreseeing approaching events. The letters of the latter part of April and of early May contain many forebodings of tragedy. "Peace? Lord knows when!" he writes to his son Arthur on May 2nd. "The blowing up of a liner with American passengers may be the prelude. I almost expect such a thing." And again on the same date: "If a British liner full of American passengers be blown up, what will Uncle Sam do? That's what's going to happen."

"We all have the feeling here," the Ambassador writes on May 6th, "that more and more frightful things are about to happen."

The ink on those words was scarcely dry when a message from Queenstown was handed to the American Ambassador. A German submarine had torpedoed and sunk the *Lusitania* off the Old Head of Kinsale, and one hundred and twenty-four American men, women, and children had been drowned.

END OF VOLUME I